THE COMEDIANS

RED SKELTON — Laughing Outside, Crying Inside

PHIL SILVERS — Up from Reform School

ART CARNEY — Talented but Tortured

JACK CARTER — He gave his analyst a nervous breakdown

MILTON BERLE — Maxi-Misery

LAUREL & HARDY — Hollywood's Biggest Losers

Jackie Gleason, Oscar Levant, Joe E. Lewis, Jackie Mason, Martha Raye, Phyllis Diller . . . 12 who suffered while millions laughed.

THE
COMEDIANS

by **TEDD THOMEY**
and **NORMAN WILNER**

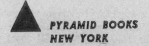 *PYRAMID BOOKS*
NEW YORK

THE COMEDIANS

A PYRAMID BOOK

First printing, July 1970

PYRAMID BOOKS are published by Pyramid Publications
A Division of The Walter Reade Organization, Inc.
444 Madison Avenue, New York, New York 10022, U.S.A.

CONTENTS

1. RED SKELTON: LAUGHING OUTSIDE, CRYING INSIDE

Red Skelton strode into the garage of his 26-room mansion in Bel Air, California. Carefully he placed a half-filled jar on the leather front seat of his $20,000 Rolls Royce and then drove to a nearby doctor's office for a medical examination. To keep from spilling the jar's contents, he drove slowly.

The jar contained what doctors call a "specimen." Most patients carry these modestly concealed in a paper bag. Not Skelton. He hadn't even bothered to put a lid on the jar.

Arriving at the doctor's suite of offices, he created a titter among the nurses in the outer section by strolling through with the jar displayed proudly on his extended palm. Told the doctor was waiting for him, he entered the inner office, where he bowed and then handed over the jar with the dignity and aplomb of a high-ranking palace aide presenting the crown jewels to his monarch.

"Good heavens," said the doctor, "you didn't bring it like this all the way in your car, did you?"

"Shucks, no," said Skelton, crossing his eyes like Cauliflower McPug. "I come on the *bus!*"

That incident illustrates several facets of the enormously complicated and entangled personality of the man who has, through prodigious applications of labor and genius, become the world's happiest clown—and one of the world's unhappiest men.

At work or play, at home or the studio, Red Skelton is constantly "on." No audience, even a one-doctor audience, is too small for a demonstration of his abilities.

He finds humor in all subjects and situations, artistic or vulgar, and is driven by a gigantic, all-powerful inner

7

compulsion which insists on producing laughter in every person he meets. His unceasing quest for laughs is so intense that his off-stage humor often has a bored, earthy streak, so Rabelaisian that it is shocking to persons used to the carefully censored brand of Skelton they see on their television screens.

The specimen jar incident is but a mild example of this.

It is more than strange that Skelton's frenzied 24-hour-a-day pursuit of laughter, while bringing joy and pleasure to millions of others, should result in continual, deep, personal unhappiness for him.

Try to untangle the fantastically twisted, looped and knotted shroud lines of this man's life and you come up with the following flatly contradictory facts:

Red Skelton is rich. He has made more than $20,000,000 in his lifetime and is one of the wealthiest men in Hollywood. Yet he acts as worried as a guy with 40 bucks in the bank who has just lost his job.

Red Skelton is poor. In emotional security, that is. He is haunted day and night by a spectre of insecurity a hundred feet tall and a hundred feet wide. He is so frightened (mostly of himself and his imagined inadequacies) that he can't sleep nights. Hollywood's greatest worrywart, he worries about his show . . . his family . . . his health . . . and whether the public will keep on laughing at him. And he worries about a thousand other things.

Red Skelton is a nice guy. When he finishes one of his TV shows he's often so exhausted from overwork (he operates on a man-killing 16-hour-a-day schedule) that he slumps into a chair backstage, eyes glazed, rivers of sweat slopping down onto his shirt, his body quivering like that of a palsied octogenarian.

But despite his fatigue he often permits children to come backstage and climb on his lap. He handles them on his knee like a kindly uncle, teases them and tells them wonderfully funny little stories about rabbits and bears, making their eyes twinkle and their cheeks dimple with delight.

Red Skelton is NOT a nice guy. His language off-stage is often filthy, and he can be ruthless. A few years ago, he blew up with rage and fired everybody on his staff, including his lawyers, agents, writers and publicity men. At first they thought he was kidding, putting on an act. Then they discovered that the man who appears so genial and pleasingly rambunctious on stage sometimes has a center of pure burning acid.

Among those he canned was Chuck Luftig, his business manager and financial adviser, a hard-working, long-suffering individual who had held Skelton's hand for years like a dutiful father, advising him on everything from how to invest his rapidly increasing millions down to what color shirt to wear.

Red Skelton has millions of friends. The millions in his TV audiences all consider him their friend, a lovable buddy who brings great warmth and marvelous humor into their homes.

Red Skelton has very few friends. Close personal pals, that is. He doesn't trust people. He is deathly afraid that everybody wants to become friendly simply to loot him out of his fortune or louse up his life in some devious way. At present, Skelton has only one really close friend, Jack Entratter, manager of the Sands Hotel in Las Vegas, who has become his business advisor and father confessor in all matters, personal and financial.

Red Skelton is a hypochondriac. A voracious gulper of pills, a sensitive-stomached man, his unusual tensions cause him to vomit even at rehearsals. He constantly seeks medical help in vain efforts to rid himself of aches and pains, real and imagined, and the tremendous frustrations and suffocating fears of audience rejection which are part of his daily routine. He admits frankly that he probably needs psychiatric help, but he wouldn't be caught within 100 yards of a psychiatrist's sofa.

"I have my problems," he once told an interviewer. In fact, I have some pips. I bet I could keep 10 psychiatrists busy. For example, I can't get into a bathtub with water in it, no matter how hard I try. I have to get in first—and then turn the water on. Crazy, isn't it?"

But Red Skelton is physically tough. This is surprising, since a legend of frailty has grown up about him in recent years, a fiction that he is a slack-muscled weakling who just barely gets through each working day. Actually, Skelton remains as strong as a draft horse, even though he is now past 50, his pink face is wrinkled and large, permanent bags half-moon beneath his light brown eyes.

Each year he has to battle harder to keep extra fat from forming on his 6-foot, 2-inch frame. But his hair is still the same dark coppery hue as when he first came to Hollywood and he is still capable of laboring at the man-killing, morning-to-midnight pace which he has maintained for decades. Although his 14- and 16-hour days appear to be the height of madness, there is method in them. Only by working himself into a state of total exhaustion can Skelton hope to be tired enough to forget his troubles for a while at night and catch a few hours of sleep.

Skelton's work schedule is so physically demanding it would make a gymnast or line-backer blanch with foreboding. Scores of times he has cut and bruised himself doing the pratfalls before the cameras which are his trademark. He has also torn ligaments and sprained his ankles, wrists and elbows.

A long-standing insomniac, Skelton has managed for years on less than four hours sleep a night. Cursed by chronic asthma, he has dragged himself wheezing to rehearsals and put in a full day's shift and part of a night before dragging himself home again. One evening in 1954, his redheaded freckle-faced daughter, Valentina, then seven, found him groaning and gasping on the floor of their home.

His redheaded wife Georgia (whom he calls "Little Red") wisely put in calls simultaneously to his doctor and a fire department resuscitation squad. The doctor diagnosed the difficulty as a combination of a heart attack and asthma, and determined that Skelton's lungs were rapidly filling with liquid. The firemen administred oxygen and rushed him unconscious to the hospital where the fluid was cleared from his lungs. He spent the night and part of the next day in an oxygen tent.

Skelton's physician, Dr. Garth Graham, later described his condition with two graphic sentences:

"Suppose there are 10 steps to death," Dr. Graham said. "Mr. Skelton had taken nine of them."

On another occasion, Skelton endured excruciating pain for weeks but refused to let his doctors make a complete examination for fear they would find something seriously wrong which would interrupt his work schedule. Finally the pain became so bad it interfered with his breathing, making it impossible for him to say his lines properly.

X-rays revealed that his repeated stage pratfalls had helped bring about a diaphragmatic hernia, a condition in which his stomach pushed against his heart and lungs, resulting in digestion troubles as well as breathing difficulties. The disorder is sometimes called an upside down stomach.

As they wheeled him off to the operating room—where he was under the knife for three hours—Skelton shook his finger playfully as his anxious wife and quipped: "Dagnabbit, Lucretia, I told you to quit baking me them upside down cakes!"

Although his furious working place alone has been enough to kill off the average comedian, Skelton has shown even greater toughness in the way he has repeatedly survived mental ordeals which would have destroyed persons equipped with less elasticity. No one can watch his often poignantly expressive work on TV without recalling the tragedy that touched Skelton and his wife when their only son, Richard, died of leukemia in 1958 at the age of nine.

In an effort to brighten Richard's final period of life, Red decided to take him on a world tour, but instead of being something wonderful to remember, the trip turned out to be a nightmare of frustration and criticism. Wherever the Skeltons turned up, they were met by staring crowds and reporters who asked ruthless personal questions.

Then newspapers in England added the final bitter blow by stating that Richard was not dying, and that his alleged illness was a shabby scheme designed to give Skelton worldwide publicity. Totally crushed by this, the Skeltons cut the trip short and returned bewildered to America.

When Richard died, the pain and heartbreak Skelton suffered was immeasurable. Perhaps because of it he was back making people laugh on TV within three weeks. While before the cameras he concealed his grief extremely well, but at home, it was a different matter. For many months after Richard's death, Skelton often locked himself in the boy's room for hours at a time, sitting there brooding and unmoving in a chair.

Skelton has always had an unreasonable fear of death, yet in a strange way Richard's demise gave Red and his wife greater understanding of one another. Unquestionably, Skelton emerged from his misfortune as an even more sensitive performer.

In a way this was peculiar and totally unexpected because for years Skelton had regularly given (and still gives) directors, producers, writers and other studio intimates the frightening impression that he was a prime candidate for a nervous blowup. His fantastic feelings of artistic inadequacy convinced his associates that it could happen imminently.

A perfect illustration of Skelton's celebrated inadequacy occured one night a few years ago at the Riviera Hotel in Las Vegas. The huge theater-restaurant was stuffed to capacity, with standees lining the walls and other scores jamming the doorway outside, eager to see Red perform.

To any other performer the size of the crowd alone would have been demonstrative proof that he was at the height of his popularity.

But to Skelton this was not important. He worried about only one thing: *Would they like him?* This fear of rejection weighed so heavily upon him that he cowered in the wings, quivering with nervousness and nausea as he waited for the great shining curtain to be drawn back.

The applause which greeted him was like a 100-gun salute and it seemed to calm his nerves almost instantly. He moved easily into the limitless collection of jokes, falls, pantomimes and characterizations which he has polished and perfected during the 39 years he has been in show business. Quickly his superb gestures, his dimples and his broad-cheeked, squirrel-like smile established the remarkable rapport which no Skelton audience has ever failed to experience.

Some of his jokes, such as "I've got a stack of blank 1918 income tax forms, and I'll make a fortune if the year 1918 comes back . . ." were familiar to his audience, but this didn't reduce their effectiveness. The chuckles became laughs, the laughs became guffaws and belly-busters.

When his allotted 45 minutes had elapsed, Skelton continued on happily for another 15—and then 15 more. When an hour and a half had passed he was still at it, and now the audience was shaking with laughter like a fat man on a vibrating machine.

The management became furious. The whole purpose of a Vegas show, of course, is to entice the customers into the hotel, entertain them briefly and then get them to the gaming tables. Frantically the manager and his assistants signaled to Red and whispered noisily at him from behind the backdrop.

"Get off the stage!" they called. "Wind things up!"

Red, relishing their discomfort, returned frantic signals with exaggerated arm motions and whispered hilarious ad libs about their frustrated antics into his microphones.

Not until two long hours had passed did Skelton consent to quit. With dramatic suddenness, he turned from comedy to his famed sentimental pantomime of "The Old Man Watching the Parade." This bit, in which Red portrays an old veteran seeing his life go by in review as he watches a parade, has been hailed by critics throughout the world as the finest silent act ever conceived. When Skelton limped out of sight at the end, the audience rose and gave him an ovation which could be heard along the famed Vegas Strip many blocks away.

Among Skelton's spectators that night was a feminine television columnist for a large East Coast newspaper. She was so emotionally moved by his performance that she asked permission to go backstage and congratulate him. The management told her that Skelton was too exhausted to see her. But shortly afterward a messenger caught up with the woman in the Riviera lobby.

"Red heard that you wanted to see him," he said. "He wants you to come on back."

In the dressing room, the columnist saw a sight she would never forget. The redheaded comedian lay on the floor in a semiconscious state, eyes closed, his cheeks pale. His wife and a doctor were struggling to revive him with smelling salts. Skelton's shivering, sweat-soaked body was wrapped in heavy blankets and his breathing was interrupted by gasps and deep asthmatic coughs.

Abruptly he opened his eyes and smiled up at the columnist. And then, although he had just heard his performance accorded two hours of nearly continuous laughter, plus a standing ovation, Red Skelton asked anxiously and with deep-rooted insecurity:

"Tell me, did you like the act? How did I do?"

Red Skelton is so afraid of failure, so fearful his audiences won't like him, that he works 10 times harder than any one else in show business and consequently earns himself 10 times as much success. To his associates, Red's strange fear of failure is a never-ceasing source of wonder and discussion because few comedians in the world have achieved as much high critical praise. His pantomimes are often called equal to Charlie Chaplin's in depth and artistic feeling.

For 11 tough years he has remained at the top of TV's ratings. During those years other top comics—Milton Berle, Jackie Gleason, Sid Caesar, Red Buttons, George Gobel—have slipped, stumbled and finally fallen in semi-disgrace, victims of overexposure on the nation's television screens. Only Jack Benny and Red Skelton remain, although both have gone on year after year with the same characterizations.

Red's portrayals of Freddie the Freeloader, San Fernando Red, Clem Kadiddlehopper and Bolivar Shagnasty, often seen in routines as familiar to his audiences as last week's scripts, continue to gain popularity. As a result, CBS doubled his time on the air this year, increasing his show to a full hour.

"Well, that ought to dood it," commented Skelton nervously when he heard CBS' plans. "It's either going to make me—or bust me up for good!"

The tangled roots of Skelton's insecurities, his fears and incredible desire to be liked by everyone he meets, can be traced directly back to the inadequacies and hardships of his youth.

Richard Bernard Skelton was born on July 18, 1913, in Vincennes, Indiana. His father, Joseph Skelton, was a part-time lawyer, elocution teacher and clown with the Hagenbeck and Wallace circus who died before Red was born. The lack of fatherly guidance and counsel scarred young Skelton from the beginning, leaving him troubled and uncertain about life and himself.

He never overcame these insecure feelings, and as he grew older they became more powerful, dominating him, keeping him permanently in mental turmoil about himself. Today he depends heavily on a man like Jack Entratter for comfort and support because in a way he serves as the father he never had.

One of four children, Skelton was raised by a tired, worn out mother who worked as a charwoman, battling grimly for every nickel she earned. The Skeltons were so dirt poor that Red began singing for pennies on the streets of Vincennes when he was seven years old.

At the age of 10 he ran away from home, not that he disliked his mother and family, but simply because there was never enough food in the house and he was hungry. He joined a medicine show run by "Doctor" R. E. Lewis, who peddled a cure-all solution of water, sugar and epsom salts called the Hot Springs System Tonic.

This was Red Skelton's introduction to show business. He sang and played the guitar for a promised salary of $10.00 a week. "The doc might as well have promised me a thousand a week," says Red, recalling those days, "because he never paid me anyway."

One night Doc Lewis accidentally bumped into young Red while they were entertaining on a makeshift stage. Skelton fell off, landing on his backside amid some old crates. This was Red Skelton's first pratfall and it produced such a big laugh from the country bumpkins that they kept it in the show.

But the lack of salary discouraged Red and he returned home to Vincennes, selling newspapers on a downtown street corner. One night a well-dressed man drove up in a car, bought a paper and asked what people did around town for excitement.

"Well," said Red. "Ed Wynn is here for a show, and the folks are all excited about that."

"Would you like to go?"

"I have to sell my papers," replied the boy, kicking unhappily at a stone on the sidewalk.

"Will a dollar buy them?" said the stranger.

Red grinned, took the money and gave him the papers. He ran home to tell his mother about his fine luck and then went to the Ed Wynn show. Like an episode in a corny dime adventure novel, it turned out that the man who had bought the papers was Ed Wynn himself. During intermission, he invited the delighted boy backstage and let him peek out at the audience through a hole in the curtain.

When Red arrived home after the show, he was so worked up he couldn't sleep. "That was the night I made up my mind," he recalls. "I decided I was going to be a comedian like Ed Wynn, lead a funny happy life and quickly get rich."

It didn't work out that way. Years of the hardest kinds of knocks were to follow before Red Skelton emerged as a master clown. When he was 13, he joined a stock company playing one-night stands. He worked on show boats, at carnivals, in tent and minstrel shows.

For a time he did a clown stint with his father's circus and seriously considered becoming an animal trainer. He changed his mind when he saw two tigers shred the arm of their owner. While still in his early teens he performed as an ill-paid clown on the Midwest burlesque circuit, lived in reeking boarding houses and cheap hotels, rode thousands of miles on rickety buses and trains, his traveling companions often including petty thieves, drunks and painted ladies of the night.

When he was 17 he met and fell in love with a pretty usherette at the Pantages Theater in Kansas City. She was 15 and her name was Edna Stillwell. They married the following year, 1931. Despite her youth, Edna had a trigger-fast mind and soon was writing her husband's vaudeville material, including all his songs and many of his skits. She also designed his costumes and managed their financial affairs.

In Montreal one night Red stumbled onto a routine which was to become the first of his many trademarks. His act was not going well and he and Edna were nearly broke, as usual. Discouraged, he dropped into a small cafe and watched a particularly inept doughnut dunker cover himself with crumbs and spilled coffee.

Red worked out a hilarious impersonation which he used at once on the Montreal stage. Night after night he stopped the show in its tracks, receiving a salary boost and laudatory notices in the papers which earned him a shot at the Paramount Theater in New York.

The lean days were now formally ended. Success on the radio followed, bringing a Hollywood film contract in 1940. Skelton's inspired, rubber-faced mugging in his first movie, *Having a Wonderful Time*, which included the doughnut dunking bit, earned him roles in eight feature pictures made at a tornadic pace in two years. Edna moved through these successes with him, serving in the mixed role of wife, manager, script doctor and financial wizard.

The marriage curdled in 1943 just before Skelton went into the Army. Red and Edna underwent what was called a "friendly" divorce.

Returning to Hollywood after the war, Red quickly developed a surprising new reputation as a tippler and an irascible character. His brief period of drinking ended, however, before doing him any permanent harm. A beautiful, redheaded starlet, Georgia Maureen Davis, was responsible for his changed attitude. Red married her in 1945.

Although happily married to Georgia, he did not end his contacts with Edna, but instead put her back on his payroll as his manager and general business chief. This unique triangle, maintained in an entirely open and above-board fashion, kept Hollywood's gossips in a stew of wild guessing and theorizing for five years.

Only once did Skelton offer an explanation and it raised more questions than it answered. "Well, shucks," he said, affably, "Edna and me have known one another since we were kids. We sort of raised each other and I guess you could say we're kind of each other's families . . ."

Under Edna's skilled guidance, Skelton—who has little business sense of his own—acquired important real estate and oil properties and began his climb to the ranks of Hollywood's multi-millionaires. And it was Edna's brilliant foresight which enabled him to win his most important battle—with the late Louis B. Mayer, head of MGM.

When Skelton made his television ambitions known, Louis B. said bluntly: "Sorry, Red. Your contract with us says you can't go into TV. So forget it."

"In that case," replied Red pleasantly, "maybe you better take another look at that contract."

Mayer and his lawyers did—and nearly choked. Tucked in an obscure paragraph was a clause permitting Red to work in television. The clause had been inserted in the contract by Edna 10 years previously, when the film studios did not consider TV a threat.

The Edna-Georgia-Red arrangement finally parted at the seams in the late Forties. Exactly what caused the break-up was never explained, but it is a reasonable guess that Georgia was primarily responsible. A former associate of Skelton's says Red was forced to pay Edna an astronomical sum to win her withdrawal.

The lights at Skelton's Bel Air mansion burn all night for the simple reason that Red is afraid of the dark. All the lights on the five and one-half-acre estate can be controlled by a single switch, located on a gadget-loaded panel at the head of the monstrous bed which fills his bedroom. Night after night, while waiting for the drowsiness which never seems to come, Hollywood's Number One Insomniac lies on the huge bed writing short stories about red-headed people. He has written hundreds, and has them bound in maroon leather albums embossed with these words in gold: "By Red Skelton." Only a few people have ever been permitted to read them.

For many years, Skelton also occupied the long hours of the night by painting—with superb skill—oil portraits of redheaded clowns. Many of these received acclaim from art experts. But after painting hundreds of them, he abruptly stopped, saying he no longer found pleasure in the pastime.

His mansion, and the unusual objects he fills it with, reflects all the contrasting facets of his personality. He roars with laughter when unwary guests are frightened by a ferocious stuffed gorilla stationed in one of his numerous bathrooms. He enjoys taking visitors on tours of his estate, pointing out features which please him, such as his badminton area, which he refers to as a "goodminton court."

"We call it that," he explains, "because we don't want anything bad around here."

Located inside his mansion or on the grounds are an antique merry-go-round, circus relics, statues of saints, 22 valuable old Bibles, a Japanese teahouse, an extensive collection of Lincolniana, numerous autographed photos of his celebrity friends, hundrels of trophies and plaques awarded him by organizations throughout the world, a macaw named Gogi, three dogs (named Paganini, Nicodemus and Half-Penny), goldfish and three wisecracking parrots.

After touring the place one visitor delighted Skelton by calling it "a Disneyland for adults," and Red has since used the term regularly in describing the estate to others.

The Bibles and statues of saints are evidence of Skelton's strong interest in religion. He has made a concentrated study of assorted Oriental and Occidental faiths and out of this has come a personal philosophy which he often mentions to friends, studio associates and occasionally even to strangers seeking his autograph. "I believe all people are placed on earth for a purpose," he says, "and mine is to make people laugh."

To some, Red's sense of religion is incompatible with another side of his character—his interest in risque humor. Others, however, find this no contradiction, emphasizing that this mixture of traits is simply another example of Skelton's basic humaneness. "Many of America's greatest men," they point out, "enjoyed raw, earthy humor. Benjamin Franklin and Mark Twain, for instance, were masters of the dirty story, told with artful good taste."

Skelton's love of the risque is most apparent at rehearsals, where his ad libs continually break up cameraman, gripmen, musicians, directors and other actors. Although some of his comments are more off-color than the roughest routines in burlesque, where he learned them, they serve an excellent purpose on the set—relaxing the nerves of co-workers struggling under the pressures of showtime deadlines and artistic temperaments.

This kind of impromptu humor has always been a part of show business camaraderie and is so acceptable that many CBS executives have Skelton's rehearsals piped into their offices so they can hear his bawdy comments while going about their prosaic duties.

His departures from the script may involve such phrases as "a pregnant cow," "a pooch in heat" or references to homosexual chickens and overly bosomed females. Repeatedly his comments will slyly allude to sex organs and the basic human excretory functions.

One afternoon at rehearsal, Skelton did a scene in which he portrayed a wacky psychiatrist giving advice to a flighty, middle-aged housewife concerning her neurotic goldfish. As she left his office, he glanced at the goldfish bowl the actress was carrying and commented:

"Don't get ahead of that thing while you're leaving here. We don't want you passing your water on the set."

The actress was embarrassed by the remark but like a good sport joined in the laughter which erupted among the technicians on the sound stage. A few hours later, when they were on the air, Skelton played right up to the same line while the actress stiffened with horrified anticipation.

Once again Red ad-libbed, but this time his remark was in perfect good taste, enjoyed by millions of families before their TV sets across the nation.

"It's raining," he said, "and you don't want to get those fish wet."

The actress was so relieved she almost dropped the fish bowl.

Across the nation the television audience that night never understood why Skelton himself laughed so hard at such a moderately funny line. Nor did the audience have the foggiest notion why the other actors in the cast, plus technicians offstage, laughed and snickered as if the joke was the funniest thing in the show, which it wasn't.

Skelton's fondness for ribaldry is not difficult to explain. It's an easy way to get laughs, and each laugh, no matter how it's earned, is inspirational music to his ears. His other peculiarities are much harder to fathom, but perhaps important clues to them can be found in the way Skelton behaves upon finishing his show each week at CBS' Television City.

Instead of being pleased with the applause which is still resounding and ringing through the studio, he is often angry and sour-faced. Instead of thinking about the jokes which went over big, perfectionist Skelton frets and curses about those which laid an egg.

He stomps to his dressing room and sheds his sweat-soaked clothes. He swallows some pink and white pills, takes a spoonful of brown medicine and gulps down a quart or two of bottled water to replace the fluids he has perspired away.

When his hands are no longer shaking and his stomach has settled down into a state of ordinary (for him) nervous tension, he shouts for his business manager. In previous years, Chuck Luftig would answer the summons and they would immediately begin criticizing and dissecting the show, line by line, laugh by laugh. Now this role of confidant and adviser is filled by Jack Entratter, who offers praise and sympathy in amounts calculated to soothe Skelton's sufferings.

Their analysis continues hour after weary hour. "I knew that lousy duck gag was a bust," Skelton moans. "I never should have let those lousy writers con me into using that lousy bit."

Ultimately they climb into Skelton's Rolls Royce and head for his Bel Air home. All during the ride, Red continues belly-aching about the show. Arriving at the mansion, they have a late snack, still talking about his performance. Finally Skelton retires. But not to sleep. All night long he tosses and twists, still worrying about the lines he should have revised, cursing himself for imagined split-second failures in timing.

Dawn finds him sitting morosely at the edge of his bed, chewing at an unlighted cigar, spitting tobacco fragments onto unread newspapers scattered across the rug.

He sits and sits, still brooding about the laughs that didn't come, straining to think of new ways to produce them.

Laughs, laughs, laughs . . .

For this unhappy, lonely man they are everything. They are his heart, his blood.

For him they are life itself.

And how he whips himself to get them is anything but funny.

2. HUNGRY COMIC

None of the coeds at Bluffton College in Ohio realized the skinny, sexless, freckled coed they were watching would eventually earn a million dollars a year. Her name then was Phyllis Driver. She was an ugly, talkative, 21-year-old senior who liked to clown around in the girl's dorm, amusing her friends with outlandish routines she made up as she went along.

One night she danced out of the shower room looking like a scrawny, plucked reject from Colonel Sanders' chicken farm. She was naked, except for curlers in her hair, a belt around her middle and a wilted rose clenched in her teeth. She cavorted up and down the hall doing an hilarious strip imitation of Gypsy Rose Lee. She concealed her bosom with her freckled arms, then uncovered one small breast slowly and suggestively, saying: "Ooooooh, look at me! Ain't I beautiful? I spent seven hours at the beauty parlor today—and that was just for the estimate!"

Soon she was surrounded by a throng of laughing coeds. "Gee, Phyllis," one said, "you're really terrific. You ought to be on the stage."

"Sure, kiddo!" cracked Phyllis, making a long, sour face. "Singing grand opera!"

She cut loose with a few exaggerated notes from *Carmen*, bowed low and then waltzed back into the shower room.

Her crack about singing grand opera was no joke. For years Phyllis had been studying classical music. Born in Lima, Ohio, she showed unusual promise as a child singer. Her mother and father, an insurance sales manager, forced her to take so many singing lessons she had arpeggios and grace notes pouring from her ears as well as her throat. When she reached her teens, she had a brilliant coloratura voice which was in great demand at church and school concerts—but nowhere else.

After high school, she attended both Northwestern Uni-

versity and an advanced school of music in Chicago. Her
parents, who were paying for her education, insisted that
she sing only longhair music. Secretly, Phyllis sang pop
tunes, hoping for a career in night clubs. When she was
20, she began to make the rounds of Chicago niteries,
asking for auditions. The impresarios took one look at her
homely, freckled pan and bony body and shook their
heads. Most of them never even gave her a chance to sing.

One veteran manager spoke what he thought was the
truth: "Look, babe. You'll never make it in nightclubs.
Never in a thousand years."

"Why not?" Phyllis demanded.

"It's like this, kid," he said gently. "It's the way you
look and the way you're built. You know what I mean?"

"I guess so," she replied.

Disgusted with her singing prospects, she quit school
and went home.

She planned to attend a business college and study
bookkeeping. "By Godfrey," roared her father, "you'll do
no such thing! I'm not going to see you throw away your
musical education, not after all the hard-earned money it
cost. You're going on with it!"

Meekly, Phyllis agreed. Her parents decided to send her
to Bluffton College in Bluffton, Ohio, for a music teacher's
degree. Late in her senior year, she met a young man
named Sherwood Diller. She took one look at his handsome physique and boyish face and decided Sherry was
for her. "That's the fellow I'm going to marry," she told
his sister confidently. "And we're going to have a big
family—at least 12 kids!"

Sherwood Diller had no chance to escape. The girl who
pursued him came on as relentlessly as a 40-ton tank. She
was no sexpot, but she had other things going for her—
personality, intelligence and wit. She was a lot of laughs,
always joking and doing crazy things. But beneath her
frisky, gabby exterior dwelt a woman who was hungry for
love and had a deep interest in the serious side of life.

They eloped in November, 1939, rented a small place
in Bluffton and Phyllis returned to her studies for two
more months in order to get her degree. Soon the first of
their five children was born. "I was an only child," Phyllis
once recalled, "and it was pretty lonely at times. I suppose
that was why I always wanted a big family of my own. I
was sorry I had to quit with just five. If we could've af-

forded 'em I would've had 20. I was like the Easter bunny, ready to lay 'em like eggs."

The Dillers were as broke as a glass anvil. Hoping to earn more money, they migrated in 1941 to what they believed was the land of milk and honey—California. For them it turned out to be a disaster area. Sherwood got a job as an inspector at the Naval Air Station at Alameda, near San Francisco. His pay was meager. The best apartment they could afford was four drafty rooms in a jerry-built war housing project.

For many years after that, there was nothing funny in Phyllis Diller's life. She scrubbed, washed, ironed, changed diapers, mended and cooked. There was never enough money, not even for such essentials as cough medicine and raincoats for the kids.

One night Phyllis and Sherry took their last dollar and went to a Clark Gable movie, leaving the youngsters with a neighbor.

"I wanted it to be a big evening out," she said, "but I was absolutely miserable. All through the movie I kept thinking about how many things that dollar could have bought for the kids. Like five quarts of milk or five boxes of corn flakes. Right when Clark Gable was in the middle of the big love scene, all puckered up over some cute dame, I started to cry. I grabbed Sherry by the coat and dragged him out of the theater. He thought I was having a crying jag because I was jealous of Clark Gable kissing that little dame. I didn't have the heart to tell him what the real reason was. All the way home he kept saying things like 'Gee, Phyllis. I'm sorry I'm not as good-looking as Clark Gable . . .' And that made me bawl all the harder."

When Phyllis' dad died, her mother moved to Alameda and invested her small inheritance in a big ramshackle house. The first floor was turned over to the Dillers. The second floor was occupied by four retired boarders, and two rooms on the third floor were turned over to Phyllis' mother. The Dillers' financial pressures were eased, but Phyllis worked herself into exhaustion.

Like a ping pong ball she bounced endlessly up and down the three flights of stairs. She was the cleaning woman who scrubbed the toilets as well as the halls. She was the cook who prepared all the meals for the four boarders and her mother, as well as for her own brood. She delivered trays of food to the boarders when they were sick. She took messages for them on the phone and lowered the boom on her kids whenever they got noisy and disturbed the tenants.

One crotchety old boarder in his mid-eighties had incredibly sensitive hearing. If someone downstairs dropped an object as small as a book, he would pound on the floor with his cane and shout, "Be quiet down there!" One afternoon, Sally, 6, and Suzy, 5 the two oldest Diller daughters, were playing with their rubber-tired doll buggy. They rolled it down the front stairs as quietly as possible, but nevertheless the sound was picked up by the old man's sonar and he bellowed, "I heard that!"

It was too much for Phyllis, whose nerves were at the breaking point. She shouted back: "Shut up, you old goat!"

The old man thumped his cane and threatened: "Just *one* more word from you, Mrs. Diller, and I'm moving out!"

For a few moments the entire house was silent. Then Phyllis screamed, as loudly as she could: "BOO!"

That did it. The old man packed his bags and moved out the same afternoon.

For days afterward Phyllis regretted her outburst because it cost the family $15, the amount of rent that was lost before a new boarder moved in. The outburst was Phyllis' last for a long time. She crawled back into the shell she had occupied as a child when she was painfully shy, starved for praise and affection, and disturbed about her appearance.

From the age of nine, she had despised her freckles because they were the most prominent symbol of her ugliness. Little boys teased her about them, making rude remarks which compared her freckles to spilled paint or animal droppings. She became an insecure child who prayed that she would somehow become a beautiful woman like her idol, movie star Carole Lombard.

It never happened. She grew into a nervous, homely adult who was, on the surface, sarcastic and flippant. Inwardly she was as troubled and full of strange fears as she had been during her school days. There was no logic to her fears. She was afraid to cross bridges. She was afraid of the dark and insisted that her husband or one of the children accompany her outdoors at night on the simplest errands. She was afraid of poverty and old age. Her fear of death was so intense at times that she refused to open up the newspaper section that contained the obituaries.

After her mother died, in March 1949, Phyllis was inconsolable for weeks. She had the feeling that more dark days lay ahead for the family. She was right. From her mother she inherited the big house in Alameda plus a residence back in Ohio. A local real estate woman suggested selling both properties and using the money to buy two smaller homes. The Dillers would live in one and gain income by renting the other.

Novices in business, Phyllis and Sherwood trustingly let the agent trick them into signing away everything they owned. In the ensuing mess, the woman was imprisoned for fraud. The Dillers scraped together what was left and made a small down payment on a house with a gigantic mortgage.

Their happiness at finally having a home of their own disappeared as soon as the first mortgage payment came due. The house became the dominant monster in a nightmare that went on without end. Each mortgage payment became harder to meet. Sherwood took a second job as a night watchman, but it wasn't enough. The children were growing up and needed more clothes, more food and other necessities.

Never fat, Phyllis lost weight from worry and skipped meals. Often she simply wasn't hungry. Sometimes she deliberately didn't eat, saving her portion of chops or dessert for the kids.

Sherwood took a third job, driving a taxi on weekends. It was too much. Dead on his feet from lack of sleep, he was caught dozing at 3 o'clock one morning on his watchman job. He was fired. It was the blow that broke the family's financial back. The mortgage company dunned them for late payments, the grocer finally refused credit and the utility companies threatened to turn off the lights and water.

The Dillers eked along by paying some bills and letting others slide. The strain on the family was terrific. Phyllis was cranky from loss of sleep worrying about the bills. Sherwood was cranky from the tension of trying to hang onto his two remaining jobs. The kids were cranky and upset because their parents fought all the time. Most of the battles were about money. But Phyllis and Sherwood were in such continual turmoil that sometimes the smallest matter—such as an argument over whether she'd put enough salt on the roast—would start another screaming, shouting clash.

Surprisingly it was in this grim period that Phyllis began to create the style of comedy which was to someday bring her fame and great wealth. She was now a woman of 35 with frazzled, bleached hair and premature wrinkles, a slattern shuffling around in worn slippers and faded cotton house dresses. To keep the neighbors from guessing how bad things were in the Diller home, she acted as if she didn't have a care in the world.

At the corner laundromat, she began cracking jokes and satirizing housework, getting laughs from the women waiting for their clothes to wash. The patter was effortless for her. Her inventive mind would take a few basic facts and exaggerate them. Instead of admitting she was a week behind in her ironing (which she was), she would lament loudly: "Oh, God, I hope Sherwood never finds out. I used to be only eight years behind in my ironing. Now it's nine!"

Then her tone would become confidential: "But I've worked out a system. I bury a lot in the back yard . . ." As the laughter mounted, she would say with a wink: "Ladies, let's face it. If you don't iron it, they'll grow out of it!"

Soon she discovered that such wisecracks and the funny atmosphere they created were doing wonders for her own morale, as well as that of the other tired women at the laundromat. They enjoyed her antics so much that she began thinking up more ambitious ways to entertain them.

One morning she leaped through the laundromat entrance with roses taped to her ears and a garland of dandelions and stinkweeds around her neck. The next morning she appeared with yards of frothy blue tulle wrapped loosely around her waist and chest. Her other props included a sauce pan and ladle which she banged together at appropriate moments while making up gags about her sad plight at home.

While she was kidding about cooking and mopping, her real problems were getting worse. One night Sherwood mentioned that he'd spent $1.49 for a new flashlight. It was money Phyllis had been counting on for something else. She began to nag at him. Soon they were arguing heatedly and saying ugly things about one another.

Suddenly Phyllis couldn't stand another moment of it. She let out a scream loud enough to sear the paint from the walls. Then she slammed out of the house and began walking. She didn't care where she went. She walked and walked, her mind spinning in frustration because there seemed to be no way out of the tragedy that her life had become. She passed a strange church. She stopped. Then she turned and walked slowly back to the church.

Many years later, discussing the incident with writer Alex Haley, she declared: "Something forced me to go into that church. As I slid down in a pew in the back, I heard the minister reading and I've never forgotten the words: 'Whatsoever things are true . . . whatsoever things are pure . . . think on these things . . .' They seemed to be addressed directly to me, as if God Himself were giving me a message."

To the dismay of her laundromat audiences, Phyllis did not entertain for the next several weeks. "I stayed home," she said, "having soul sessions with myself and reading self help books from the library. One was *The Magic of Believing* by Claude Bristol, who said a person can do almost anything he sets his mind to. Before, I had always ridiculed claims that anyone could change his life by positive thinking. But considering the shape Serwood and I were in, I was willing to try anything.

"I didn't change my life overnight, but at least I got a glimpse of what I had to do. I had to stop wallowing in negative thoughts about what a hard time we were having. I knew I had to think and work in positive ways with the good things I had—my healthy, obedient children and my hard-working husband. As a start, since we absolutely had to have more money, I knew I needed to go out and get a job."

To take care of her children and house while she was away, Phyllis hired a friendly Negro woman, Mabel Bess. Then Phyllis began making the rounds of office buildings and employment agencies. Repeatedly she was turned down because she had no professional training other than her musical education, which was now useless to her. She had never used her teaching degree, and so many years had passed since her graduation that she was no longer qualified.

She decided she would have to depend on her wits and bluffing ability. Wangling an interview with the editor of the *News-Observer*, published in nearby San Leandro, she told him the paper needed a shopping column and that she could write it.

"Have you ever done any writing?" the editor asked.

"Sure," she replied brashly. "I've been writing for years."

It wasn't exactly a lie. For years she had been writing funny, interesting letters to relatives back in the Midwest. She got the job and wrote a successful column. Soon she obtained a better paying position writing ad copy for a department store. Then she moved up to writing continuity for Oakland's radio station KROW, and from there to San Francisco's KSFO as head of merchandising and press relations. Whenever there was time, she cut up for the benefit of her fellow workers, doing the old laundromat routines and new ones she developed.

At home she clowned around night after night for her family. Things were much improved now in the Diller household. Her salary helped pay the bills, she had more confidence in herself and didn't nag at Sherwood and the kids. Time and again after one of her spontaneous gag sessions in the kitchen, Sherwood said, "Phyllis, you're getting awfully darn good. I think you're ready to turn pro."

She shook her head, frightened. She insisted that a chasm lay between her kitchen acts and smooth, professional comedy. But inside the old dream was rekindling, her hunger for a nightclub career which she'd first felt 16 years previously at Bluffton College. She wondered if she might pull it off now. Her new positive thinking had helped her succeed in writing jobs she would never have dared apply for previously. Why couldn't it work in show business?

While window-shopping one lunch hour, she amazed herself by plunking down $75 for a silver-sequined dress. It was the ostentatious kind of thing an actress or singer might wear. She had it in a drawer. Weeks of doubt and indecision passed. Then one night she said to her husband: "Sherry, I think you might be right. Maybe I could make it as a gal comic."

"You're ready right now," he grinned. But they didn't rush it. A drama coach helped her develop skits. He concentrated on her own natural delivery and sarcastic style. Each night she locked herself in her room with a full-length mirror and tape recorder. She made faces at herself and rattled off gags till she was hoarse. Then she went out in the living room and studied the techniques of Milton Berle, Red Skelton and Lucille Ball on TV.

After 10 months of such practice she obtained an audition at the Purple Onion, a small popular San Francisco basement club noted for encouraging new talent. Fortunately she auditioned just before the club's regular comic went to New York for a TV show. Hired as a substitute for two weeks, she quit her job at KSFO and began frantic preparations for her opening night.

On a chill and blustery evening in March, 1965 Phyllis Diller walked out under her first night club spotlight. She was 38 years old and nervous as a mouse in an elephant stampede. Fighting her fears with prayers, she draped herself over a piano and spoofed Eartha Kitt's hit song *Monotonous* with her own version, *Ridiculous*. She satirized the high-octave singing of Yma Sumack flailed away at a zither and delivered topical jokes based on newspaper items.

The Purple Onion audience clapped politely. Offstage, in the sour glances of bartenders and waiters, Phyllis saw the real verdict, which she knew she deserved. In her dressing room she wept bitterly and told Sherwood: "I'm just not good enough. I've got 10,000 things to learn."

She had only two weeks to learn them, scarcely enough time. Each night she tested new gag lines, new props and zany faces to see which made her listeners laugh the most. When the regular comic returned, the Purple Onion's manager told her truthfully: "Phyllis, you're not the greatest. But you've got something. We'll try you again soon."

A few weeks later she offered the Onion's clientele a revised act. The audiences loved her. She won top billing and San Francisco's columnists began quoting her original wisecracks:

"I wore one of those topless swimsuits to the beach the other day. It took me 20 minutes to get arrested—and then it was because I was parked by a fire hydrant. That night I had a phone call from a Peeping Tom. He asked me to pull my window shades down!"

After a record 89 weeks at the Onion, Phyllis signed with an agent who booked her into clubs on the East Coast. Stashing the kids with relatives in St. Louis, she and Sherwood—now working as her manager—drove from city to city and from club to club. She appeared mostly in small niteries until hooking on at the swank Fontainbleau Hotel in Miami Beach.

"This is it!" Sherwood told her jubilantly. "This is the

break we've needed. Once you knock this crowd over, the other big clubs will start begging for you!"

Exactly the opposite happened. When Phyllis strolled onto the Fontainbleau stage, she suffered a return of the opening-night jitters that had plagued her at the Purple Onion. The audience consisted of sophisticated tourists who refused to warm up to her. The harder she tried, the less they applauded. Near the end of the show, frenzied and close to panic, she began rushing her delivery, trying to force the laughs. Nothing worked. As she stumbled to the wings, she heard boos and jeers.

When she reached her dressing room, she was bawling like a baby. But worse was to come. The door slammed open and in came the hotel's manager, his face grim. "Mrs. Diller," he exploded, "that was the lousiest show I've ever seen. You're fired! I'm flying a guy down from New York to replace you!"

He refused to give her a second chance. It was the beginning of a long streak of rotten luck. Other big night clubs refused to hire her, having heard how she'd bombed in Florida. A Hollywood screen test fizzled. A TV show signed her for an appearance, then canceled her after one rehearsal. The verdict: "Diller isn't really funny. She tries too hard. She's too frantic."

Jack Paar heard the negative reports, but invited her onto his show anyway. It was her first nationwide audience. Her garish, outrageous costume, wild ad libs and cockcrow laugh were an instant hit. Paar invited her back again and again, her popularity soared and the big night clubs began clamoring to sign her.

She was a tremendous hit at New York's *Bon Soir*. Dropping the songs and impersonations which slowed her act at the Fontainbleau, she relied strictly on jokes, fired with blazing speed, ridiculing family life, household drudgery and American morals. "Nowadays," she declared, "insecurity explains everything. If your kids dynamite the house, it's because they're insecure. It's all muzzie's and dadsie's fault. Honey, let me tell you about a real childhood shakeup. When I was three, my folks sent me out for bubble gum. While I was out, they moved!"

She discovered that bursts of one-line jokes, switched swiftly from topic to topic, worked best. Scribbling gags on a pad between shows, she turned out incredibly large amounts of fresh, original material. She got her ideas from the people and things she encountered every day. She described the smoke-filled *Bon Soir* as an underground cigarette oven, so sophisticated "that a nine-year-old boy came in here the other night and when he left he was 38."

Waving a bejeweled cigarette holder longer than a sword, she strutted around on ostrich legs, popped her eyes and worked her mouth into weird shapes. She kidded herself more than anyone else: "You know what keeps me humble? Mirrors!" Tugging at the jagged spears of her dyed blonde locks, she cackled madly: "You think this is hair? It's nerve ends! Aha . . . haa . . . HAA!"

Some of her most successful gags were razor cuts at her own hubby, whom she nicknamed Fang. "I call him that," she explained, "because he has only one tooth in his old head and it's two inches long. The first time I met him I set fire to it. Thought it was a Lucky Strike. I realized on our first wedding anniversary that our marriage was in trouble. Fang gave me luggage. It was packed. My mother damn near suffocated in there." Sherwood himself supplied her with a lot of the Fang jokes. Sometimes he laughed harder at her jibes than the audience.

For years she and Sherry had wondered what they would do if they ever hit the really big dough. It had been a long time coming. At the Purple Onion, her salary had been $60 a week to start. On the Paar show, despite her success, she'd been low on the salary scale, drawing little more than enough to meet expenses. During her first Paar appearances, the Dillers had been so broke they stayed in a cheap New York hotel. Phyllis cooked their meals on an electric plate and washed the dishes in the bathroom.

But now that was all changed. Her salaries hit $2,000, then $4,000 a week and more. The Dillers began eating filet mignon and lobster in *haute cuisine* restaurants instead of hamburgers in hash houses. Phyllis went on shopping sprees, buying all the things she had despaired of ever owning when she was a slattern back in Alameda. She wasn't satisfied with one mink coat. She bought four, plus a full length sable and a chinchilla. She bought diamonds the way she once wished she could buy eggs—by the dozen, in rings, brooches, necklaces and wrist bands. Just for laughs, she purchased a score of unset diamonds and let them roll around loose on her dressing table. "A nice homey touch," she giggled.

On stage she continued to show up in ludicrous costumes that made her resemble a beat-up housewife utterly lacking in taste. In private life she tried to look like a glamour goddess, a hopeless prospect. Her wardrobe consisted of sleek Dior gowns, costly lingerie and slinky, lacy lounging ensembles. She spent a fortune on dental work, glamorizing her crooked, stained teeth with caps. When she and Sherwood went out, they were chauffeured in her silver cloud Rolls Royce. They stayed in plush, $80-a-day hotel suites and tipped bellboys and waiters lavishly.

One night, noticing a skinny, impoverished-looking busboy in a Manhattan restaurant, Phyllis impulsively thrust a $20 bill into his hand and said, "My God, you look half starved. Go back in the kitchen and have a feast."

Sherwood chided her, arguing that restaurant employees didn't starve because they received meals as part of their pay. "I don't care," she replied. "I'll never forget how it feels to be poor. It's the worst, scariest feeling in the world. Anyway, I can tell if people are hungry just by looking at them. And I just *know* that boy hasn't been eating enough."

She was right. Later, the busboy, a Mexican, shyly approached their table and thanked Phyllis for the money. He explained that he'd been hired only a few days before and had been taking part of his meals home in a paper bag for his young wife. Tears poured from Phyllis' eyes, blurring her green contact lenses. Opening her huge rhinestone-studded purse, she dug out another twenty and gave it to the boy.

With their financial goals achieved, the Dillers—for the first time in their lives—began to argue seriously about subjects other than money. Big time showbiz created tensions and pressures no less nerve-wracking than the problems of poverty back in their Alameda hovel. After nine years of ceaseless traveling, staying up all night, fighting impossible time schedules, Sherwood and Phyllis began to battle like never before. They found that luxury and a surfeit of cash emphasized their basic incompatibility instead of relieving it.

They argued about her career goals and how all the traveling kept them away from their children, now 15 through 24. They also traded angry blasts about her inlaws. Sherwood's mother and sister complained regularly about how Phyllis insulted them on her TV and club shows, referring to them bitterly as "Moby Dick," "Captain Bligh" and "the great white whale."

Sherwood had never been able to convince them that

Phyllis was talking about mythical in-laws, just as her sharp references to him as Fang and her cracks about their children were also supposedly about fictional persons. Her in-laws eventually sued her for $100,000, claiming invasion of privacy. Phyllis, admitting that maybe she had overdone it, settled the case out of court for an undisclosed amount.

After a blazing clash in July, 1965, the Diller marriage of 25 years ended in St. Louis. Phyllis charged that Sherwood had subjected her to certain indignities which her attorneys declined to reveal in public. He denied the allegations but did not contest the divorce. She was awarded custody of the children. Later it was revealed that Sherwood had pleaded with her for a reconciliation, but had been turned down flat.

It appeared that Phyllis, now that she was wealthy and famous, had developed a swollen, Hollywood-type ego and short memory. It seemed that she had coldly and selfishly turned her back on the man who had struggled at three jobs to feed her and the kids, the man who had begged her to overcome her fears and become a stage success. Asked about these matters during an exchange with reporters in Los Angeles, Phyllis mixed sarcasm and evasiveness in her replies.

"Are you cutting Fang out completely, now that you're in the big money?" a correspondent asked.

"We're working that out," she answered.

"Is it true," asked another, "that you're planning to marry again? And your new husband will be someone you think will help your career more?"

Shaking her head, she cackled boisterously and said: "What kind of LSD have you guys been smoking? Who the hell would marry an old broad like me? Look what I did to poor Fang. Drove him to drink. Made him so shaky he couldn't shave. One morning he cut himself and lost so much blood his eyes cleared up."

When the interview ended, the reporters discovered she had neatly parried their questions with gags, successfully withholding the information they sought about the changes in her personal life. She used the same technique a few weeks later to rebuff reports that she had rushed into a secret new marriage. Eventually the news leaked out. It was revealed that only a month after divorcing Sherwood she had wed Warde Donovan, a tall actor-singer with flowing blond locks. Warde supposedly had all the glamour that stodgy Sherwood lacked. He was handsome as a story-book prince; witty and knew all the right people in Hollywood.

For four months, Phyllis, working with Bob Hope in the film *Boy, Did I Get a Wrong Number,* dodged all inquiries about the new marriage. Finally, badgered into a press conference, she met reporters in her 22-room, $200,000 mansion in Brentwood, a high mucky-muck suburb of Los Angeles. Punctuating her remarks with bursts of window-rattling laughter, she disclosed that her marriage to Donovan had fallen apart while the glue was still wet.

"The crying is all over now," she declared. "Warde and I were married for all of 25 horrible minutes. How's that for contrast? My first one hung on for 25 horrible years. Aha, ha . . . HA HAA!"

She pointed to a red velvet-lined frame on the living room wall containing a large calendar page with the date of October 7, 1965. "That's the day Warde and I got married," she explained. "It's the first of a series of disasters I'm going to hang on that wall. The others will be Lincoln's assassination, a picture of Hitler, the *Titanic* going down and the *Hindenburg* in flames. Ah, ha . . . HA, HAA! You realize, of course, that I was so busy getting a divorce I didn't have time to open the wedding present. But I've figured out how to handle the problem of the monograms on my silver. Paste-on initials! Ah, ha, ha . . . HAA!"

Unhampered by matrimonial problems, Phyllis enjoyed her biggest financial year in 1966, when her TV series and night club earnings ballooned to slightly over a million dollars. It was also the year of her most momentous flop as a comedienne. From the beginning she had warned the producers of her series, *The Pruitts of Southampton,* that the character she portrayed in the show was all wrong.

She argued until she was purple in the face. "Are you out of your flaming brains?" she demanded. "Why make me a glamorous society type? Who needs that? It's as phony as a $12 bill and isn't going to work—not for me!"

The producers insisted that the role would be terrific because they would include dramatic action that would provide depth and pathos. "If you play it right, Phyllis," they said, "you'll be mixing laughs and tears the way Chaplin did. You'll be fantastic!"

"Oh, my God!" she wailed, holding her head. "You

said it. Yes! Any time people start CRYING at Diller that'll be fantastic! It will *never* happen!"

It didn't. The audiences watching her series didn't laugh very much either. The sponsors, meanwhile, wept floods. Midway through the season, the producers admitted they had made serious mistakes. They gave her greater control of the show and let her revise the Mrs. Pruitt characterization into a bedraggled, frantic housewife more like her real self. By then it was too late. The program sank in the ratings like a gangrenous whale. ABC mercifully killed it.

As a result of that whopping pay cut, Phyllis has since been forced to eke along on from $450,000 to $650,000 annually, income received from TV guest appearances, film work and night clubs. Now a prune-faced, sack-shaped woman in her fifties, she travels less than previously, trying to spend as much time as possible at home with her children.

She maintains cordial relationships with Warde Donovan, who co-stars with her occasionally during her Las Vegas and Los Angeles niterie engagements. Sherwood Diller however, remains an outcast. She hasn't seen him since their divorce.

3. HOLLYWOOD'S TWISTED GENIUS

The world's most dedicated enemy of the number 13 arrived in Buffalo, New York, to give a piano concert.

Oscar Levant—wit, hypochondriac, insomniac and genius—was delivered by taxi to the door of Buffalo's finest hotel. Waiting to greet him was its manager, an unfortunate gentleman not aware that Levant will have nothing to do with 13 in any shape or form. Levant is so superstitious that he will not even speak the dreaded word, referring to it darkly as "that number."

The hotel manager bowed low. In a flowery welcoming speech, he told Levant that the hotel was so honored and flattered by his presence that it had made special arrangements to give him the best suite in the house. This was no small accomplishment, since it was then the middle of World War II.

"We want your stay to be perfect, Mr. Levant," gushed the hotel manager. "There will be complete quiet. We've managed to get the piano you asked for, and it is now in your suite—rooms 1301, 1302 and 1303."

The hotel manager, his fawning assistant and several assembled bellhops were astounded by the change which came over their respected guest as soon as he heard the room numbers. One moment he was Oscar Jekyll, smiling and nodding as he listened to the hotel manager's buttery phrases. The next moment he was Oscar Hyde, his swarthy face twisted with torment, his racoon-like eyes protruding with fear.

"That number!" he cried. "That terrible number!"

The hotel manager recoiled as Levant clenched his fist and pounded the desk. His thick lips loosed a torrent of shouts which echoed through the large lobby. "You've spoiled my entire day! You've ruined my concert! I'll never be able to come to Buffalo again! Why did you do this to me?"

Levant's reaction was so bizarre that for a few moments the hotel manager and his aides thought he was staging a practical joke. But their attempt at laughter was erased as Levant—muttering like a victim under a witch doctor's spell—strode from the hotel. He spent the remainder of his Buffalo visit in the concert hall, where he slept nervously on a cot in his dressing room.

The self-styled "world's oldest child prodigy," fears the number 13 with such a child-like simplicity that one bad contact with it can affect him for days at a time. It doesn't matter how remote the contact. Once he hears that number he turns into a blob of quivering jelly.

One day Oscar Levant arrived in Oklahoma City for a concert. Traveling with him was Larry Fitzgerald, a patient, understanding assistant whose duties included keeping the temperamental pianist free of hexes. The day started out especially well. Levant had awakened in buoyant spirits after a few hours sleep in his compartment on the train. He liked the coffee in the dining car and made small jokes about passing scenery. He had no physical complaints that day—no pains in the head, chest or stomach.

Levant was still in an ebullient mood when they reached the hotel in Oklahoma City. He liked his suite. The tone of the piano was satisfactory. He put in four and a half solid hours of practice during the afternoon, playing with gusto and expression. Fitzgerald began to relax, telling himself that everything was really going nicely and it would be an outstanding concert.

Thirty minutes before show time, a woman from the local music-lovers' committee arrived to drive Levant to the auditorium. As they were cruising along, Levant noticed a large neon sign—JULIUS OULP, INSURANCE. Strange names are one of Levant's diversions. He once composed a lengthy polka simply so it could be titled *A Polka for Oscar Homolka.*

"Julius Oulp," murmured Levant over and over. "What a beautiful name. Such rhythm. Such distinction." Chuckling he turned to the woman. "I suppose Julius Oulp is coming to the concert tonight?"

"Oh, my yes," she replied. "He's got four seats in the thirteenth row."

Thirteenth! Levant covered his face with his hands. "I'm ruined!" he cried. "Why did Julius Oulp do this to me?"

The concert was not a great success. Levant played in a

protective crouch over the keyboard, looking as if he expected the stage to collapse or a bolt of lightning to strike him from above.

The number 13 is only one of numerous hexes which grip the mind of Oscar Levant, one of the most troubled, most tormented and most unpredictable talents ever born in this country. He is afraid of so many things even his closest friends can't keep track of them because new ones are always being added. When last tabulated, his taboos included the following, all of which he considers unlucky: hats, flowers, hummingbirds and sunshine. (Like Dracula he refuses to go outside of his Beverly Hills mansion in the daytime.)

The word "lucky" must not be used in his presence because he feels it is a reversible jinx which can bring only bad luck. If he is traveling with somebody, he always wants them to go first into elevators, cabs, trains, hotel lobbies and restaurants. Born in Pittsburgh, he regards the town as unlucky and flies into a rage if anyone mentions it even casually in a conversation. The word "death" agitates him even further. Nor can he abide mention of anything connected with death, such as coffins, wills, funerals, inheritances and cemeteries.

Now near sixty and quite ill, he lives in near-seclusion, a jittery individual who refuses to give concerts, compose, act in movies or in any way display the talents which have made him a legend. During the last two years he has ventured into public view a few times on Jack Paar's TV show, and these have been agonizing appearances during which he has trembled and stuttered like a man about to suffer a fatal heart attack or lose his head by guillotine.

Despite his obvious deterioration and constant references—only half in jest—to his stays in mental hospitals, Levant has provided some moments of rare entertainment on the Paar show. Flashes of the old Levant wit have shown through—charming, exasperating, rude and brilliant. Even though it was plain that Paar was carefully cueing each witticism from a prepared list, and then coaxing Levant to respond, the effects were noteworthy because they showed that Levant—troubled as he is—is still one of the world's funniest humans.

Among his cynical, stuttering cracks were these, some of which were cut from the show by TV censors:

Discussing his clothes: "I apologize for not being formally attired for tonight's show. My usual dress is black tie and straitjacket."

Concerning Zsa Zsa Gabor: "She has discovered the secret of perpetual middle age. She not only worships at the golden calf but insists on barbecuing it for lunch."

Cigarettes: "When the surgeon general made his dreary announcement on TV, he was so nervous they had to take the cigarette out of his clenched fist."

David Susskind: "He's still mad at me because I said all his prose is dipped in chicken fat."

Mental Illness: "When you suffer from deep depression you cannot make a decision. I just had a deep apathy and then relapsed into deep depression. Gee, how I longed for those deep apathy days."

Dinah Shore: "I can't stand seeing her on account of my diabetes."

Some of those quips seem contrived compared to off-the-cuff remarks Levant made during the years when he was a sought-after concert artist noted for his hostile moods and bitter impoliteness. During the Forties his income was in the $120,000 to $200,000 per year range, and he was such a successful egomaniac that playwright S. N. Behrman summed him up with these words: "If Oscar weren't real, you couldn't believe him."

Levant agreed, thoroughly. "I'm a controversial figure," he admitted. "My friends either dislike me or hate me."

His rudeness helped his lucrative career in the movies, where in such films as *Humoresque* and *American in Paris* he merely played his impudent, sarcastic self. After he appeared in *Rhythm on the River* with Mary Martin, she told him delightedly: "I just saw the first showing of our movie and you were charming."

"Charming?" said Levant, blinking his heavily lidded eyes. "Then I'm through in pictures."

Once a friend told him: "Oscar, you sound happy."

"I'm not myself today," he replied.

When Al Jolson greeted him with, "Oscar, I've been hearing a lot of nice things about you," Levant scowled and said: "They're all lies!"

Levant's first wife, a dancer named Barbara Smith, divorced him after three months. Asked what caused the breakup, he explained airily: "Incompatibility. And, besides, I had a definite feeling that she loathed me."

Many years afterward, discussing his first wife on TV, Levant described her as an absolutely beautiful girl and said they had remained good friends after their divorce. Recalling that she later married Arthur Loew Sr., of the movie theater chain family, he grinned impishly as he told how he phoned their suite at 2 A.M. on their wedding night.

"I asked for Mrs. Loew," he smirked, "and when she answered I said, 'What's playing at Loew's State and what time does the feature go on?' "

Levant's twisted sense of humor is a basic part of his personality, which first showed signs of abnormal strain during his childhood. He came from a secure and loving Pittsburgh family. None of his three brothers—Oscar was the youngest—showed any signs of neurosis. People who know him well say that Oscar was always a nervous, spoiled little boy who cried a lot and demanded his own way in everything. This could have been caused, they feel, because he had arrived many years after his brothers and was overprotected by his doting mother.

Oscar's father, Max, ran a hole-in-the-wall watch repair shop at 1420 Fifth Avenue, where the family had living quarters in the rear. Intensely interested in music, Max encouraged his sons to study it from the time they were small. Oscar, born December 27, 1906, was the prodigy. By the time he was 10 he had already convinced his teacher that he would some day be a great artist. He could learn a long and complicated piano piece after merely hearing it twice.

When Oscar was 16 and in his junior year at Forbes High School, his father died and the family was left without funds. Oscar quit school and went to New York to pursue a career in music. He wanted to be another Rachmaninoff. To support himself and pay for lessons with classical teachers like Sigismund Stojowski, a colleague of Paderewski, Levant got a job playing piano in a ballet school where little girls practiced arabesques and entrechats. "My work was child's play," he once remarked.

Despite his obvious technical ability and the great warmth of his piano style, Levant went nowhere in the concert field. He was an unknown and nobody wanted him. Certain he was better than such concert stars as Rubinstein and Horowitz, he burned with frustration and bitterness. He was reduced to taking jobs with small dance bands that played music he detested in minor supper clubs and hotels. He tried to be a Tin Pan Alley composer to earn enough to support his serious music, and churned out 40 pop tunes, including one hit, *Lady, Play Your Mandolin*. But the financial returns were not great enough to offset the suffering of his musical ego, which yearned for the concert stage.

In his mid-twenties, Levant became a close friend of George Gershwin. He was so impressed with Gershwin's talent and work that he nearly destroyed his own personality and ability as he tried to imitate the composer. For over six years he played only Gershwin music, practiced with Gershwin, was Gershwin's companion on trips, ate with Gershwin and agonized with Gershwin through the composition of such work as *Porgy and Bess*. He tempered his worship with occasional insults. Once he asked: "Tell me something, George. If you had it to do all over again, would you fall in love with yourself?"

When Gershwin died, Levant, grief-stricken, went into a period of inactivity during which he refused to work, establishing a parasitic existence in the homes of such friends as playwright George S. Kaufman and lyricist Ira Gershwin, George's brother. Describing that debt-ridden era of his life, Levant once cracked: "I was a penthouse beachcomber. Everything I touched turned to pennies."

One evening, feeling sorry for himself, he told Ira Gershwin how unhappy he was, how he suffered each time he had to borrow money from a friend, how he loathed his inability to hold a steady job.

"Good Lord," interrupted Gershwin, "how long can you go on like this, Oscar?"

"Another 10 years," retorted Levant.

While walking on a Manhattan avenue one warm day in August, 1938, Levant met Dan Golenpaul, a young radio producer who was aware that Oscar had achieved an informal fame in theatrical circles for his sardonic, cutting jibes. Golenpaul asked Levant if he would be interested in appearing on a new program he was planning called *Information Please*. Levant quickly accepted.

The job was his first steady work in years. He started at $100 a week but his acid quips were such a hit that eventually he received $500 per appearance. He became nationally famous for his fabulous memory. Innumerable times he identified symphonies and concertos with only a scrap of melody as a clue.

Levant grew temperamentally difficult to work with as his fame increased. After being on the show six years, he became involved in a series of bitter diputes with Golenpaul. One night Lefty Gomez, the Yankee pitcher, was a guest on the show. Levant, a devoted baseball fan who idolized Gomez, felt that Golenpaul's remarks had been disrespectful to the hurler.

After the show he halted Golenpaul in the hall outside the studio. "You practically called Gomez a bum," said Levant hotly.

"I did not," replied Golenpaul.

"Well, you certainly slighted him," rasped Levant.

"I certainly did not," said Golenpaul.

As Golenpaul turned away abruptly, Levant became so incensed he seized him by the shoulder and spun him around. Then—to Golenpaul's amazement—Oscar punched him in the nose.

It was a wild punch thrown by a flabby, 5-foot, 10-inch, 155-pound man singularly lacking in fistic prowess. It was not hard enough to draw blood, but it rocked Golenpaul's head back and stung enough to bring tears to his eyes.

Golenpaul fired Levant from the show. Levant didn't care because, by then, his publicity from *Information Please* had created a demand for his concert performances. This peculiar turnabout in his fortunes delighted Oscar. For years concert impressarios had ignored him. And now —long after he'd given up hope of becoming a concert star—they begged him to go on tour.

He created musical history. His undeniable piano wizardry and surly, egocentric behavior combined to make him one of the hottest attractions in the classical field. He outdrew all rival pianists, earning as much as $3,000 and $4,000 per concert. He made over 120 recordings for Columbia Records and his sales were extraordinary in the long-haired field. His recordings of Debussy, Chopin, Gershwin, Tschaikovsky and Grieg regularly sold between 500,000 and 750,000 copies annually. His brilliant interpretation of Gershwin's *Rhapsody in Blue* became Columbia's all-time best-selling classical disc.

After listening to Levant play, writer Maurice Zolotow analyzed him with the following comment: "All the tenderness and gentleness that Levant is unable to express in his living come out when you hear him do a Chopin nocturne or perform an emotional passage in the Tschaikovsky concerto."

Levant added to his income with choice movie roles written expressly for him. He was paid as much as $1,000 per sneer, often idling about a set for a week or more waiting for his call to perform. Then he would stroll before the cameras, twist his thick lips sardonically, insult somebody and return to his dressing room for a few more days of wise-cracking idleness. He fitted so perfectly into Hollywood's wacky atmosphere that he soon became a citizen, purchasing a 10-room mansion in Beverly Hills. There he led an elegant, occasionally turbulent existence with his second wife, a redheaded ex-actress named June Gale, and their three small daughters.

His reputation as a wit continued to grow with perceptive quips which were quoted and requoted at Hollywood parties, including:

"There is a thin line between genuis and insanity. I have erased that line."

"Suicide is the longest sleeping pill I know of."

"An atheist is a person with no invisible means of support."

Levant's career boomed until 1952. Then disaster struck in the form of a heart attack. He had always been a devoted hypochondriac, taking countless pills for a variety of imaginary aches and miseries. Although he made an excellent physical recovery from the heart attack, he suffered constantly from the fear that he would have another, with fatal results. For years he visited his Beverly Hills' psychiatrist once a week. Then he increased his visits to three a week, but they didn't help. He became moody, deeply depressed and used so many sleeping pills that eventually his system became nearly immune to them. All night long he prowled nervously about his mansion waiting for drowsiness that never came.

For four years he stayed out of the limelight, giving no concerts, refusing all radio, TV and film offers. Only once during that period did he pop back into the public eye, creating embarrassing headlines when it was reported erroneously that he had attempted suicide. The incident began one morning in February, 1954, when Levant awoke in a black mood and quarreled with June. He went back to bed, dozed until noon and then began looking around again for his wife. Unable to find her, he decided she was at her mother's house.

He tried repeatedly to phone her mother's home, but the line was busy. When he asked an operator for assistance, she suggested that he wait half an hour and then try again.

"Half an hour?" said Levant. "In half an hour I'll be dead."

He explained later that he was merely joking, but admitted he might have put more self-pity into his words than he intended. At any rate, the operator thought he was serious and about to kill himself. Quickly she set the phone company's emergency procedures into action. While she continued to speak soothingly to Levant, other operators traced his phone and notified police.

The operator's words were so comforting that Levant went to sleep. When two police officers burst into his bedroom a few minutes later, they found him lying on his bed, his eyes closed, still holding the phone to his ear. One of the officers noticed a bottle of paraldehyde on the nightstand, sniffed Oscar's breath and exclaimed: "My God, he's taken poison!"

Now the farce swung into high gear like a scene in a poorly directed TV medical drama. The officers slapped Levant's cheeks to keep him awake. Groggily he protested that he was all right but the officers ignored his explanations. They trundled him off to an emergency hospital where Levant suffered the rude experience of having his stomach pumped out.

Newscasters broke into Los Angeles radio broadcasts with bulletins that Oscar Levant had attempted suicide. Later, as the full story came out, it was explained that the episode had been a series of comical misunderstandings.

"Of course I took the paraldehyde!" snapped Oscar angrily. "It's a sedative from my doctor. I've been taking it ever since my heart attack. All I took was my usual dose. As for that operator, I thought she was being very kind and sweet—but all she really did was spoil my sleep. I am very unhappy about all this. It was certainly no fun being routed out of bed by those policemen. I am not a very pretty person at best and I need all the beauty rest I can get."

During the next two years Levant hid in seclusion, taking an acid delight in snubbing promoters who tried to get him to return to the concert stage or to appear in films or TV. But in the spring of 1956 he changed his mind and agreed to appear on a local panel show over a Hollywood television station. His pungent, corrosive comments made the program a hit for 18 weeks. At the height of its popularity Levant quit in disgust when the station's management tried to censor his anti-Nixon barbs.

Once more he went into seclusion, drawing a shroud of secrecy about his personal life. His refusal to permit interviews with the press sent rumors flying about his mental health. He was said to be so disturbed that he had been a patient in one or more sanitariums where he received intensive psychiatric care and shock treatment.

In March of 1958 Levant returned in triumph to television with his own show on one of Los Angeles' smaller stations, Channel 13. He dazzled the viewers with his daring. His quips were the work of the vitriolic Levant of old—but now a new ingredient had been added: sickness. Levant, often unshaven and bleary-eyed while on screen, was obviously an ill man. He wore unpressed suits. His hands trembled. He gasped for breath and clutched his chest. His wife June appeared with him on the show and it was apparent that she was there as a controlling factor—to soothe his rages, ease him away from too-controversial subjects and perhaps to pick him up if he should faint.

During his broadcast Levant reveled in his various illnesses, imagined and real. He delighted his audiences with revealing quips about his health, mental as well as physical. Once he introduced himself by saying: "This is Oscar Levant speaking. It's an identification I have to make because I suffer from amnesia." He snapped at his guest stars, who ranged from actors and producers to intellectuals like Aldous Huxley and Christopher Isherwood. He snarled at the cameras, referred to the 20 members of his tiny studio audience as "out-patients," blinked his eyes incessantly and squirmed and twitched while playing the piano.

"I am," he declared with utmost sinceserity, "the study of a man in chaos searching for frenzy."

Asked why he continually clutched his chest while on camera, he replied: "If I didn't hold it, my heart would fall out."

After eight weeks his show was such a success that the big TV networks began angling for Oscar's talents. In an interview with reporters for *Time* and *Newsweek*, he made starting revelations about his mental health, confirming the reports that he had been in and out of an assortment of hospitals and sanitariums during the previous six years. He admitted that after his heart attack in 1952 he had tried recuperating with liquor and had deteriorated rapidly.

"But I'm off the bottle now," he added. "I don't drink liquor. I don't like it. It makes me feel good."

He also admitted that he had been on drugs, but did not go into detail as to what kind. He said this occured after he was temporarily kicked out of the Musicians Union for missing a concert.

"I first went on drugs," he said, "because I was deeply hurt. I had always been a good union man. After that I lived on drugs for a time. My withdrawal was a rejection of life and myself. I loathed my musical past. I made up my mind never to play the piano again. What I rejected most was the sensational aspect of my musical life."

Levant paid tribute to his wife, saying that she wisely refrained from urging him to play the piano during his months of depression.

"That's the whole secret of how I returned to my music," he explained. "My wonderful wife tricked me. She took me to Mt. Sinai Hospital but didn't tell me I would be in a closed psychiatric unit. I was miserable. My musical life returned there weeks later. There was a piano in the day room and people playing it drove me mad. One night I was lying down and I heard someone playing a waltz by Fritz Kreisler from *Apple Blossoms*. It was a charming, banal piece.

"I sat at the piano. My hands trembled. I played eight bars of the waltz. The sound was terrible. A patient asked if I would play the *Appassionata* by Beethoven. I had lost all my humility. I played two pages of it for her. During the days after that I played badly. I was relaxing."

Levant concluded the interview by saying perspectively: "I learned a great deal in the hospital. It takes a sick man to know some of the secrets of life."

Shortly after this he showed how far he had climbed from the depths by playing the piano at the opening of the Los Angeles Music Festival. He rattled off Shostakovich's *Piano Concerto No. 2* with so much stylish fire that one critic referred to him as "very nearly the Levant of old."

Meanwhile, Oscar continued his unpredictable, controversial antics on TV, sometimes carrying his insults to amazing extremes. One night the guest star was talkative Art Aragon, a former boxer. Levant started to introduce him, changed his mind and began a charming, polite discourse on the life and times of Debussy. While Aragon fumed, Levant played Debussy.

Levant leaned one elbow against the piano and propped his head with his hand. He sighed. "Playing a piece like that," he said, "makes a man very tired." For a minute he said nothing. Then he closed his eyes.

There was dead silence in the studio as the audience waited in suspense to see what Oscar would do next. He did nothing. For four extremely long minutes the entire show consisted of Levant apparently sleeping at the piano.

A feminine hand appeared in one corner of the screen, hovered, then touched him lightly on the shoulder. "Dear," said the voice of his wife. "Your guest, Art Aragon, is here. He's waiting."

Without opening his eyes, Levant snarled: "Wake me up when he leaves."

Aragon left the studio in a huff.

Inevitably Levant's rude ways and balky temperament had explosive consequences. One night Channel 13 brought in a beauty queen to do a Philco commercial in place of Mrs. Levant, who had been ill for a few days. Oscar had expected to do the commercial himself. He told the viewers that the station's actions humiliated him from "id to toe." He was surly toward the embarrassed young beauty queen and hustled her off-camera before she could make her sales pitch.

While the show was still on the air, Levant received notice that Philco was quitting as one of his sponsors. Outraged, Oscar launched into a shocking assault on Philco, urging his audience not to buy Philco until the company returned to the program. "Let's fight the power game with the power game!" he cried. "I don't need Philco! Who needs Philco?"

The station immediately suspended him. This action produced the greatest deluge of phone calls and mail in Channel 13's history. "We've never had such literate and highly abusive calls before," admitted one harried official. Telegrams poured in, including one from architect Frank Lloyd Wright, himself an iconoclast of some distinction. "Have just canceled order for my 15th Philco," he wired. "I don't need anybody either. Oscar, you are a good deed in a naughty world."

Snorted Levant: "My leaving Channel 13 is a catastrophe for the community. The channel will now revert to its cloacal status with such intellectual pursuits as hypnotism and bingo."

Oscar won his point. Caving in under the weight of

the complaints, Channel 13 reinstated him. Philco also surrendered and returned as a sponsor. Commented Oscar shrewdly: "I thrive on humiliation. That's why I'm willing to return to Channel 13. I couldn't get that much humiliation anywhere else."

Two days later he sprang another surprise. He announced that he was switching his show to Channel 9, which only a few days previously he had scathingly called "the Skid Row channel." For 10 days Levant was his happy, rude, sarcastic self on the show and then, abruptly, his personal life blew as high as a Titan rocket. Police were called to Levant's mansion to settle a violent squabble between Oscar and June.

"She tried to kill me!" Levant screamed to the investigating officers. "She tried to stab me with a pair of scissors!"

He fled to the home of friends, where he continued to rant, declaring: "I'm never going back to her. I wouldn't go back to that house with an armed guard!"

Mrs. Levant presented a different version of the battle to reporters. "I just threw a shoe at him," she said. "It missed—and that was all there was to it. It did not have the scissors anywhere near him. I don't know why Oscar wants this kind of publicity. Doesn't he have any regard for our three lovely daughters?"

When told of his wife's comments, Oscar replied bitterly: "She tells the children everything, especially while she's choking me. Why doesn't she think of shielding them then?" After a pause he added generously: "She's one of the most wonderful women in the world and should do very well without me."

A few days later the Levants patched things up and Oscar returned quietly home. His TV appearances continued for another month, but he was increasingly nervous, too easily irritated and showed signs of being near physical collapse. It was clear that he wouldn't be able to go on much longer. In August, Channel 9 reluctantly canceled his show, announcing that Levant—pleading extreme fatigue—had requested an indefinitive leave of absence.

That was the end of Oscar's regular public appearances. Since then he has spent half a dozen years in semi-retirement, coming out of his shell only for his nerve-wracking, shuddering exhibitions with Jack Paar. More than once he has thanked Paar for "taking me out of the darkness of the sick room," implying that his present life consists of prolonged, boring stays in his bedroom broken only by dreary visits to psychiatrists and hospitals.

While gathering material for this article, I became intensely curious about Levant's current existence, wondering how he passed the long days and sleepless nights. Hoping to obtain an interview with him, I phoned his Beverly Hills home one afternoon. Mrs. Levant told me Oscar was out and wouldn't return for several hours. She said she would ask him about the interview when he returned, saying she doubted that he would agree "because he hasn't permitted an interview for years."

I phoned back in the early evening. Mrs. Levant said she was sorry, but Oscar had flatly refused to be interviewed either in person or on the phone. "He's not feeling well," she said, adding pleasantly that she would try to supply me with some of the information about him that I needed: We then had a lengthy conversation during which she revealed the following details of his daily routine:

He rarely goes to bed before 2 A.M. He sleeps very little, getting no help from sleeping pills, which he says are "like marriage—after a while they don't work." He stays in bed until past noon, dozing and reading sporadically. He chainsmokes cigarettes and drinks from three to six cups of coffee a day. He used to drink 16 to 20 cups daily, but a painful stomach ulcer has forced him to cut down.

He has no financial problems, receiving substantial royalties from the sales of his records, which in recent years have been reissued in stereo. Mrs. Levant and their three daughters, Marcia, Lorna, and Amanda, occasionally coax him to play the piano but he refuses. He has no hobbies. He spends his time restlessly reading newspapers, magazines or books and fiddling with the TV dial, angrily protesting the triteness and banality of the few programs he is willing to watch.

"When was the last time he played the piano?" I asked.

"I can't remember," Mrs. Levant said. "It's been so long. I think it was on one of the Paar shows. I'm very sad about his reluctance to play. But, of course, he—"

She was interrupted by a man's voice which abruptly came on the line. It was Oscar himself, his voice raspy, nervous and high-pitched. I realized he had been secretly using an extension phone to listen in on the conversation between his wife and myself.

"Who are you?" he demanded.

He scarcely listened to my reply.

"I know what you're going to do," he said quickly and resentfully. "You're going to steal my old gags and reprint them, aren't you? And you'll be paid money for them, won't you?"

I declared that I intended to quote some of his quips, but that I didn't consider this stealing since they would be properly credited to him.

His reply was a wrathful snort. Not wishing to make him any angrier, because he might hang up on me, I switched the subject, asking if he had any writing or composing plans.

"No," he said. "I've been sick and haven't been doing anything. I haven't composed for over 20 years."

"Do you write letters?" I asked. "Do you think about writing your autobiography?"

He sighed as if under a great strain. "I'll let my wife answer. I'm not used to talking to people." He paused and then added very politely and apologetically: "You'll have to forgive me."

Mrs. Levant came back on the line. I repeated my question about his autobiography, saying that I'd heard he'd been planning a new version for several years.

"It's still in the planning stage," she said. "He hasn't been doing any writing."

Mrs. Levant and I continued to chat for several more minutes. While discussing their three daughters, she mentioned that Oscar lets her make most of the decisions regarding the girls' training and upbringing.

"What about their boy friends?" I asked. "Is he concerned about what kind of young men they meet?"

"Yes," she replied, "but he lets the girls choose for themselves. If he has any objections, he keeps them to himself."

"Do the girls like their father's late hours?" I asked. "Do they stay up past midnight the way he does?"

"Not on school nights," she said. "But now that they're older, they rather like the late hours too."

Suddenly Oscar cut in again. He sounded extremely agitated, his voice crackling with hostility and suspicion.

"That's enough!" he shouted. "I resent this intrusion!"

"I'm not trying to intrude," I replied.

"But you are!" he cried. "You're asking secret things about me. And I don't like it!"

His wife tried to soothe him, saying she thought my questions were reasonable and proper.

"But they're not!" he shouted, his voice ringing in my ear. "They are most private questions!"

For a moment there was silence on the line. Then Mrs. Levant asked: "Oscar? Hello?"

He did not reply.

"I don't think he's there," she said. "I do hope you'll excuse me, but I think we've talked enough."

She hung up.

Despite its abrupt ending, it had been a productive interview, confirming that Levant, withdrawn from the outside world, lives in a state of continual jitter, his brilliant mind handicapped by a neurotic pattern of anxiety, torment and mistrust of others.

I regretted that in my brief conversation with him I had not been privileged to meet the other side of his mind—the waspish wit, the sensitive, perceptive reasoning which have made him one of the great intellects of his day.

Pondering the enigma of Oscar Levant, I recalled that he had once defined himself with a perception far more penetrating than any appraisals offered by his intellectual contemporaries. Shortly after his turbulent misadventures on TV in 1958, when he sulphurously scorched every target in sight, including sponsors, guest artists and politicians, he offered this candid view of himself:

"In some situations I was difficult, in odd moments impossible, in rare moments loathsome, but, at my best, unapproachably great."

4. UP FROM REFORM SCHOOL

When Phil Silvers strode on stage, he seemed his usual, supercharged self. Noisy as a string of firecrackers, frenzied as an opera star with laryngitis, he exuded enough self-confidence for a dozen comics.

But, unknown to him or the Broadway audience, a frightening medical reaction was about to strike his spot-lighted figure, to attack him without warning.

Silvers had been building up to it for many weeks. He was such a success in *Top Banana* that he thought he could do no wrong. The Broadway show wasn't the great-est: It had no terrific songs, no remarkable scenery, but it had laughs, hundreds of them, mostly wisecracks by Silvers.

Because of those laughs, Silvers had fallen into a familiar celebrity trap. The reviews, accolades about his performance, went to his head. He began to believe there was no talent quite like his anywhere else in the world. His head, bald as a balloon, swelled beyond any normal hat size. He thought he was Super Comic, a marvel with unlimited mental and physical prowess.

When he finished the show one Thursday, around 11:30 P.M., Silvers felt so good he decided he didn't need any sleep that night. He walked over to a hotel room near Times Square where he knew a perpetual poker game was conducted by half a dozen actors, press agents and Broadway sharpies.

"Gladda see ya, Phil," said the others, grinning at him through dense blue cigar and cigarette smoke. "How was the show tonight?"

"I must be modest," declared Silvers. "I was merely sensational. Who's dealing?"

It was an intense game, played by experts who con-centrated on every card despite the continual banter. At six o'clock the next morning, Silvers was $250 ahead.

But at noon his luck went sour and stayed that way. At two in the afternoon—after playing for nearly 15 hours straight—he was 450 clams in the hole and decided to call it quits.

Bleary-eyed and unshaven, he stumbled to his hotel suite for a nap of a few hours. Awakening shortly before show time, he cleaned up, dressed and hopped a cab. He was hungry, having had nothing to eat since the night before, but there wasn't time for more than a pineapple milkshake, grabbed on the run at a drugstore around the corner from the theater.

He'd gulped half the milkshake before he realized it was rancid. When he reached the theater, his stomach felt like a ball of hot grease. When he made his first stage entrance, wearing a T-shirt with a sheet draped around his middle, his body seemed to be aflame from head to toe.

Other members of the cast looked at Silvers strangely, wondering what was wrong with him. And at that moment terror struck the comic . . .

Silvers looked down and saw his heart jumping under the T-shirt like a fish out of water. Certain he was suffering a heart attack, he panicked.

"I don't wanna die on stage!" he thought. "Why shock all these people?"

He staggered to the wings and collapsed. While an understudy finished the show, Silvers was examined by a physician in his dressing room. He was white as an egg-shell and shaking.

"Doc," he pleaded, "tell me the truth! How much time have I got?"

"Mr. Silvers," replied the doctor, "I think you're going to be all right. But you're going to need all the rest you can get. Six weeks at least, without working. Maybe more."

When they heard the bad news, the show's producers knew that if Phil were out of the cast for even one week, it would mean the end of *Top Banana*. It was strictly a one-man production, based on Silvers' ability to milk his lines for extra laughs.

A thorough physical exam the next day revealed that Silvers' heart action was satisfactory. The doctor reluctantly agreed to let him return to work.

On his first night back on the stage, Silvers panicked again—with reason. His breath was short. His heart pounded. He felt certain, despite the doctor's findings, that he was going to die before the shocked eyes of hundreds in the audience.

Night after night the terror continued. Night after night Silvers wanted to quit, but he never walked off the stage again.

Telling me about his ordeal during a recent interview, Silvers was a bundle of hyperthyroid nerves as we lunched in a rear booth at the Brown Derby in Beverly Hills. He gestured repeatedly and quickly with his hands, his plumpish face perspired copiously although the room was air-conditioned, and he seemed to relive in sharp detail every moment of the panic he suffered on that New York stage back in 1952.

"Yeah, I boobooed," he said. "I thought I was the greatest, one of God's elite. And I paid for it. Through here." He pointed to his pink, shiny snout. "People don't understand the special kind of hell a comic goes through. They think it's all one big happy yukkety-yuk. But every night when I walked out on that stage, it was like being in the blitz, waiting for death to strike. I got through it by making a bet with myself that I could stay. And I did. But it used up everything I had."

During *Top Banana's* long run, Silvers developed chronic insomnia which kept him on the edge of physical exhaustion. After finishing his show each night, he would have a late supper, including a glass of warm milk which was supposed to induce sleep. It didn't work. He tried whiskey, but it didn't work either. Hour after hour through the long dark nights he lay in his hotel room, waiting frantically for sleep that wouldn't come, using up his last reserves of energy worrying about the heart attack that he knew would destroy him.

"I was a crazy hypochondriac," he said. "Every time my ticker speeded up, I thought to myself, *'This is it. Here it comes!'* When the show finally closed, I was a pitiful wreck. I crawled off by myself to die. I went to a hotel as far from New York as I could get, a quiet place for retired people out in the sticks at Ojai, California. I'd stay in my room and then go down to the dining room for each meal, alone, trying to look nonchalant, debonaire.

"A few days of that and I was so bored I was balmy. 'Schnook! I said. 'You've trapped yourself good this time.' I lit out of there and went to L.A. But by then I was beginning to be able to laugh at myself again, and that meant I had rounded the corner."

During our talk, Silvers revealed many of the characteristics which have given him his reputation of being the most frenzied star in show business. A nervous, bespectacled man, wearing a natty $250 suit, he was unable to sit still in the restaurant booth for more than a minute at a time. He bounced repeatedly to his feet to say "Hi, ya" and chat briefly with a steady stream of pals from the worlds of show biz and sports who came by to swap friendly insults.

Between visitors he talked freely about his bitter career failures as well as his successes, such as the Sergeant Bilko role which earned him a king's ransom on TV. When I steered the conversation around to his boyhood in Brownsville, the tough Jewish section of Brooklyn, he made no effort to conceal his juvenile expeditions into crime and violence. With a touch of pride, he told me that Brownsville, which Silvers pronounces Bronzville, was a vicious, rat-infested tenement slum from which many kids were never able to escape to better lives.

"It was a stinking place to raise a family. Really rotten." Silvers shook his head so hard his plump chins wobbled. "Bronzville was electric-chair country for sure. It was the home base of the gangsters who ran Murder, Inc. Half the kids from my neighborhood wound up in prison or on the hot squat at Sing Sing. In Bronzville, it was kill or be killed, steal or go hungry. When you're a kid, you have no choice. You go with the mob. If there's a fight, you fight. If there's stealing going on, you steal."

With a shrug, Phil admitted that he went on forays into Brownsville's pushcart section, stealing fruit, vegetables and roasted chestnuts from peddlers' wagons . . .

"There was nuthin' to it," he said. "The big kids would run up first and knock over a pushcart by bumping into it, spilling stuff into the street. Then us little kids would run in and start filling our pockets. I was lucky I never got caught. With a bad break here or there, I could have gone permanently into crime like many of the kids that I grew up with."

Silvers lived with his impoverished Russian immigrant parents, five brothers and two sisters jammed into a third-floor flat on Pennsylvania Avenue near Blake Avenue. He was the youngest child in the family. His father, a tinsmith, and his mother, a small workworn woman, were religious Jews who reared their children in an atmosphere of warm affection.

"It was that family love," said Silvers, "that kept me from turning into a punk."

Nevertheless young Phil admired the tough kids of Brownsville and tried to keep up with their hoodlum antics. His moment of greatest glory came at school one morning when—quite by accident—he was elevated to the ranks of hardened juvenile delinquents. It began when some toughs scuffled near Silvers on a crowded staircase. A student monitor who tried to restore order was slugged and knocked down the steps.

As the monitor bounced past him, Phil—quick with a quip even then—commented: "Hey, look, a human football!" His remark stirred laughter among the throng of watching boys.

When two teachers rushed up to stop the fight, they were told about Silvers' wisecrack and decided erroneously that he was involved in the slugging. He was seized by the arm and marched off to the principal's office. The principal, noted for dealing out harsh punishments, listened to the teachers' charges against the boy, glared at Phil and roared:

"What's the matter with punks like you? You think it's funny to hit someone and then make a wisecrack about it? Well, it's *not* funny—and I'm making an example out of you!"

Silvers was expelled on the spot and reassigned to P.S. 61, a reform school. He was given no chance to explain what had really happened on the stairs. He knew the identity of the boy who had struck the monitor but, following the code of his gang, refused to be a squealer. He gladly went off to reform school.

"Amoung the kids it was an honor to be sent to P.S. 61," he told me. "It was a distinguished badge of merit. After that I was one of the heroes on my block. I was pointed out as one of the real tough guys of Brownsville. I swaggered around like a young Dillinger or Capone."

Phil described P.S. 61 as a "come home" reform school whose young inmates were released each evening to the custody of their parents. For several weeks he managed to keep his mother and father from discovering where he was going each day. When his father found out, he raged at the only one of his six sons ever to wind up in that kind of trouble. After thrashing the boy with his leather belt, raising large red welts across his thighs, the elder Silvers vowed to move his family out of Brownsville as soon as possible.

Because of their poverty, the family was forced to remain another year. Phil spent half of the eighth grade at P.S. 61, thrown in with hardbitten kids who were already veteran thieves, pimps, pickpockets and muggers. One of these, an acne-scarred teen-ager, much taller and stronger than Silvers, insisted that Phil participate in a bakery shop burglary.

"His name was Maxie the Twist," said Silvers. "Nobody liked him because he was such a creep. He said he'd knock my brains out if I didn't go with him, so I went. It was just a little Jewish bakery with maybe a few bucks in the till. The first night we went the place was too lit up, with somebody working in the kitchen, so Maxie called it off. But he said we'd try again the next night. I couldn't sleep a wink, worrying about what might happen.

Silvers grimaced nervously, then smiled. "But it turned out OK. The cops came to P.S. 61 the next day and grabbed Maxie for picking pockets. He never came back. After that I kept my nose clean, which was no problem because by then I had other interests. I always had a good singing voice and I picked up small change warbling at social club events. By the time I was 13 I was the most prominent boy soprano in Bronzville."

Phil won prizes in every kiddie show for miles around and volunteered to sing to the audiences at the Supreme Movie House each evening, performing only when the film broke. He became a regular entertainer at numerous smokers and parties given by the racketeers and hoodlums of Brownsville who had first heard him sing for boxers training at Willie Beech's gymnasium.

Silvers was 14 years old when his big break came. Fantastically, he jumped from nowhere, which was Brownsville, to New York's Palace Theater, biggest of the vaudeville big time.

"I went to Coney Island one night with a bunch of kids," he explained, "and, of course, I was the life of the party, showing off and telling jokes down on the beach.

"When the kids asked me to sing, a crowd gathered on the boardwalk and listened. One of the men leaned over the railing and threw a card down to me. He hollered, 'Come and see me, son!' The name on the card was Gus

Edwards, and when I saw it I leaped about six feet into the air!"

Phil showed up early the next morning at the office of Edwards, whose "School Days" act had long been a Palace headliner. Edwards had given a start to countless youngsters, including Eddie Cantor, Georgie Jessel and Walter Winchell. Two weeks after his audition, Phil was accompanied to the contract-signing by his father, who found it difficult to believe that such astonishing good fortune could come to his family. Phil was given $40 a week (his father made only $27.50) and opened at the Palace.

His high, clear soprano was such a smash hit that Edwards signed him for a lengthy tour of the vaudeville circuit. Phil was one of the show's stars for a year, attending a special school for professional children when he was in New York and taking a correspondence course when the act was on the road.

"I remember the joy of it." Silvers said. "There's nothing else in the world like having a fine voice. It's an exalted feeling. But for me that feeling was too brief. I was hit by a terrible calamity. My voice changed. Just like that," He snapped his fingers. "In the middle of a song, it suddenly cracked."

Gus Edwards sent him back to his family to recuperate. For months Phil moped around the Silvers' home, which was now in Bensonhurst, a better-class Brooklyn suburb. Desperately he tried everything to restore his voice— special gargles, exercices of the vocal chords and surgery on his tonsils.

"Nothing helped," he said. "But in a year I sprouted from a pudgy kid built like a pudding into a six-footer weighing 200 pounds. It was crazy. The kids in our new neighborhood kept coming around, staring at me and wondering about what kind of magic oatmeal I ate."

Silvers, certain his professional career had been smothered in its infancy, was rescued by a top vaudevillian named Joe Morris, whose act needed a tall boy. Phil stayed with Morris and his partner Flo Campbell for five years, playing the Palace eight times in one year at a salary of $150 a week.

"I loved the pay," he said, scowling, "but I hated what I was doing. I was 21 years old, as big as a giraffe—and still wearing knee pants. I felt ridiculous. Also, I knew nothing about acting. I wasn't getting anywhere. So I quit."

For a while he played in an act with Herbie Faye and Mildred Harris, Charlie Chaplin's first wife. Then he made two-reel movie shorts and worked the borscht circuit. In 1934 he went into burlesque, working for most of the next four years in Minsky's Gaiety Theatre on Broadway. Times were bad in the theatre during those Depression years and top-ranking actors were willing to take any kind of work in order to survive. Silvers discovered that the cracked voice which had torpedoed his singing career was a golden godsend for a comedian.

The rough and tumble action at Minsky's developed his timing and self-confidence and he became one of the fastest-thinking, fastest-cracking comics in the business. But at times he was secretly ashamed of the things he had to do and say.

"You hear a lot of guff these days about burlesque," he said. "About what a great school it was for comics. But who do they think they're kidding? Guys went to burlesque to see the strippers take their clothes off. When the comedians were on, most of the audience would read newspapers. A comic had to be real dirty to get them to stop reading."

Silvers shrugged and glanced down at his half-empty coffee cup. "Let's face it," he went on. "I was just as dirty as the rest of those shnooks. But you know, even then, I was envious of the class. When I'd throw out a line that was particularly raw, I used to step up to the footlights and say, 'Just a little thing I picked up from the Theatre Guild.' I didn't know anything about the Theatre Guild, except that it was real classy, and the jerks out in the audience knew even less. But it made me feel better to mention it, so I did."

In 1938, when he was 27 years old, Silvers broke out of burlesque into the legitimate theater, thanks to the help of Hy Gardner, then a press agent. Gardner had long admired Silvers' work in burlesque. When he wrote some material for a musical called *Yokel Boy,* Gardner touted the producer into using Silvers in a secondary role. After the show opened in Boston, its star, Jack Pearl, thought it stank and angrily quit the cast. Silvers was promoted to Pearl's spot and promptly revamped the whole show, working in dozens of pages of his burlesque routines, cleaning up the gags so they would be acceptable to Broadway's more sophisticated audiences.

Yokel Boy was a great success, and it made Silvers a

celebrity. One night L. B. Mayer, head of Metro-Goldwyn-Mayer Studios, saw the show, and invited Silvers to work in Hollywood for $500 a week.

Rushing to California, he immediately banged head-long into apathy and disinterest. Silvers not only couldn't crash the movies, he couldn't even talk MGM into giving him a three-minute screen test! For six months he drew his $500-a-week salary without lifting a finger to earn it. He was such a nobody that he had to have a pass to go through the studio gates.

One morning his phone rang. He was summoned to the office of an MGM director who said: "Phil, we want to test you for a picture. We've tested several others and if you get the role it will be a feather in your cap."

"Give me a crack at it!" Silvers replied eagerly.

Phil took home four sheets of paper on which his lines were typed. Reading them, he was dismayed by the horribly pompous part he'd been given. He was supposed to portray a stuffy British clergyman in *Pride and Prejudice*. His stilted opening lines were: "My dear Dame Elizabeth, you can hardly doubt the purport of my discourse. Please forgive this outburst of passion. Your modesty does you no disservice."

The part was so wrong for him that at first Silvers thought it was a practical joke. But he couldn't be sure. If he'd been back in New York, he would have phoned some of his pals backstage and got the lowdown. But in Hollywood he had no such contacts, and like everyone else, he was in such awe of L. B. Mayer that he didn't dare question the great man.

Silvers decided the role was on the level. After carefully practicing his monstrous lines before a mirror, he arrived at MGM the following week letter perfect in the role. He began to grow nervous, however, during the four agonizing hours he spent being costumed and made up. Nothing went right. His black coat and white rector's collar just didn't go with his comic's face. The make-up man cursed as he fitted wig after wig to Silvers' bald noggin. No matter how hard he tried, Silvers wound up looking like a Halloween caricature instead of a dignified English pastor.

When Phil reached the sound stage, he found the director of the test in a tizzy because of mechanical snafus in the sound equipment. "Phil," he said, "We're late getting this thing started. We won't have much time to rehearse. The main thing is that I want you to be British in a very subtle way."

Silvers broke out in a sweat. On his first run through his lines, his Brooklyn accent came out like cannon balls dropping on a steel floor. He said "outboist of passion" and "does you no dissoivice." On his third try he got rid of the Brooklynese and the director ordered the cameras to start turning.

When the test film was run the next morning, Silvers felt ill. In his frenzied efforts to be subtly British, he practically had fire spouting from his nostrils. When he said "My dear Dame Elizabeth," he looked like Rudolph Valentino rolling his eyes at a sexy harem girl in *The Sheik*.

It wasn't until months later that Phil learned the test had been a deliberate plot to discredit him. Certain officials at MGM resented the fact that Silvers had been brought in by Mayer himself and had started out as a potential star instead of working his way up slowly through the proper channels.

In desperation, Silvers began to entertain as a non-salaried comic at Hollywood parties and benefits. He was so good that he obtained bookings at such top night spots as Ciro's and the Copa. Film producers and directors began catching his act. Convinced that Silvers was the hottest thing they'd seen in years, they called MGM and asked if he'd ever been tested. Shown the British clergyman film, they turned away with disgust, saying, "Hell, he's only funny at Ciro's."

Silvers didn't tumble to what was going on until Harry Kurnitz, a screenwriter with contacts in MGM's upper echelons, stopped him on the street one day and explained why he was getting the run-around. Phil rushed back to the studio, sprinkled a few bribes among certain minor employees and had the test film burned.

After that he obtained good-paying roles in a score of pictures, but none gave him artistic satisfaction. Again and again, he played the part of the hero's devoted pal who supplied inconsequential comedy relief. After three years of such muck, he was so nauseated he leaped enthusiastically at the chance to make a USO tour of the Mediterranean area in 1945 with Frank Sinatra.

When he returned to the United States, Silver was offered a top role in a Broadway musical, *High Button*

Shoes, he thumbed his nose cheerfully at Hollywood and flew to New York.

"They gave me a wonderfully fat role to start with." Silvers recalled, "and I made it even fatter."

After romping through 700 performances of *High Button Shoes,* Phil rested for a few months, spending his time on such valued bachelor activities as dating pretty girls, betting on horses and cheering on his favorite baseball team, the Yankees. Then he signed for his third and most successful musical comedy, *Top Banana,* which established him firmly as a star. The show was a spoof based on the brash, overbearing personality of Milton Berle, then known as "Mr. Television."

While the show was in rehearsal, Silvers played golf one week end with Berle, who kept asking questions in an effort to learn what *Top Banana* was about. Silvers was afraid to tell him, certain that Berle would fly into a rage and file suit to halt the production. For most of the afternoon Silvers evasively changed the subject, but finally Berle pinned him down and demanded to know what kind of a character he was going to play.

"Well, Milton," explained Silvers with a weak smile, "he's a comedian who can't stand to have anyone else get a laugh. He carries a whistle on a cord around his neck and blows it whenever he wants the attention of his cast at rehearsal. And he's always being accused of stealing material from other comics."

When Phil finished, Berle looked him in the eye and said very seriously, "You know, Phil, I've *known* guys like that."

Instead of getting sore, Berle was delighted with the idea of a show based on him. He invested money in *Top Banana* and became Phil's most zealous booster. One night, when the audience wasn't receptive as usual, Phil met Berle at Lindy's after the show. "Brother," said Silvers disconsolately, "did they hate *you* tonight!"

When *Top Banana* closed, Phil suddenly found himself among the unemployed. He phoned an old friend, Hubbell Robinson, program manager for CBS, and said he was looking around for a TV series.

"Terrific," replied Robinson. "You couldn't have picked a better time because one of the best comedy writers in the business is available. Nat Hiken. Ever hear of him?"

"And how!" Silvers smiled. "When do we start?"

Silvers knew that Hiken had been a comedy writer for

many years for Milton Berle, Fred Allen and Martha Raye.

"I was sure we'd make a good team," Phil told me during our interview. "But the great thing was that Robinson left Hiken and me alone. He put us on good salaries and turned us loose. He never bugged us, never asked, 'What did you do today?' Nat and I went to ball games and discussed a lot of show ideas. We thought of 101 plots, but Nat kept coming back to his Bilko idea. I couldn't warm up to it for a long time. I could see nothing but phony drills and flimsy facetiousness, so we also worked up complete formats for over a dozen other shows."

Six weeks after their original meeting with Robinson, Silvers and Hiken returned to his office. Robinson sat patiently and listened to each of their ideas. Then he said, "Fellas, they're all damn good. But I definitely like the Army one best."

From that collaboration grew the character of Master Sergeant Ernie Bilko, the smartest wheeler-dealer in the U.S. Army. A great deal of effort was also devoted to delineating the characters of Bilko's barracks buffoons, such as Private Doberman, Corporal Barbella and the bumbling colonel, played by Paul Ford.

As brisk speculation hit the Broadway columns and advertising agencies as to who would sponsor his show, Phil called up his pal Jackie Gleason, who had just signed a multimillion dollar contract with CBS-TV.

"Hey, Jackie," said Phil, "how's about *you* sponsoring my show?"

Gleason thought a moment and answered, "Well, Phil, it sounds like a pretty good idea, but what would we say in the commercials?"

"Oh, that's simple," declared Silvers. "We'll just say, 'Jackie Gleason Is Good For You.' "

Silvers was a sensation, as Bilko. He won six Emmy awards and commanded a weekly salary that put him in the millionaire class. Several of the episodes, such as the time Bilko and his buddies succeeded in having a monkey inducted into the Army, have become classic comedy art.

For five years he worked at a frenzied pace, filming 142 Bilko episodes which left him exhausted and nervous. Finally the pressure hit Silvers so hard that he realized TV was devouring him.

"I've had it," he told his stunned sponsors one night

in 1959. "I'm turning in my chips. If don't, I'll be a babbling crazy man."

After lengthy negotiations, Silvers went into semi-retirement, doing only TV specials and night club shows which gave him more time for his burgeoning family. After a brief, unsuccessful marriage in 1945, he had been a bachelor for 11 years until he married Evelyn Patrick midway through his Bilko period. Evelyn was a tall, gorgeous, green-eyed brunette, half his age, who had done cosmetic commercials on TV. She led 45-year-old Silvers into a state of domestication which flabbergasted his pals on the bachelor circuit.

A year after their wedding, Evelyn and Phil had their first child, a daughter named Tracey. In rapid succession they had four more daughters, including twins in 1961.

But Silvers began to miss TV's mad gyrations. Moving his brood into a rented mansion in Beverly Hills, he signed for a new series he had planned in secret for several years. He had long dreamed of trying his hand at being a real "top banana," owning 100 per cent of his own show, doing all the producing and directing a la Gleason and Berle. "The New Phil Silvers Show" made its debut over CBS in 1963, featuring him in the Bilko-like role of Harry Grafton, a scheming factory foreman.

Once again, forgetting the lesson he'd learned the hard way back in 1952, Silvers developed a chronically swelled head. As "top banana," bossing everybody within sight, he lost his perspective, becoming firmly convinced that other people made mistakes but everything he did was 100 per cent right.

His daily routine became even more frenzied than during the wild years on the Bilko show. In addition to his own frazzled performances as the foreman, Silvers revolved in a non-stop pandemonium of story conferences, writing checks for every expenditure, okaying this, disapproving that, directing his co-actors and guest stars, lambasting their failures and then being forced to soothe their real and imagined hurts. Instead of relaxing at home after his 12-hour days on the set, Silvers continued at a mad pace, romping with his lively young daughters until he was purple in the face and wheezing like a leaky basketball.

It was too much for one man—and the series showed it. "The New Phil Silvers Show" was a turkey, largely because of Phil himself. The character he played seemed unbelievable, lacking the funny finesse-in-depth of Bilko. In addition, many of the stories were so badly contrived that their falseness was obvious to most viewers. After 38 episodes, CBS dropped the show. It was the first bitter failure Silvers had suffered in over a dozen years.

When I asked him how he reacted to the sniping of the critics, he replied: "I didn't deserve everything they said, but I had most of it coming to me. I made an awful lot of mistakes. Isn't there a cliche that covers it, something like 'you can't win 'em all'?"

As Phil Silvers talked, I couldn't help but contrast the self-assured millionaire comic of today with the different street urchin of 40 years ago. No, you can't win them all. But I thought of a story Silvers had related to me earlier, about a fight he had won. With his fists . . . but more important, with a realization why he was different from the hoodlums in his Brownsville gang . . .

The beef was over nothing. A kid from a gang named the Red Royals claimed a member of the rival Bronze gang had swiped some marbles at school.

Young Phil Silvers, fattest member of the Bronzes, got the urgent whispered message during lunch recess: "Four o'clock. The vacant lot. Be there!"

Silvers was 13 years old, ruddy cheeked and as round and soft as a baby hog. He didn't like gang fights. But he lived in teeming Brownsville, where a boy's heroes were prize fighters, thieves and murderers, and gang rumbles were a way of life.

A kid learned to swing his dukes there as soon as he could toddle. And if his gang scheduled a rumble, every member was sworn to be there and to engage viciously in the blood-letting.

Half a dozen strong, the invading Royals arrived on time and found the Bronzes waiting for them. There were no preliminaries, except for an exchange of spat-out oaths and obscenities. Then they went at it, each combatant picking out an opponent he though he could clobber. Within 10 seconds dark clouds of billowing dust hung over the vacant lot, kicked up by boys rolling in the dirt, banging away at one another with brass knucks or fists clenching short lengths of heavy lead pipe.

Young Phil found himself paired off with a slender hoodlum named Pete. Silvers had tangled with Pete previously and knew his favorite weapon was a fake gold ring set with a piece of jagged brown glass from a broken beer bottle. Pete wore it prominently on the first finger of his right hand.

The ring had lacerated Phil's forearm the month before. This time, seizing the initiative, he leaped upon Pete, knocked him flat and straddled his chest, his superior weight keeping the other boy pinned down. Pete twisted his body, the whites of his eyes showing wildly as he tried to escape, his ring slashing away at Silvers' leg but unable to pierce the thick brown corduroy of his trousers.

Silvers threw his plump fist against Pete's nose. Pete's proboscus exploded like a mushy tomato, spattering blood on Silvers and two other combatants wrestling nearby. Pete's face became such a mask of dripping red that it made Silvers' stomach turn over. Unable to gaze any longer at the mess he had created, he stumbled into a nearby alley. Doubled up behind a fence where the other boys couldn't see him and taunt him, he was violently ill, suffering and vomiting.

"That was the end of the battle for me," recalled Phil. "I could never stand the sight of blood, mine or anybody else's. I guess that's where I was different from the other kids of Brownsville. If they drew blood, then they really went to work on a kid, finishing him off. I just wasn't cut out for that kind of viciousness. So maybe that's why I escaped the electric chair."

5. SUFFERING COMIC

It was one of the quickest "demotions" on record. On the evening of March 14, 1944, Art Carney imitated General Eisenhower and other war leaders on a CBS radio news show, *Report to the Nation*. The next morning he was drafted.

A few days later, Private Arthur William Matthew Carney—a tall, slim, blue-eyed Irishman—began accelerated Army training at Camp Bland, Florida. During his 17 weeks of basic instruction he tried hard, but lacking aggressiveness and hostility, he just wasn't much of a soldier. Nevertheless, because of his age (he was 25, several years older than most of the men in his unit), he was offered a promotion to acting corporal.

Private Carney turned it down, telling his company commander: "I don't want to kid you or myself, sir, I'm just no leader. I'd just as soon spend this war as a dogface soldier in the ranks."

On the troopship going to France, Carney delighted the other dogfaces with his perfect imitations of President Roosevelt, Sir Winston Churchill and Adolf Hitler. He also demonstrated his ability to reproduce, with uncanny accuracy, the snarling Brooklyn voice of his top sergeant and the soft Alabama drawl of the private in the bunk above his. When the other soldiers insisted on knowing his civilian background, Carney admitted modestly that he had been a professional radio entertainer.

Pressed for more details, he revealed that he had been making $225 a week before being drafted. Since $50 weekly was a generous salary in those days, his Army pals were properly impressed, one commenting: "Good Lord, Art, what the hell are you doing in a fighting outfit? Why don't you volunteer for a soft billet in Special Services entertaining the troops?"

"Not me." shrugged Carney. "I'm not the volunteering type. I'll just keep on doing what they tell me."

"Yeah," was the reply. "And you'll wind up getting your butt shot off."

The remark was far more prophetic than Carney realized. Since the landings in June at Omaha and Utah beaches, Americans had been killed by the thousands as General Patton's Third Army broke through the German left flank at Avranches and began a determined drive for Paris. Fresh troops were desperately needed. Carney and other green replacements were jammed into every available truck and raced to the front.

On August 15—only five months after being drafted—Private Art Carney found himself in the middle of a German artillery barrage half a mile from the Normandy fighting lines. He and the other replacements jumped from the trucks and sprawled in thick, powdery dust at the side of the road.

"I was scared silly," Carney recalled later. "It was my first day in combat and I didn't know what the hell I was doing. I kept lying with my face down in that damn brown dust, sucking it up my nose and into my throat, coughing until I nearly strangled."

When the barrage lifted, Carney stopped to fill his canteen from a water tank trailer behind one of the trucks. He never heard the explosion of the artillery shell which cut him down.

One moment he was listening to the gurgle of water from the trailer spigot. The next, he found himself flat on his back, half a dozen yards away from the trailer. There was a tremendous ringing sound in his ears from the shell concussion, and his right leg felt numb.

Twisting his head, he looked at his leg and realized it was angled away from his body in a grotesque way. The angle was so peculiar that at first he thought the leg had been blown off. He tried to move his foot. It didn't budge. He tried again, forcing all his energy into the brown Army boot.

This time it moved slightly. *Thank God*, he thought, *it's still attached*. Turning his body gingerly, he saw a dark red stain spreading on the upper part of his trouser leg. It was blood, in large amounts, and he began shouting: "Medic! Medic!"

The barrage had wounded many men along the roadside and it was half an hour before a medic arrived to examine Carney's injury. It had been given a rough dressing by two of Carney's buddies who had been forced to leave him behind as orders had been shouted for the truck convoy to start moving again. By the time the medic showed up, the numbness had worn off and Carney's leg was burning with pain. It was the most excruciating agony he had ever known, so overwhelming that in frustration and helplessness he'd rubbed his fists against the ground, scraping his knuckles raw.

"Easy," said the medic, opening his kit. "Easy, fella."

He gave Carney an injection of morphine. It relieved his pain so magically that Carney wept tears of joy and lay still while the medic attended to his thigh. The wound wasn't large, but it was deep, and the flesh was burned black where the fiery shell fragment had entered. The medic applied a tourniquet, dusted the hole with sulpha powder, bandaged it and ticketed Carney for quick removal to a field hospital.

During the monumental confusion of the next few days, the German Seventh Army was chopped to pieces as the Allies won the decisive battle for northern France. U.S. Army tent hospitals overflowed with wounded and dying men. Communications became fouled up and the telegram dispatched to Carney's wife Jean, in Mt. Vernon, New York, listed him erroneously as "missing in action."

For almost three weeks Carney's family—including his mother, father and five older brothers—suffered in suspense, fearing the worst while waiting to learn his fate. Then on September 6 came great news. Three of Carney's letters arrived simultaneously. Written from a hospital in England, they were chipper and cheerful, revealing that he was recovering well from bone surgery on his right leg.

"They took out a chunk of German steel," he wrote. "Looks like I'll be back on my feet in no time."

Carney's words were overly optimistic. The shell fragment had shattered his thigh bone and he spent nine weary months in the hospital, undergoing repeated surgery. The doctors found it necessary to shorten his leg—removing three-quarters of an inch of bone in order to get the remainder to knit properly.

It was during his hospital ordeal that Art Carney made the moral decision destined to have a profound effect on his later life in show business. Looking at the wounded around him—the blinded, the maimed, men with missing legs, paraplegics who would never walk again—Carney realized he was one of the lucky ones. He would walk again, though with a limp, and he would probably have a chance to resume his interrupted show business career.

Discussing this some years later with friends, Carney admitted that there were times while working in night clubs before the war that he had done things for which he'd been ashamed.

"I'd been a heel now and then," he said. "I scooted around the way people do in showbiz. I dropped a few hints here and there with the boss and got him to demote or fire somebody who was lousing up the show. But while I was lying there in that British hospital I made up my mind that I'd never do it again. I realized that the Lord had spared me. I hadn't been killed, I hadn't been maimed, and I was so grateful that I made up mind that I'd never pull any mean tricks again. I promised myself that never again would I louse up the chances of some poor slob, no matter how he was messing up the show."

That promise to himself was to have unexpectedly disagreeable side effects in the Fifties and Sixties when Art Carney rose to national prominence as a TV comic and sensitive dramatic actor earning from $250,000 to $350,000 a year. His vow subjected him to extra pressure as he worked in the weekly madhouse of the Jackie Gleason Show, where his portrayal of Ed Norton, the dopey sewer worker, and other wacky characters earned him the reputation of being the nation's best second banana.

Off-camera, however, Carney was often as funny as a funeral. He was a worrier and a fumer, nervous and irritable. But he refused to criticize openly the way the show was being run or the performances of any of the other actors, no matter how bad they were or how they loused up his own lines. If something went wrong, Jackie Gleason would get rid of his tensions by storming and raging on the set, firing an actor or two, and having a few drinks to calm himself.

Carney, however, couldn't get rid of his tensions that way. He suffered in silence, damming his frustrations deep inside. He rarely drank on the set. But in the solitude of his home he drank plenty.

Eventually he became an alcoholic. And this added immeasurably to his inner torment as he battled to keep the booze from wrecking his career. Sometimes he would stay on the wagon for months, during which not one drop of whiskey touched his lips. Then there would be periods in which he drank heavily every day. But no matter how much he consumed he always managed to show up sober on the set, taking an intense pride in his record of never having ruined a performance by being drunk.

An example of Carney's battle for self-control occurred one day in New York's NBC studios while he was rehearsing with Hermione Gingold, the fiery, temperamental English comedienne. The show was *Small World, Isn't It?*, one of a series of high-budget spectaculars starring Carney. Miss Gingold created an uproar on the set by stopping the rehearsal with outbursts during which she assailed the quality of the script.

"These lines are horrid!" she wailed at one point. "I simply can't say them!"

Carney waited in patient silence while her lines were revised.

They continued the scene for a few minutes. Then Miss Gingold blew up again. This time she hurled her copy of the script on the floor. She jumped on it with both feet and then—in most unladylike fashion—spit on it several times.

If Gleason or any other top star had seen his show subjected to such abuse, he would have reacted with retaliatory emotional fireworks which would have set Miss Gingold back on her tail feathers. Carney, however, merely blushed and walked away. He went to the water fountain and had a long drink, doubtlessly wishing he had something stronger to settle his nerves.

David Susskind, the show's producer, walked over and said: "Art, she's ruining the rehearsal. You want me to fire her?"

"No," said Carney. "I wouldn't want that on my conscience. I've got enough to worry about as it is."

A similar incident occurred on another of Carney's spectaculars. During rehearsal, it was obvious to everyone that a certain secondary actor was woefully inadequate. Writer Alfred Bester spoke to Carney during a lull, saying: "My God, Art,——is terrible. Aren't you going to raise hell?"

Carney shook his head. "Not in front of the cast. I'll keep after the director. It that doesn't do any good, we'll switch him around to a smaller part."

"Wouldn't it be easier to fire him?" asked Bester.

"Sure," said Carney. Then he paused and made the same statement he had given Susskind. "But I wouldn't want that on my conscience."

"Have you ever fired anybody?" asked Bester.

"Nope."

"Ever wanted to?"

"Yep. Hundreds of times."

Carney's pale blue eyes suddenly flashed sparks, showing the depth of his feelings about inadequate actors.

"I hate 'em," he said. "And I hate this business that we get all the time from directors: 'Never mind if he's bad in rehearsal, wait for the show. He'll come up with a great performance . . .' "

Carney shook his head bitterly. "To hell with that jazz. We're all working like Trojans on these shows. And that means we've *all* got to produce."

Then Carney uttered one of the few criticisms he ever made about his former partner, Jackie Gleason. "Gleason used to do that," he said. "Sometimes he wouldn't go all-out. And he'd never rehearse. He'd wait until an hour before the show to learn his lines. He's a very quick study and has a fantastic memory. But that was unfair. Not to me and Audrey Meadows, our co-star. Audrey and me knew Jackie and *The Honeymooners* cold. We could always mug or ad lib our way out of tough spots. But some of the minor actors didn't work well without rehearsals. So Jackie was murder on them."

The millions who watched Carney's wacky performances on *The Honeymooners* made the mistake of assuming that Carney is also a comic and cutup in real life. Once in a while he is. He can wisecrack when in the mood and even attempt a practical joke. But basically he is a loner. He has a few close friends in show business, preferring the company of ordinary folk, such as his neighbors in the New York suburb of Bronxville, where he lives in a fairly large but not fancy home.

Carney likes to picture himself as just an ordinary guy who hit it lucky. But he is in no way ordinary. Seriously introverted, he has an astonishing lack of self-confidence for a man who has risen so high in an occupation where ego is everything. He is never satisfied with his performances. When he finishes a show, he worries about its imperfections instead of remembering the things which earned him the most applause.

At the end of a performance most actors or comics are emotionally supercharged. Carney, however, is usually down in the dumps, convinced he was rotten. After every show he gets a haircut, whether he needs it or not. "It's a compulsion," he explains. "I feel sort of dirty from the show—and I want to start off clean again."

In addition to his compulsions about haircuts and booze, Carney is nagged by other peculiar, contradictory habits. Before going to bed he arranges his change in a neat stack on his dresser, all the coins heads-up. He is neat to the point of obsession, constantly arranging objects around him in piles. Letters, magazines and books must be stacked with no overlapping edges; if not, Carney fidgets with them until the stacks are even.

"I have to know where everything is," he says. "Otherwise I go nuts. What do you suppose Freud would say about that?"

He has an almost fanatic fear of facial perspiration. On the Gleason show, Carney's constant dousing of his face with water became a standing joke. He kept a plastic squeeze bottle handy and sprayed himself whenever he perspired too heavily under the hot lights. Afterward he would dry himself carefully with a small hand towel. One day Gleason brought a seltzer bottle to rehearsal and hid it beneath his chair. When he saw Carney reach for his little squeeze bottle, Gleason snatched up the seltzer bottle and spritzed him with a blast of carbonated water.

It bubbled and dripped in torrents from Carney's face, practically drowning him. Everybody in the cast laughed, except Carney. Mopping his face off, he said quietly:

"Thanks, Jackie. I really needed that. Now shall we get on with the rehearsal?"

Carney is a hypochondriac who jams his medicine cabinet with bottles and jars of every cold and cough remedy ever patented. Excessively devoted to sweets (they help diminish his craving for alcohol), he is a connoisseur of chocolate sodas, chocolate milk shakes, Hershey bars, Mallomars, chewing gum and Necco wafers.

When on the wagon, he is also a prodigious eater of beef, potatoes, eggs and Italian food. During dinner he often has two huge helpings of everything, topped off with dessert of two large gooey chocolate sundaes. Because of his nervousness and high metabolism, he doesn't get fat no matter how much he consumes.

Carney's quirks, his chronic introversion and lack of ego have been part of his personality since he was a small boy. Born in Mt. Vernon, N.Y., only a few miles from where he now lives, he was the youngest of the six sons born to newspaperman Edward Carney and his wife Helen, Irish Catholics who hailed originally from Boston. Young Art was a shy, retiring boy who did poorly in school because of a lack of interest rather than brains.

His brothers, all eager-beavers, were school leaders who later did well in business and the professions. They regarded Art as a lazy, spoiled brat who would never amount to anything. His brother Phil, four years older, couldn't stand to have Art in the same room when he was entertaining his chums.

"I always tried to get rid of him," Phil recalls. "All he ever did was hang around making stupid faces and noodling on the piano. So I'd say, 'That's Arthur, my dumb little brother. We don't think he'll ever finish school.'"

By the time he was 12, Art had lost some of his reticence. At DeWitt Clinton grammar school, just across the street from the Carney home, his moods ranged from long periods of silence to sudden outbursts of show-offy humor. One day he grew bored while standing in line with other boys waiting to sharpen their pencils. Nearby stood a life-sized bust of Beethoven, noble and severe. Suddenly Art darted from the line and unfurled a billowing white handkerchief. In a gesture of inspired insanity, he blew Beethoven's nose—"honk! honk!"

He broke up the class and was sent at once to the office of the principal, who punished him by making him sit rigidly at attention for 30 minutes. Instead of being cowed by this experience, young Carney found that he got a secret thrill out of the attention he had received.

For many months he'd been aware that he could imitate the voices of the boys and girls in his class. He didn't know where the ability came from; it was simply something he could do effortlessly without much thought. He began mimicking the voice of one of his teachers, Miss Trinity. For a week he kept the class in an uproar, saying, "Open your English books to page 47." Or: "Now, children, let us write a theme on the mating habits of hedgehogs."

One day in class young Carney went too far. Everybody heard "Miss Trinity" say, "Miss Trinity is a dope!" This made her so angry she dragged two pupils out in the hall and threatened them with a variety of dire penalties unless they revealed the name of the culprit.

Told that the culprit was Art Carney, Miss Trinity was flabbergasted because up until then he'd been such a quiet, withdrawn boy. She hauled him to the principal's office where he was whacked across the knuckles with a ruler. The punishment apparently was too mild, because in subsequent weeks Carney was caught mimicking other teachers. Finally the principal, a stern Scotswoman named Minnie S. Graham, threatened to expel him unless his conduct improved.

Many years later, when he was an established TV star, Carney attended a reception honoring Miss Graham on her retirement. He made her laugh by imitating the way she had repeatedly scolded him when he was a boy: "I had all your brothers before you. I had Jack, Ned, Bob, Phil and Fred and they were fine boys. But you, Arthur —you are a *bad, bad boy*. You'll never amount to anything. Never!"

In high school Art was such a poor student that he had to repeat two semesters. This was a unique disgrace; none of his brothers ever failed a subject. In his junior year, however, Art finally achieved his first favorable recognition. At a school amateur night he went on the stage and —despite a bad case of nerves—delivered his vocal impressions of Lionel Barrymore, Edward G. Robinson and Franklin D. Roosevelt.

To his astonishment, and that of his teachers, brothers and parents, he won first prize. As a result, the school drama club invited him to join, but Carney modestly declined, saying, "Naw, I'm no actor. I'm too dumb."

After graduating high school at the hoary age of 19, Carney got a job peddling newspapers and then switched to sweeping out a jewelry store for the grandiose sum of $11 a week. Six miserable months later, his big brother Jack came to his rescue. Jack, a brilliant Rutgers University grad, had become an agent with MCA, the huge talent booking corporation. One of his clients was band leader Horace Heidt, who needed an entertainer.

"My kid brother does imitations," Jack told him. "How about an audition?"

Heidt agreed. But then Jack encountered a new problem. The thought of talking over a microphone frightened young Art half to death and he refused to go to the rehearsal hall.

"You idiot!" stormed his brother. "You stubborn fool! You want to spend your life sweeping out that damn store?"

Carney decided that prospect was more frightening than the mike. Trembling like a man on his way to the gallows, he went up on the rehearsal hall stage and began an impression of radio comedian Fred Allen. Despite his nervous stuttering, it wasn't bad. Then he did Al Smith, James Cagney and President Roosevelt. The latter was so perfect that Heidt and the members of his band broke out in applause.

Heidt hired him for $50 a week. During the next three and a half years, Art toured with the band, doing novelty songs as well as mimicry, acquiring technique so quickly that Heidt raised his salary to $150. In 1940, when he was 22 years old, Carney married Jean Myers, a girl he'd known in high school. They decided life with a traveling band was too haphazard, so he quit and began a new career as a night club comic on the New York circuit.

He stuck it out for a year. But he knew from the beginning that he was a failure. His imitations were the only things which went over well, but there was a limit as to how far they could be stretched. He simply was not a stand-up comic. This was partly because he refused to tell the dirty jokes that night club audiences demanded, and partly because he lacked the aggressiveness to deal with drunks and hecklers.

One night when Carney's act was particularly flat, a belligerent drunk kept bellowing, "Brother, you stink!" When Carney ignored him, the drunk climbed on the stage, grabbed the microphone and told an exceedingly filthy story. He drew more laughter than Carney had been getting.

Art finished his act. He went to his dressing room and locked the door. "I sat down and cried," he told his wife later. "I bawled like a baby—and then I told the manager I was quitting. He wasn't surprised. He said if I didn't quit—he'd fire me!"

Ashamed to tell his brother Jack what had happened, Art went into hiding for two weeks, living with Jean in a seedy hotel. When their money ran out, he tried to get a job as a shipping clerk or janitor. After Macy's, Gimbel's and two other stores turned him down, he reluctantly went to a pay phone, dialed Jack at MCA and confessed that he was broke and out of work.

"Jack," he said, "how about getting me a job as an actor?"

This time Jack was not encouraging. "You boob!" he said angrily. "You're no actor. A night club act is a commodity I can sell. But an actor is just another name in a file. We've got 10,000 actors on file here—and only a handful ever work!"

Nevertheless, Jack lent him $50 and Carney began making the rounds of theaters and radio studios. Jack, as usual, was right. Nobody wanted to hire a shy, perplexed-looking actor named Art Carney.

Then Jack heard about a CBS radio program called *Report to the Nation* which dramatized news about World War II with reproductions of the voices of generals, politicians and statesmen. He sent Art over for an audition.

"My friends . . ." began Carney.

"Good Lord!" exclaimed a CBS executive. "He IS Roosevelt!"

For good measure, Carney added in a rich British accent: "Blood, sweat and tears . . ."

"My God!" exclaimed another executive. "He IS Churchill!"

Within minutes Carney was signed to a contract for $225 a week. He stayed on the show two and a half years, until he was drafted.

After the long hospitalization for his wound, Carney went through weeks of Army rehabilitation, during which he was trained to walk on a leg that was nearly an inch shorter than its mate. Then he was discharged and began drawing $55-a-month compensation. Returning to radio work after the war, he found that the leg troubled him a lot when he was nervous or tired. It was then that he was apt to limp more noticeably, and he discovered that a few stiff belts of whiskey eased the pain.

In 1949 Carney broke into TV, appearing on Morey Amsterdam's show as a stooge and mustached waiter. His antics caught the eye of gag writer Arnold Rosen, who recommended him to Jackie Gleason. It was Carney's big break.

In his first sketch with Gleason, on the Du Mont network, Carney portrayed a nitwit photographer posing playboy Reggie Van Gleason for a Man of Distinction whiskey ad. Since Reggie was unable to drink the booze properly for the picture, Carney kept showing him how to do it. Both ended up hilariously crocked.

Gleason signed Carney to a long contract, commenting, "The first time he opened his mouth, I knew he was what I'd been looking for. I also knew I'd have to work twice as hard for my laughs, because he was funny as hell."

During the next seven years Gleason and Carney revealed a unique genius for working together. Wearing a dirty undershirt and crumpled hat, Carney won his loudest guffaws as Ed Norton, the *"va-va-va-varoom"* sewer bum. He was almost as great as he simmered and bubbled with outrage as aristocratic Sedgwick Van Gleason, helpless parent of no-good Reggie. As Clem Finch, Carney was the unlucky victim of "Loudmouth" Gleason's back-slapping, pie-in-the-puss humor.

In all those sketches, Carney was the stooge, Gleason the dominant buffoon. They performed well together because they were nearly the same in real life. Gleason, an overpowering extrovert, was the wild monarch of the set, running everything, shouting, wisecracking, demanding blind obedience to his whims from all his co-workers. Carney, the meek introvert, allowed Gleason to dominate him totally, accepting his orders and suggestions without question.

If Carney disagreed with Gleason, he kept it hidden. But by refusing to argue, he built up tremendous tensions within himself that could be relieved only by a few belts of booze. Whenever Gleason offered him a drink on the set, however, Carney would shake his head quickly and say, "No thanks, Jackie. I'm on the wagon." Often he was. If he wasn't, he controlled his thirst until he got home.

Throughout their long years together on the air, Carney kept his private life separate from Gleason's. He rarely attended any of Gleason's drinkathon parties. Nor did he like to drop into Toots Shor's old restaurant, where Gleason often held court after work, showing off and boozing it up with his pals. When the broadcast was over, Carney headed for Bronxville and the company of Jean and their three children.

Sometimes he gave co-star Audrey Meadows a lift in his car because her apartment was on his route home. Asked about Carney's mood after a show, Miss Meadows replied, "Art didn't talk too much as we drove along. Usually he was pretty negative, saying he'd been lousy on the show and grumbling about ways he could have improved his performance."

During his last two years on the Gleason show, Carney's

family and friends began to bug him, urging him to strike out on his own. He heard this constant refrain: "Art, you're more than a No. 2 clown. You've got sensitivity, you've got depth. You could do so much more with your talent than Ed Norton and those other bits. You've got to get away from Gleason!"

When his agent, Bill McCaffrey, began making the same pitch, Carney resisted, but not too hard. Since his earliest days in radio, he'd always had a yen to be a dramatic actor, but lacked the guts to try it. His Gleason contract permitted occasional roles in outside TV dramas, but those did not require the artistry and discipline of a Broadway play.

In 1957 Carney took the plunge. Breaking away from the Gleason show, he agreed to play a weak, wayward husband in *The Rope Dancers*, a heavy drama of sex and guilt. The transition in some ways was as difficult as if Carney had suddenly decided to fly to the moon or walk on water. As soon as he began rehearsals, he discovered that his co-star, blustery Irish actress Siobhan McKenna, was going to be a problem. A woman of great will and skill, she was—like Jackie Gleason—an extremely forceful person who tried to dominate those around her.

She made it clear from the beginning that she regarded Carney as her intellectual inferior. Aware that he'd had no training in the legitimate theater, she felt he was unqualified to play opposite her. During their first meeting, Carney tried to break the ice by joking and doing comic imitations of Arthur Godfrey and Milton Berle. Miss McKenna sniffed with displeasure and indicated that she was more interested in discussing psychological motivations for characters and other serious theatrical topics. Such subjects left Carney tongue-tied with embarrassment, since he'd read little literature and had never mingled with the Broadway intelligentsia.

But as they went deeper into *The Rope Dancers*, Miss McKenna's attitude changed. She became aware that Carney, despite his comedy background, was an actor of sensitivity and insight. Both claimed later that they had become good friends, but one of Carney's closest associates commented: "Don't you believe it. If you really want to know how Art feels about her, you ought to hear his imitation of her. He rolls his eyes and talks with tremendous intensity, the way she does. He cuts her up into little pieces."

The play was given its tryout in New Haven, Connecticut. Opening night was a disaster, for a totally unexpected reason. Carney's role was that of a man who, after visiting a prostitute, goes home and makes love to his wife (Miss McKenna) with tragic consequences. Except for a few wry lines, there was nothing funny about the story, but as soon as Carney stepped on the stage the audience began to laugh.

No matter what he did or said in the role of the tortured husband, the audience chuckled. So far as they were concerned, he was still TV's Ed Norton, the bumbling sewer man, and they'd come to see him do some slapstick "va-va-va-varoom" stuff. During the first and second acts, they laughed in all the wrong places. They didn't stop laughing until the final depressing scenes in the third act. Then they applauded, but they were disappointed and puzzled.

It was the worst night of Art Carney's life. Convinced he was a failure as an actor, he went out and got sloshed. While the play was being reworked the following week, he drank a lot, but showed up cold sober for rehearsals. After the show closed in New Haven, Carney, Miss McKenna and other members of the cast traveled to Stratford, Ontario, one night to see Christopher Plummer's performance of *Hamlet*. Carney got loaded, dropped off to sleep in his seat and snored like hell through Plummer's most dramatic scenes.

When *The Rope Dancers* went to Broadway, Carney suffered opening night agonies. His suffering was needless. The sophisticated Broadway audience, aware from the beginning that Carney was portraying a tragic figure, loved him. So did the critics, who gave him superb reviews.

Carney, however, remained in doubt about his work. Commented Morton Wishengrad, the play's author, "Miss McKenna and I told him repeatedly how good he was. But I don't think he ever believed us."

Although not a smash hit, the play was an excellent success, enjoying a run of 189 performances. As a result, Carney became one of the hottest talents in show business. He and his agent received hordes of offers, including starring roles in more Broadway plays and half a dozen TV comedy series. Carney rejected most of them and then astounded the theatrical world by agreeing to do not two, or merely three—but nine TV spectaculars in a row.

For a performer whose lack of self-confidence had become legend, this turnabout was a staggering achievement.

Carney did all nine shows in fast succession during the 1959-60 season. Each spectacular cost around $175,000 and his take-home pay for the lot was a whopping $350,000. The shows were a kaleidoscope of Carney's versatility. *Small World, Isn't It?* was a revue; in *Our Town*, he was the philosophical stage manager-spokesman; *Very Important People* was a political satire which earned him a fourth Emmy award (he'd won three previously for Ed Norton).

He also did *Man in the Dog Suit, Best of Anything, Three In One, Victory, Moon Over Brooklyn* and *Call Me Back*. The latter fulfilled Carney's long-held desire to portray a bedeviled alcoholic. When his associates protested that such a portrayal might hit too close to the truth about his own problem, Carney replied, "If it does, let it. I've got the background for it and I damn well want to use it."

Despite intense pressures, Carney remained on the wagon throughout the season of his chain of spectaculars. He was also a model of sobriety while appearing the following winter in a new and largely unsuccessful Broadway play, *Take Her, She's Mine*. After that he made his first trip to Hollywood where he appeared as a sympathetic gangster in *The Yellow Rolls Royce*, and then he returned east for more TV roles and a new Broadway comedy, *The Odd Couple*.

That play was by far the best thing Carney had ever attempted. He and his co-star, Walter Matthau, portrayed two miserable men who, kicked out by their wives, found that they couldn't live with each other either. Carney played a character very much like himself, a fussy fellow who tried to keep everything around him neat and orderly, while Matthau depicted an untidy slob. The resulting conflict enabled Carney to display outrageously hilarious comedy as well as moments of touching sensitivity.

The Odd Couple was a smash from the moment it opened in March, 1965. Night after night for seven months, Carney had such an emotional ball on stage that it looked as if the play would run forever. And then—with shocking abruptness—he was dropped from the cast one night in October and replaced by an understudy.

At first it was assumed that Carney's absence was merely temporary and that he would return to the show after a short rest. Then his manager, Bill MacCaffrey, revealed that Carney was hospitalized with ailments so serious that he had been forced to quit the play for good.

"Art's not in the best of shape," McCaffrey said in a brief statement to the press. "He's suffering depression and nervousness for a lot of reasons I won't go into."

McCaffrey then slammed an iron curtain around Carney's problems, refusing to divulge the exact nature of his illness or the location of the hospital where he was being treated. This action stirred a storm of rumors, most of them centered on the theme that Carney's ailments were related to his alcoholism and that he had been taken to a sanitarium to dry out.

For many weeks Carney's condition continued to be a national mystery. Then McCaffrey put an end to some of the rumors by revealing that Carney had suffered a nervous breakdown and was under treatment at the Institute for Living, a sanitarium at Hartford, Connecticut.

"He's making good progress," McCaffrey said, "but we don't know how long he will have to remain at the Institute."

McCaffrey declined to go into detail about what had caused Carney's breakdown, but what had happened was obvious. The pressure of appearing on stage night after night before a live audience in a difficult, emotional role had driven Carney to the brink of physical and mental collapse. Fearing he would disgrace himself with a bad performance, he had decided to remove himself from the cast before such a catastrophe could occur.

His reasons for making such a decision had been revealed by Carney a few years earlier, during an unusually candid conversation with writer Alfred Bester. Discussing the fact that he occasionally suffered attacks of great nervous tension while working, Carney disclosed that he was subject to severe nosebleeds at such times and that his bad leg would pain him and break out in a rash.

Then, without offering any excuses, Carney talked frankly about his alcoholism.

"When I was a young man," said Carney, "I could drink like hell. When I got older and worried with responsibilities, I found the remorse made the hangover terrible, so I figured I better quit. I don't like to drink regularly, because it means I'm headed on the road for a lost weekend. It's a question of body chemistry. Sometimes I can go along with the usual drinks and nothing happens. Another time they hit me different and then I get the message: 'Art?' 'Yes, I hear you.' 'You're getting loaded.' 'OK,' I say. 'Thanks.' So I quit."

Carney grinned his familiar perplexed grin.

"Look," he added, "when you talk to yourself, you have to tell the truth. I could have a couple of drinks now, and nothing would happen. And tomorrow. And maybe all week. But sooner or later I'd start drinking and never stop, depending on the mood or the chemistry. I'm the kind that can't drink."

"What do you fear the most?" Bester asked.

"Hitting rock-bottom," Carney replied. "But there isn't any single rock-bottom for a drinker. It isn't being a bum on the Bowery only. There are all kinds of rock-bottom. Rock-bottom for me would be seeing my wife and kids crying because I came home drunk. Or it would be missing a performance because I was drunk . . ."

From those statements it was clear that Carney would quit a show, even a hit like *The Odd Couple,* if he feared he was about to hit the "rock-bottom" of missing a performance.

In December, during the second month of Carney's stay at the sanitarium, his manager reported that Jackie Gleason had invited Art to do a guest appearance on his TV show. "Art wants to do it," McCaffrey said. "And he will as soon as he's able."

During Christmas week, Carney flew to Miami Beach for a gleeful reunion with Jackie Gleason and Audrey Meadows. Art had never looked better. There was bounce in his step, his blue eyes gleamed and his cheeks had the pink glow of restored health. With Carney once again portraying dopey Ed Norton, the three taped a musical comedy version of *The Honeymooners* which was broadcast in January. When the ratings came in, it was discovered that the show had been an incredible triumph, topping anything Gleason had done for years. It was so successful that Gleason—who only the week before had said he was sick of TV and was quitting—did an abrupt about-face. Beaming like a fat pussycat who had just swallowed a couple of canaries, he announced that he had signed Carney and Miss Meadows for a whole new season of weekly *Honeymooners* shows.

Carney, who in the meantime had returned to the seclusion of his New York home, declined to discuss his future plans with reporters. His manager, however, exuded confidence for him, declaring he was certain that Carney would be able to withstand the mental and physical rigors of working in Gleason's frenzied weekly nuthouse.

"Hell's bells," said McCaffrey. "If he wanted, Art could do a lot more than that. We're working on deals for more spectaculars and we've got enough movie offers to make Art a millionaire two or three times over."

But with his next breath McCaffrey admitted that Carney would refuse most of the offers, particularly those from Hollywood, which he detests.

Asked whether Carney had finally licked his drinking problem, McCaffrey—who has been Art's manager for a dozen years—refused to make a prediction. Instead, he offered the following analysis of Carney's basic problem, from which his other problems spring:

"The trouble with Art is that he just doesn't know how good he is. And he won't believe you when you try to tell him. He is totally lacking in ego, which is unheard of for an actor. Why, if he had just an average amount of ego, he could be the greatest actor on Broadway and the greatest comedian on TV. Instead, he suffers from a disease which can be fatal in show business."

"You mean chronic alcoholism?" he was asked.

"No!" snorted McCaffrey. "Something far worse. Chronic modesty . . ."

6. THE FRENZIED WORLD
OF JACK CARTER

I was sitting in a Miami nightclub with Jack Carter and his beautiful blonde wife when Jimmy Durante introduced Carter as "Pound fuh pound, America's greatest entertainer . . ."

Then Durante sniggered coyly. "Next tuh me, of course."

A shy, abashed look came over Carter's face. He stood up to acknowledge the applause and knocked the table over, inundating everybody within a three-foot radius with celery, shrimp cocktails and whiskey. "Oh, my God!" he quavered.

The audience howled under the erroneous impression that it was part of the show. Carter smiled weakly and slunk out under cover of the darkness. Paula Carter and I followed him outside where he stood muttering to himself. "As an encore, I should have blown my brains out," he said. He hailed a cab and we all got in. Carter dusted off the seat and sat down, daintily hitching up his pants. The Fontainebleu," he said.

The cab shot off into the heavy traffic. We heard what sounded like a kitten mewing. Carter started nervously. "What the hell is that?" he grumbled.

The cab driver turned around and grinned at us. "That was me. I'm learning how to be a ventriloquist. Pretty good, huh?"

"Turn around, you idiot, you'll kill us all!" Carter bellowed. "Watch where you're going! . . . That's a red light . . . You're going too fast! . . . Watch the taxi on your right! . . . Where'd *you* learn how to drive? . . . Look at that meter, 80 cents already! The bastard's got one of these trick meters! . . . Ten dollars a day I'm paying for a rented car, and I won't use it because it costs 10 cents a mile." Carter struck himself on the forehead. "Oh, how I hate myself!"

As Carter nervously harangued him, the cab driver kept mewing like a kitten. At the red light, he turned around and evidently recognized the comedian. "Hey!" he said delightedly to Carter's wife, "You know who that is?"

"I hope so," she smiled.

The cabby leaned out the window and shouted at the driver of the adjoining cab as Carter fussed and fumed at him. "Hey, guess who I got for a fare, what's his name?"

"Chakrin's the name," Carter snapped.

"Go *wann*, your name ain't Chakrin. I know who you are. You're uh . . . uh . . . ," he kept snapping his fingers. "I got it on the tip of my tongue."

"Tongue," Carter said. "That's my name, Jack Tongue."

The light changed and the cab started again. Carter dabbed gloomily at the shrimp cocktail sauce on his jacket. "Twenty-five years I've been in show business and they still don't know my name."

"They know your name, darling," Paula said, comfortingly. She turned to me. "Sammy Davis, Jr. says Jack is the greatest crowd pleaser in the business—"

"I don't please me. I'm very dissatisfied with me." He took out his immaculate white handkerchief and absently began to wipe the window. "Nobody knows me. For a performer, I'm very untheatrical. Milton Berle steals gags, Joe E. Lewis drinks, Buddy Hackett talks out of duh side of his mout' like dis in that beautiful nasal voice. What have I got going for me? I'm masochistic. I'm depressive. Somebody up there doesn't like me and I think it's me."

To what did he attribute this unhappy frame of mind?

He shrugged. "It's the fashion nowadays to blame your parents. I blame me. I'm the kind of guy, if they crowned me king of England, I'd be *furious* because they didn't make me prime minister, too."

I said he sounded like a stereotype of a neurotic comedian. Had he ever been analyzed? "By three different analysts and I gave them all nervous breakdowns. The last one took off for Europe and is doing my act in Vienna."

The cab pulled up at the Fontainebleu. The cabby turned around. "I got it. Jackie Mason, right?"

Carter looked pained. "The name is really Chakrin. In Russian, that means 'philosopher.' and that's what you've gotta be in this business."

We got out and Carter said, "It's a good thing he didn't

know me. When I play New York or Miami or Vegas, the word gets out, 'Jack Carter's in town.' It's like jungle drums. The bastards refuse to take me in their cabs because I drive them crazy. All right, I'm the first to admit it. I'm tough to live with. Thank God, my wife understands me and puts up with me."

As we walked into the Fontainebleu lobby, a middle-aged woman in a mink stole rushed up with an autograph book. "I saw your show last night and I never laughed so much in my whole life. So many jokes. You really work very hard!"

Carter smiled wanly and signed her book. In the elevator, he said, "I resent it when people come up to me and say, 'Jack you work very hard.' What am I, a truckdriver? Sure I work hard," he added incongruously. "I have to *crush* an audience or I'm not happy. I swarm all over them, give them 40 jokes instead of four, even though I know it's wrong. I should give them the charm routine like Danny Kaye, not 196 jokes a minute."

"Don't you like Danny Kaye?"

"Certainly I like him!" Carter said indignantly. "I admire the man. He's a cool worker and he lays the language in well."

We got off on the sixteenth floor and went into his luxurious suite. "Jack isn't the average run of comedian," Paula said.

"I speak 12 languages," Carter said proudly. He began ticking them off on his fingers. "English, Spanish, French, Italian, German, Hebrew, Yiddish—" He paused.

"That's only seven languages."

Carter fixed his hooded blue eyes on me with hostility. "What are you, a certified public accountant?" He turned to Paula. "Why is the whole world against me?"

"The whole world is not against you, darling," she said patiently.

"I just got hungry or thirsty, I don't know which. You feel like a drink or a sandwich or something?"

"I'll have a Screwdriver," Paula said.

"Bourbon, hot water and orange juice," I said.

Carter scowled at me. "What kind of a drink is that? I'm *dying* for seltzer."

He talked about his childhood when he, his two sisters and mother and father lived somewhat less than luxuriously in three rooms in back of a candy store his father owned in Coney Island.

"My father had a Jewish still in the basement, a seltzer machine. It always scared me. I never liked to go near it. The damn thing was almost human. It had metal arms and coils and wires like a Rube Goldberg invention and it made a dull, humming noise—*mmmmmm, mmmmmm.* One night, my father sent me down to the basement for a box of Tootsie Rolls. It was dark down there and I stumbled against the seltzer machine and the arms grabbed me!" He let out a hoarse scream. "I've had seltzer trauma ever since."

Paula said, "Sometimes we're watching a horror movie on the Late Show and I'll say 'Boo!' and he jumps."

"I still sleep with one eyeball open," Carter said.

He phoned room service for the drinks and a hamburger for himself. "Make sure you bring sliced tomatoes with the hamburger," he emphasized.

"Jack ad libs a totally different show every night," Paula said.

"I really make a tough job tougher," Carter frowned. "I enjoy torturing myself. I do a bit where my mother keeps hitting me in the head. 'Where's your brains? Where's your brains?' She hits and she hits and finally, I say, 'Keep hitting, Mom, they'll be right out.'"

He excused himself and went into the bedroom to change his clothes. I asked Paula whether her husband was difficult to live with. "Jack drives me crazy but I can't imagine being married to anybody else. He's the most unpredictable person I know, and that's part of his charm."

She told about inveigling him into accompanying her to an auction at the Parke-Bernet galleries in New York. Carter had never been to an art auction before and he viewed the proceedings with a jaundiced eye. He sat there, grimly silent, while she bid on a grotesque cigar store figure of Punch that was well over six feet tall. When the auctioneer knocked it down to her, Carter leaped up, his eyes blazing, leveled his finger at the gargoyle and bellowed, "Not in *my* house!"

"It took Jack weeks to get over it," Paula said. "He would close his eyes and make horrible faces every time he looked at it. Then somebody offered me double what I had paid for it but Jack had a fit. 'What are you, crazy?' he screamed. 'I *love* that Punch!'"

The bedroom door opened suddenly and Carter's head popped out. "That's the story of my life," he rumbled. "I have to hate something before I love it." He came out, fumbling with the buttons on the jacket of a new tuxedo. "It's warfare when I get dressed. Even my clothes are against me. Buttons pop, zippers snag. Some of my worst battles have been against clothes hangers. I've never won a fight yet."

"When we're home," Paula said, "he hangs around all morning driving me crazy. He finally gets all dressed, kisses me goodby, goes to the door, and as he's on his way out, he changes his mind, comes back and drives me crazy for another hour. Then he'll go downtown and call me 20 times to look in the pocket of his suit for his cigarette lighter. 'Which suit?' I ask. 'The gray suit.' He has maybe 15 suits in different shades of gray hanging in the closet. I look in the pockets of his gray suits, his brown suits, his blue suits, I look through all his suits and finally he finds the lighter in the suit he's wearing."

Carter stared in the mirror with a curious mixture of admiration and loathing. An impeccable dresser, Carter insists on buying not only his own clothes but his wife's as well. For some mysterious reason, however, he invariably brings home dresses that fit tall, emaciated girls and Paula is not, by the wildest stretch of the imagination, emaciated. I asked her if he had good taste.

"I have excellent taste!" Carter shouted. "I could have been the Jewish version of Christian Dior!"

I asked if he had any physical idiosyncrasies. "What the hell kind of an insulting question is that?" Carter roared. "What are you, a goddamn Peeping Tom?"

Paula gave me a funny look. "I didn't mean Krafft-Ebing," I explained. "All I meant was—oh, let's strike the question."

"He's ambidextrous," Paula said.

"That's right," Carter said. "I can talk lefty or righty."

"He punches me lefty."

"But she bleeds righty."

He strode around the room restlessly, hacking and clearing his throat. He sounded very much like a seal barking for herring. "They gave me a —— air conditioned virus room!" he suddenly shouted. "Did I come down to Miami to freeze or to get a little sunshine? I don't know how I can do the show tonight, but if I lay down, I'm dead. If I keep moving, I'm better off. Maybe I better go in the bathroom and take steam for my throat, huh? What do you think?"

He looked at his watch and turned pale. "It's almost

time for me to go down and make a fool of myself. God, I hate this business!"

"Can I watch the show tonight?" Paula asked.

"Paula, for God's sake, you *know* how I feel about that."

Carter does not like his wife to be in the audience while he is performing. During a recent engagement, she sneaked into the nightclub disguised in a brown wig and horn rim glasses and hid behind a pillar. There were 3,000 people in the nightclub, but in the middle of his frenzied gyrations, Carter suddenly halted. "I see you, Paula! Out! *Out!*"

"And he refused to go on with his act until I left," Paula said. "I don't know why he did it. I'm his greatest audience."

"You stink," Carter growled affectionately. "Where's my hamburger? I'm starved and I gotta go on in 10 minutes."

Red Buttons came in and Carter fell upon him like a tiger. "Red, you gotta help me! I'm all out of material!"

Buttons laughed. "Last year, Jack was opening at the Copa and he got panicky. He phoned me and said he had nothing to say, nothing new to offer the audience. I come over, thinking I'll help the poor guy out. He's done it for me and other comics countless times. Jack sits me down in a chair and for four solid hours, he rattles off his nothing to say. I give him maybe one joke. He was a bloody riot at the opening—"

"You think so, Red? I thought I was lousy that night."

" He started 8 P.M. and got off the floor like three shopping days before Christmas." Buttons chuckled. "And then he tells the audience *I* wrote his entire act."

Carter gazed moodily out the window at the Miami lights glittering in the dusk. "I was a strange child. I had a constant fear of being left out and I had to be the best."

Carter considers himself physically grotesque. "I'm 5 foot 11 or 11 foot 5, depending on my mental state. I weigh 185 stripped . . ." He leered. "I have a very strong, weak chin. My eyebrows are bowlegged. I've got 20-20 vision in one ear . . ."

"We call him 'Brillo-Head,' " said Buttons.

"That's right. I don't comb or brush my hair, I scrub pots with it. I'm so ugly I should be fined and sent to jail."

He was joking and yet he was serious. "You're crazy," I said. "Why, you're handsome!"

He shook his head. "I don't believe it. I would have done me over." He brooded a moment. "Whenever I drive out to the suburbs, all I see are beautiful children. You don't see ugly kids any more. They must throw the ugly ones away."

Buttons turned to me. "Jack is a very bright, nervous kind of guy. He hasn't changed a bit in the 17 years I've known him. He drives everybody nuts but everybody loves him."

"I've got enemies in this business, Red."

"You're your own worst enemy," Paula said.

"And who has a better right?" Carter bellowed. "I'm Jack of all trades, master of nothing. I'm not me, I'm not Jack Carter. I'm a chameleon. I'm potpourri. In Texas, I say, 'Ah reckon' and I walk like I've got saddle sores. In Miami, I use Jewish routines even a Nazi would laugh at. In Boston, I used to talk like J.F.K. . . . It's almost like I'm ashamed of my own talent."

"Jack is so talented he could be anything," Buttons said. "When I got back from Japan after making *Sayonara*, I brought a scroll with me. Jack made up a poem on the spur of the moment and hand lettered it on the scroll for me—

CLEAN FLOOR
DIRTY STREET
PLEASE REMOVE
SHOES FROM FEET.

"I have a terrible phobia about cleanliness," Carter said gloomily.

"He waxes and polishes every inch of the apartment the day before the cleaning girl comes," Paula said. "When people come to our house, he makes them take their shoes off before he lets them in." For his thirty-ninth birthday party, one discerning friend brought him 1,000 pairs of paper slippers. Lucille Ball and Gary Morton presented him with a mop and pail and 14 large bottles of Mr. Clean. Knowing that Carter entertains a morbid interest in medicine, one physician friend brought him a moldy dissecting kit.

"Jack is the kind of guy who steps out of the shower to take a leak," Buttons whispered to me.

"He loves his carpet more than he loves me," Paula said. "Once I fell down the stairs and he hollered, *'Look* what you did to my beautiful carpet!' It drives him crazy when I walk on my high heels on that damned carpet. He follows me sniffing like a bloodhound on the trail with a vacuum cleaner picking up every last tiny particle of dirt—"

"But my entire life is disheveled," said Carter running his finger over the windowsill and inspecting it.

"We went for a drive the other night and had to stop for a red light," Paula said. "Don't you think he jumped out with a cloth and began polishing the hood?"

Carter is the fretful owner of a 1956 Thunderbird which is as spotless as the day he bought it and still has the original plastic covers over the seats. He has driven in it perhaps a dozen times. "I curse the dealer who sold it to me, I curse the insurance company for letting me have insurance on it and most of all I curse the State for issuing me a driver's license."

The phone rang and Paula answered it. "It's your press agent."

"I don't want to talk to him," Carter snarled.

"What shall I tell him?"

"Tell him I died and I'm not expected to recover."

Paula murmured her apologies into the phone and hung up.

"That character," Carter rumbled. "One thousand a month I'm paying him and he can't even get me into the *Christian Science Monitor*." A look of intense anguish came over his face. "And he has the *chutzpah* (nerve) to charge me extra every time he uses a six-cent stamp! He'll probably send me a bill for this 10-cent phone call."

The waiter came in wheeling a tea cart. Carter threw his arm around Buttons and asked if he would join us. "You know I only touch organic foods," the diminutive comedian said.

"I forgot! A glass of balsa wood for my friend!" Carter shouted. With elaborate, ceremonious gestures, the waiter took the serving plate and lifted up the large silver cover, disclosing a dried-up little hamburger.

"Where's the tomatoes?" Carter asked, his voice shaking with rage. "I *distinctly* said tomatoes. Did you hear me say tomatoes?" He looked at me.

"You distinctly said tomatoes," I said.

"A dollar-seventy-five for a stinking hamburger plus a dollar extra for room service and I can't get a lousy slice of tomato," Carter said, visibly trying to control himself.

"I bring you tomato, yes?" said the waiter, bowing obsequiously.

"You bring me tomato, no!" Carter roared. "By the time you bring me the goddamn tomato, I'll be on the plane back to New York!"

The waiter cringed. Carter tipped him $5 and pointed majestically to the door. "My compliments to the chef and tell him to drop dead." The waiter scuttled out, a broad grin on his face. Carter bit into his hamburger savagely. "Either I overtip or I undertip. There's no in-between," he mumbled, his mouth full.

"Jack is the bull and the bear of our business," Buttons said. "He's either way up or way down, there's no happy medium."

"Jack E. Leonard says I'm the only guy he knows who sends back restaurants," Carter said. "I should have had my mother cater this hamburger, only she drives me nuts too. She makes 'watch-out' food. With every dish, you get a warning—'Watch out for the bones; watch out, it's too hot; watch out, it's too spicy; watch out, don't eat too fast.' My father is the umpire. 'Let him alone, let him burn his tongue, who cares?' "

Carter glanced nervously at his watch. "Red, pray for me. I got a feeling in my bones I'm not gonna make it tonight. I got a feeling the audience is gonna rise up and walk out on me tonight."

"That's about par for the course." Buttons said. "All the little Carter enzymes are waving the flag. Don't worry, Jack, you'll knock them dead the way you always do."

"I'm an actor, damn it!" Carter roared. "What am I doing telling jokes for a living?"

"Are you a Method actor?" I asked.

"No, but I've read Stanislavsky and all these inwardly-within guys . . ." Carter's mouth contorted suddenly. He clutched his hands to his stomach as though he were in pain. "You mus' sufferrrr!" he bellowed in a pseudo-Russian accent. "*Them,* not me. I do enough suffering on my own time."

Carter's closest friend, Mickey Hayes, a Miami haberdasher, shudders when the comedian bestows his patronage upon him. He has, on various occasions, diplomatically suggested that Carter take his trade elsewhere but the latter is adamant in his loyalty. Says Hayes: "Jack can come in for 30 fittings on a suit before he's satisfied. He pulls at the sleeves and the crotch and the lapels until the suit is all out of shape. Then he says. 'See? I *told* you it didn't fit right.' "

Hayes was best man when Carter married Paula and, since it was impossible for him to come to New York for the wedding, Carter impulsively chartered a plane and flew the entire entourage, bridesmaids, rabbi and all, to Miami.

I met Hayes the next day in the Poodle Room of the Fontainebleu. A four-piece Cuban band was clattering away noisily, waiters scurried around with drinks, amorous couples clutched at each other and everybody seemed to be whispering at the top of his lungs. Sodom and Gomorrah, I couldn't help thinking as I furtively regarded a redhead with a spectacular bosom dancing with a wizened old man.

"To me, he's a fantastic guy," Hayes said. "When I opened my new store, Jack flew from Los Angeles just to cut the tape. It was in Winchell's column. Jack likes to hang around my store and wait on customers. The other day, he fitted somebody for a suit and the guy happened to see Jack perform that very same night. The guy was amazed. 'Hey!' he said, 'This comedian's a *tailor* in the daytime!' "

Hayes fingered the ice in his Scotch reflectively. "Jack has the most immaculate wardrobe hung away in his closet, maybe 75 suits like brand new he's too nervous to wear."

Hayes is friendly with all the big-time comedians but feels closest to Carter. Why Carter? "This is the kind of guy Jack is," Hayes explains. "I've seen him turn down an appointment with an important Hollywood producer because he was going over to his parents' house for supper. Jack has no faith in himself. He'll be the last one in the world to find out how great he is. The funny thing is, in spite of the public image of him as a loud, brash comedian, actually he's a very shy person."

Hayes stubbed out his cigarette. "If he were here, this ashtray would be cleaned out already.

Carter came over wearing jazzy pink cotton slacks, a yellow zebra-striped polo shirt and red loafers. He didn't look particularly shy. The Cuban band began to play again, the bongos thumping and the maraccas chattering. Carter looked back over his shoulder. "Did something fall down?" He sat down, took a napkin and meticulously wiped off his side of the table, then emptied the ashtray into a nearby wastebasket. Hayes burst out laughing. "See what I mean?"

Carter grinned self consciously. He crumpled up the napkin and threw it away. "The Vegas bit came out like pure gold last night," Hayes said. "I can't even remember the *shtick* (bit) I did," Carter said pensively. "If I'm on a venom subject, I get vicious funny."

"You couldn't be vicious if you tried," said Hayes.

"I'm the most vicious sonofabitch that ever lived," said Carter, nudging the crumpled napkin with his toe.

"I was with Jack one night when a total stranger came up and said. 'Here's that $100 I owe you.' Jack looked at him. 'What $100?' He didn't even remember the guy. He's always doing things like that. Vicious," Hayes snorted affectionately.

The band played an Afro-Cuban jazz number and Carter jumped up suddenly and began jitterbugging. "The first dance I went to, everybody was Lindy Hopping all over the joint. I didn't know how to dance so I went home and for two weeks, I practiced. When I came back, I was a Jewish Fred Astaire. I was born with this crazy gift for mimicry, so I mimic dancing and singing and acting and eating and even living. I'm not me. I'm not Jack Carter. I'm 14 other people." He sat down just as suddenly, breathing hard.

"How do you relax?" I asked Carter. "Or aren't you able to relax?"

"I was a basket case for four years on the golf course. I got so angry at myself once, I threw a wood and wrapped it around one of the Strafaci brothers' neck. Frank or somebody. That's when I decided to give up golf. I'm too competitive."

"Are you a poor loser?"

"I'm a *born* loser."

"Have you arrived at a philosophy of life yet?"

Carter looked amazed. "Here? You want the Lin Yutang bit *here?*" He had to raise his voice over the infernal din of the chacha band and the cocktail glasses clinking. "Thou shalt not fart!" he snarled.

Carter's leather-lunged voice has been likened to a bullfrog suffering acute dyspepsia. He attributes this to his humble beginnings, one summer, when he was a towel boy at the Washington Baths in Coney Island. He stood around naked and shivering all day, assiduously scrubbing the customers' back and hoping for a nickel tip. The bathhouse employed a regular barker who fell temporarily ill and Carter, eager to get back into dry clothes, volunteered to substitute for him.

In order to attract more customers, Carter prayed toward Mecca, bellowed crude insults at the gaping yokels and developed the machine-gun attack that characterizes his present work.

He attended Public School 100, where he was walloped regularly because of his imitations of the principal. He didn't do too well scholastically but graduated with more welts than any other student. At Brooklyn's New Utrecht High School, he specialized in art and dramatics. Carter is privately convinced that he might have been another Rembrandt except for his unfortunate proclivity for drawing caricatures of those in authority. Art, however, did not satisfy his lust for theatricals, so he accepted the leading role in a school production of Cyrano de Bergerac.

("I make over $300,000 a year in nightclubs and television, but the guy with the nose is buried deep inside me and I can't get him out. Anthony Quinn would give his right eye to be a nightclub performer, and I would give both of mine to be a dramatic actor.")

In 1939, Carter won first prize in a Major Bowes amateur hour. He did a raucous imitation of Jimmy Durante, pigeon-toed around the stage in a glassy-eyed facsimile of Boris Karloff as the monster in Frankenstein, and rattled off jokes. Through the peculiar logic of show business, this won him a dramatic scholarship in the summer stock company run by Christopher Morley.

The famed author told him, "My dear boy, you are that rarity—an actor who can clown and a clown who can act." Morley took a fatherly interest in the young comic and even went so far as to write some rather literary jokes for his act which Carter stealthily discarded.

Carter's first professional engagement was a one-night stand at a saloon not too far from the Swift slaughterhouses in Manhattan. "I got seven bucks and all the blood I could drink." The patrons, a singularly uninhibited lot cheered him to the rafters when they discovered that he had neglected, in his stagefright, to zip up his fly.

Emboldened by his success, Carter demanded a fee of $8 for his next engagement. A somewhat spirited argument ensued. The proprietor, a large, burly individual, hoarsely informed Carter, "I don't wanna have to lean on you, kid." Carter hastily agreed to work for $7 but was cancelled, nevertheless, when the disenchanted patrons discovered that he was mouthing Henry Youngman's routine, word for word.

Carter played a number of smaller niteries and was then booked with a Major Bowes unit along with Frank Sinatra, Robert Merrill and other hopeful unknowns on a cross-country tour. "I was just a kid and I had never been away from home before. I cried all the way on the bus to Syracuse because I was so scared." The sight of Carter so unnerved Sinatra that the emaciated crooner sat on the other side of the bus and refused to have anything to do with the blubbering comic.

After a stint emceeing for the Les Brown band, Carter was drafted and served in the Medical Corps. The young comic, who turned queasy at the sight of a hangnail, was soon transferred to a radio quiz show under Air Force sponsorship. Among other phobias, Carter had a fear of height. For the next three years, ashen faced with fright, he flew the Pacific war stations, while starring in a military review, *Flying Varieties*.

It took Carter many years to overcome his aversion to airplanes but he appears to have mastered his fears.

Actually, Carter's most vivid memories of the war center around the town of Needles, California, which enjoys a mean temperature of approximately 130 degrees. "We would come out of a cold shower, drenched with perspiration. I took my O.C.S. test standing at attention, stark naked. Four officers sat at a desk, reviewing my case, stark naked too. I mean it was *hot!*"

When the war ended, Carter returned to nightclubs and vaudeville and began to earn important money. His bright, fresh monologues caught the attention of the TV tycoons and in 1948 he was starred in a variety minstrel show.

"I was only 26 and didn't even know how to blow my nose, but I ran the whole show. Berle used to watch me in action and smack his writers—'Why can't you write sketches like that?' " Berle was so enamored of the whirlwind technique that he signed Carter to pinch-hit for him on the famous Texaco hour.

In 1950, Carter was signed by NBC to star in the hourlong segment before Sid Caesar's 90-minute show. Although Carter got a towering 48.7 rating, he immediately ran into difficulties with the NBC brass.

"They would tell me, 'You can't wear a robe because Caesar wears a robe. You can't have an opera bit because

Caesar has an opera bit.' You can't do this, you can't do that. I, like a *nebbish* (nothing), stood at attention and saluted. 'Yes sir. Yes sir.' Finally, my sponsor, Campbell Soup, got mad. Hell, they were spending *millions* and they said, 'Goddamit, if Jack wants to wear a robe or do an opera bit or anything, he'll do it and nobody's going to order him around.'"

Carter shrugged philosophically about the financial aftermath. "Caesar was protected for 10 years by his lawyers and agents, Berle was protected for life, Gleason they hadda give the building and I ended up with heartburn."

During the ensuing decade, Carter landed starring roles in Broadway musicals, *Mr. Wonderful, Top Banana,* and *Call Me Mister.* In 1958, with his unerring sense for disaster. Carter turned down the Robert Preston role in *The Music Man* to play Sganarelle in a musical flop based on a play by Moliere.

"I was flattered because the producers auditioned for me, little Jack Carter, the guy with the biggest inferiority complex in the business bar none. Opera singers were in the cast. Wright and Forrest, who wrote *Kismet* and *Song of Norway,* wrote it. It was one of those Alfred Drake-type musicals—"

Carter leaped up and propped one foot on a couch, stroking his imaginary beard lustfully. He began to sing a melody from the show in a rich baritone, leering at the imaginary soubrette as only Alfred Drake can leer. I was surprised at the quality of Carter's voice and asked if he had ever tried opera.

"Robert Merrill once said to me, 'Idiot, let me take you to my voice teacher. You've got a voice big enough for opera. All it needs is training.' But I wouldn't go because I only do the things that are wrong for me. When I was 25—it sounds like the beginning of a Robert Frost poem—'When I was 25 and terribly young and alive'—Guy Lombardo said to me, 'You have a terrible, driving ambition to be a star, wait 10 years, you can't hurry up success.'"

Carter squinted one eye up at the ceiling musingly. "Settle for something less than your ambition. I read that somewhere."

"The thing Jack doesn't realize is that he *is* a big star," Paula said.

Carter looked pleased, but he loftily ignored his wife. "Success is a step backward in the right direction. I read that in a book."

"Do you read a lot?" I asked.

A dreamy, poetic look came over his face. "Everything that comes out," he said.

Paula giggled. "Don't let him kid you. He makes me read all the latest books and review them for him. Jack is like a Hollywood producer—he's too busy to read."

Not too long ago, Carter made a movie for MGM entitled *The Horizontal Lieutenant*. Before the screening, there was a party and everybody commented on the delicious hors d'oeuvres. What might be tactfully described as an awkward silence prevailed when the picture ended. It had evidently not been one of the studio's more notable efforts. Carter stood up and shouted, "But wasn't the *food* wild?"

Paula laughed as she told the story. I said, "You enjoy your husband, don't you?"

"I *kvell* (thrill)."

"Don't be a phony," Carter said. "You're only half-Jewish."

"The only reason we stay married is because its cheaper than getting a divorce," Paula said.

"Many's the time she's threatened to go home to her mother, only her mother is divorced and living with *her* mother," Carter said. "That's no gag, either. Paula's grandmother just got married at the age of 85 to a kid of 70. Can you imagine anything like that happening with *my* parents? They're so old fashioned, to them divorce is something you read about in the papers that happens only to Hollywood actresses. My father, God bless him . . ." Carter shook his head lovingly.

Carter's father owned a small candy store in Coney Island and eked out a precarious living. Many of the freaks who appeared in the Coney Island side shows came into the store. "My big thrill was when Houdini's dog bit my sister. I have two sisters and we get along fine."

Carter recalls that he once timidly sidled up to his father and whispered, "Hey, Pop, it's my birthday." His hard working parent, absorbed in his own private woes, fixed him with a malevolent stare and said, "We should break out the American flag maybe?"

Paula reminisced about the first birthday party she threw for him. "He stood in the corner like a shy little boy. He couldn't believe it. He was positive nobody would show up."

He was wrong. A Carter party is a show business attraction.

"Jack is the funniest present opener in the business," says Ed Sullivan. "People have parties nowadays just so Jack can open the presents. You can't imagine what belly laughs there are in three silk hankies when Jack opens the box. I literally fell down on the floor laughing and pounding my fists, begging for mercy. Jack is funny on my show but he's 10 times as funny at home. Paula and he once did a double on my show and he upstaged her. His own wife. Jack goes on to win," Sullivan chuckled.

"How'd we get on the birthday kick?" Carter said. "We were talking about Pop." Carter smiled. "My father is a peculiar man. He loves Paula, but he's still testing her. If she tells my mother she doesn't feel like gefilteh fish, he'll say, "See? *See?* A *shikseh* (gentile girl) wouldn't eat that." Carter chuckled. "Even my mother, good natured as she is, I'm the original 'No One's Good Enough For My Son' momma's boy. Years ago, every girl I would bring home, my mother would say, 'She's not for you. She's not for you.' Finally, one day I got mad and I hollered at her. 'Mom, for God's sake, is there a girl walking around with a sign 'This Girl Is For Jack'?"

"My folks *live* to be hurt. They pray that I don't phone, so they can go around and tell all the neighbors, 'See what a rotten son we've got? He never telephones.' "

Carter told about recently kissing Miss America, Mary Ann Mobley, on the lips. The following day, she contracted the mumps and the doctor told him to check with his parents to see whether he had had it as a child. He phoned his mother. "Mom, did I have the mumps?" "Who remembers?" "Mom, you've only got one son. It's important! Try to remember up to age 12, I'll take it after that." Meanwhile, his father was rumbling in the background, "Who? What? Where? Tell Jack not to give him his right name."

"My pop really believes in the old joke where the doctor says, 'Stick out your wallet and say Ahh' He never tells anybody he's Jack Carter's father because he's afraid he'll be overcharged. This is the first year I couldn't get my parents to come down to Florida. Their apartment was robbed so all winter long they sat by the door waiting for 12 Puerto Ricans to come in. The place looks like Langley Collier moved out 30 years ago. They leave the plugs out of the sockets because they're afraid to waste electricity. I laugh but I'm the same way."

He lighted a cigarette, took one puff and grimaced. "What am I doing with this" he said, stubbing it out. "I hate cigarettes."

"I bought him that cigarette lighter just to light my cigarettes," Paula said. "Some smoker . . ." She giggled. "He puffs but he doesn't inhale. He can't *stand* cigars, the smell drives him crazy. Jack is very sensitive to odor. He's got a whole closetful of men's cologne but he doesn't even use it—"

"I never sweat unless I'm onstage," Carter said. "Then I *giss*. There's something cockeyed about my sweat glands." A gloomy expression came over his face. "I can't even have B.O. the way any normal, average guy has it. I only shower every other day. I don't know, maybe it's a psychological reaction from my Washington Baths job as a kid in Coney Island."

The following day, I met Carter at his cabana. He was stretched out on a beach lounge. He blearily opened one bloodshot eye and glared at me. "I took one of those sleeping suppositories at five o'clock in the morning," he croaked.

"Were you able to fall asleep?"

"No, but my ass yawned all night."

He closed the eye, his face twitching slightly in the burning sun. "Let's forget about the interview today. Have lunch but not near me. The thought of food makes me nauseous."

"Relax. I promise not to ask any questions."

"You're a liar. You're going to sit there and stare at me with your pen." He lay there, gasping at regular intervals, then mumbled. "Go ahead, ask me some more of your stupid questions."

Just then Paula came over, looking voluptuous in a polka-dot bikini. I asked her if Carter is a hypochondriac.

"He's the opposite, He doesn't even know if he's sick. He never wears rubbers or a scarf or anything."

Carter suddenly sat bolt upright as a redhead undulated by, and he leered at her. "Get a load of that shape, will you?"

"Uh huh," she said, unenthusiastically.

"How much do you give your wife as a weekly allowance?" I asked Carter.

"$150." He paused. "Actually, I give her $100 but I enjoy lying."

"One hundred dollars isn't much for a big star like you."

"That's just for her bobby pins, you idiot!" Carter roared. "She spends $1,000 a month just for long distance calls."

Jack Tirman, one of Carter's many press agents, later told me. "He's frugal but *crazy* frugal. Once he raised hell with Paula for throwing out three cents worth of soup greens, then in the next breath he went out and bought her a $10,000 mink."

A jeweler-friend sat down on the adjoining lounge and Carter began to haggle with him. He loves to buy gifts for anybody even remotely associated with him. A nightclub dishwasher was astonished when the comedian came charging in one night and presented him with a handsome wristwatch. The dishwasher, a Puerto Rican, was properly grateful but had difficulty making out the numerals. They were inscribed in Hebrew.

Last Christmas, Carter was shopping in Bergdorf-Goodman for lingerie for his wife when a well-dressed stranger approached him. Talking out of the side of his mouth, he informed Carter that he would be willing to part with his $1,200 diamond ring for a mere third of the cost because he was temporarily strapped. Leading the amazed comedian over to a nearby phone booth, he gently pressed him down in the seat and delivered a persuasive sales talk. To prove beyond a shadow of a doubt that is was a perfect diamond, the impeccably dressed charlatan began to rub the ring against the glass door.

"Now he's got the glass of the phone booth door cut to shreds," Carter reminisced. "I'm saying 'Yeah, yeah, yeah' even though I *know* he's conning me and I end up buying the ring for 80 bucks cash. I've even convinced myself it's worth $1,200. I quick run over to a jeweler who's a friend. He takes one look at it and says. 'What's with the crackerjack?' I tell him, 'You're *crazy*. That ring is worth thousands.' He brings his partner over and the partner squints at it through his jeweler's loupe and says, 'Nice cheap stone you got there, but somebody ruined it by rubbing it against glass.'

"Not only did I forget to buy Paula the lingerie, but

when I got home that night what do you think she bought me for Christmas? A diamond ring!"

Carter shook his fist at a cloud that had covered the sun. "All right, we saw you. Stop showing off. Move. Beat it. One hundred dollars a day I'm paying for sunshine. Paula, why don't you sit in the sun and get some color? Any color. Get blue." It became increasingly cloudy.

"How do you like that," Carter raged, "an anti-Semitic cloud!"

"What is this green ring I see on your pinkie all the time?" I asked.

"It's a green ring you see on my pinkie all the time."

The waiter came with food on a tray. "Excuse me," Carter said, heaving himself to his feet. "It's time for my swimming lesson. I may drown just to get a laugh." He walked down to the pool.

I asked Paula how she met her husband.

"Every time I saw Jack, he was with a different beautiful girl. Not just beautiful but intelligent, so I couldn't help but be impressed. When he asked me for a date, I wouldn't go out with him at first. He kept phoning and phoning, and finally I said to him, 'All right, but you'll have to take my mother, too.' I was a little afraid of him. He had the reputation of being a playboy—"

"You mean a wolf?"

She laughed. "Some wolf. We were going together four months, and finally I told him, 'If you don't kiss me tonight, I'm never going out with you again!' "

After two years of seeing each other constantly, Paula asked whether his intentions were serious. Carter turned pale and changed the subject. She then wrote him a letter saying she thought they ought to get married. Carter's first panicky impulse was to leave the country. He wrote back that he was impossible to live with. Paula countered with another letter stating that she wouldn't dream of letting his little peccadilloes come between them. She received a letter several days later stating that he loved her too much to make her unhappy.

The impassioned correspondence built up to the inevitable climax when Carter reluctantly permitted her to announce their engagement. Paula wanted to get married immediately but Carter blushed modestly and insisted on a long engagement so they could get to know one another better.

"Jack was thinking in terms of 14 or 15 years, but I wouldn't let him get away with it."

It was a war of nerves and almost a foregone conclusion that Carter, who has always been a nervous individual, would lose the uneven battle. At the last minute, however, Carter left her waiting at the synagogue. Undaunted, Paula went to work on him again. The end came one morning at four o'clock when she was awakened from a sound sleep by Carter calling from Los Angeles, where he had a nightclub engagement. He sounded a trifle hysterical.

"Listen, Paula," he said tensely, "Something terrible has happened—"

"Oh my God! Are you all right, darling?" Paula inquired anxiously.

"Me? I'm fine but I forgot to water my plants before I left. Will you run over like a good girl and water them?"

"Now?" Paula inquired in a dangerously restrained voice. "At four o'clock in the morning."

"Paula, I swear I'll marry you when I get back from the Coast. Only please, *please* water my plants or they'll die!" he blubbered. True to his word, Carter married her when he got back, but he was so angry at himself for giving in, he virtually ignored her for one solid month afterwards.

For a while, they maintained their own apartments because Carter was convinced the marriage wouldn't last. The Broadway columnists called it "Carter East" and "Carter West."

At the time, Paula was playing the ingenue in *Wildcat,* and Lucille Ball refused to give them a wedding present until they moved into one apartment. "Your marriage isn't a real marriage until you live together, you silly kids" she told them. Again, Paula had a tough job convincing him, but they finally gave up their individual apartments and moved into a luxurious eight-room apartment on Central Park West. Carter took one look at the opulent furnishings and snarled, "I hate this crummy joint!"

According to Paula, the reason Carter doesn't like the apartment is because it's on the nineteenth floor and he can't lean out the window and scream at strangers. This is one of the few pleasures he has in life.

One day, he unwillingly accompanied her to the showroom of the company that makes furniture for the White

House. Paula selected a blue couch and for once he liked what she had selected. When it was delivered six weeks later, he glared at the inoffensive couch and demanded, "What's this hunk of junk?" Paula reminded him that he had given his okay.

"I don't like it! Send it back!" It reminded him of a couch his family had in the old days when they lived in back of the candy store. After some rather heated words, Paula gave in and sent it back. The following day, Carter went to Bloomingdale's and ordered another blue couch. "It's almost exactly the same couch, but to this day Jack won't admit it."

Several weeks later in New York I phoned Carter just as he was about to leave for Palm Beach to star in *A Thousand Clowns*. He told me he had fired the public relations firm that represented him and re-hired his former press agent, Jack Tirman. I was to get in touch with him for any further biographical material. I phoned Tirman and told him what Carter had said. There was a stunned silence, then Tirman laughed uproariously.

"How do you like that crazy bastard? He never told *me!*"

I met Tirman the following Saturday at the Friars' club. A slender, balding, rapid-talking man, Tirman said Carter had been his most eccentric client. He told me about the time the comic had just concluded a big TV spectacular and scored a personal triumph. "Jack was secure for maybe 25 minutes."

Tirman persuaded the TV editor of New York's *Daily News*, the country's biggest newspaper, to interview Carter. They met in Sardi's restaurant. The TV editor told him what a marvelous performance he had given and various show business friends came over to the table to congratulate him. Carter stared at the caricatures of actors on the walls and became increasingly gloomy.

"Jack had just played to something like 20,000,000 people," Tirman explained, "but he was terribly upset because he didn't make the walls at Sardi's."

According to Tirman, Carter is a highly sensitive man who lives in perpetual fear of offending people. "Jack screams at you, and five minutes later, he forgets why. I liked him so much I did publicity for him for nothing even after our contract ran out."

Tirman signaled the waiter for some more coffee.

"Worry. That's his middle name. I've seen him on his way to a date in the old days. He'd telephone and make another date for later that same evening, just so he shouldn't be hung up. Once he went out with six different girls in one night. In the middle of a handball game with me, he'd be worrying what he was going to be doing a half-hour after the handball game.

"Jack is a great comedy star," Tirman added, "but that's not enough for him. He wants to be a big dramatic star. But if he ever got to be another Barrymore, say, he wouldn't be happy because he'd want to be another Caruso.

Tirman stopped a plumpish man in his early forties and asked him to sit at our table. "This is Jay Burton, the gag writer. He can tell you a million stories about Jack Carter."

"This is a nut of nuts," Burton said, recalling an occasion 10 years ago in Miami when he, Carter and Sid Caesar, another notoriously indecisive personality, felt like having a bite to eat at 2 A.M.

For 15 minutes, they couldn't make up their minds whether to take Jack's car or Sid's car or a taxi. Then Burton was seized by inspiration. "Fellas," he said, "I tell you what, let's take Jack's car." Grateful that Burton had made the big decision for them, they all piled into Jack's car and drove off.

"Jack drives around the safety island," Burton recalls, "cursing and screaming like a madman at the other cars. Then he drives right back to the hotel and says, 'I can't take this Miami traffic, let's grab a cab.' They went to six restaurants and never even touched the food. Either they didn't like the looks of the headwaiter or the menu was too fancy or the hatcheck girl was blonde instead of brunette," Burton recalls. "Finally at four o'clock in the morning, they're still arguing about where we should eat and I said the hell with it. I lost my appetite and went to bed."

Tirman told me that Carter enjoyed an exceptionally busy year in 1961. He was booked every week for 50 solid weeks and earned considerable sums of money. During the two free weeks Carter grew increasingly nervous and began to gnaw at his nails. He pestered his agent every day until the latter finally secured him a booking. Carter turned pale at the news.

"My God, I've forgotten how to talk to an audience. I say hello to the people, right? *Then* what do I do?"

When the Carters returned from Palm Beach several weeks later, I met them at the office of Bullets Durgom, the comedian's manager.

I asked Carter how he liked Palm Beach.

"It's a disaster area," he said. "The youngest couple is 90. Two of them died while the show was on. We didn't tell them because we didn't want to spoil their evening."

At the conclusion of the play, as the audience was filing out, Carter yelled, "Come on back! There's a fourth act!" Carter chuckled. "They couldn't believe their ears. They never heard a play talk back."

He told about introducing actress Penny Fuller to the audience. Miss Fuller, who hails from North Carolina, played the part of Sandy Markowitz from the Bronx. Carter said. "B'nai Brith made her a retroactive Hebrew. She's entitled to 25 years of retroactive persecution."

Carter willingly sacrificed a month of lucrative nightclub bookings to work in *A Thousand Clowns* for $2,000 a week. "After taxes and agents and managerial fees, I maybe had a dime left for a cup of coffee, but I was happy."

I asked if he had somebody who watched his money.

"I watch my money," Carter rumbled. "I watch it go."

"I never know what we're going to do any evening until positively the last minute," says Paula. "God forbid I should make plans. Jack *hates* to make plans. Either we have dinner at the corner delicatessen or in Hong Kong, there's no in between."

"We'll be having dinner in Las Vegas next Thursday," Carter said. "I'm booked for six weeks there." He brooded for a moment.

"There's not much dignity in the nightclub world. I have a terrible tendency to put it down myself. I remember we were rehearsing *Mr. Wonderful* and Julie Styne, the producer, said about a certain bit, 'That's no good. That's *nightclub*' like it was a dirty word. Sammy Davis, Jr. who was in the show with me—or rather, I should say I was in the show with him—tore off his jacket and flung it on the floor, he was so mad. For 30 solid minutes, he told poor Julie off about the wonderful heritage of nightclubs, how so many big-time performers have started in nightclubs.

"The trouble is, we all yearn for the legitimate stage

because it has prestige. I worked a solid month in *A Thousand Clows* in Palm Beach for peanuts when I could have made 10 times the money in nightclubs . . ."

Carter glowered at me darkly. "That——David Merrick knocked me out of a play once just by saying, 'Carter isn't Equity.' You know what he meant, don't you?"

"Let's go somewhere for cocktails," Paula interjected.

"I feel more like seltzer," Carter said.

Carter drinks sparingly and is probably the only performer who wakes up in the morning suffering a hangover without benefit of alcohol. Says Red Buttons, "I've never seen him drunk in my life. He has a mental high going all the time." He enjoys, if that is the proper verb, a simple Spartan breakfast of coffee and self-flagellation. The coffee is almost but not quite as black as his mood and is rarely hot enough to suit him.

One morning, annoyed by his constant carping at the temperature of the coffee, Paula invited him to stick his finger in the cup and test it. Carter's eyes almost popped out of his head as he dipped his finger into the scalding coffee. Manfully restraining a scream of pain, he kept his finger in the coffee and smiled at her nonchalantly.

"See? I told you it wasn't hot enough."

Paula didn't say anything but gazed at his submerged finger, which was slowly but inexorably blistering. Carter held out as long as he could, then pulled his boiled finger out and ran, screaming and cursing, around the house.

I met Carter and Tirman backstage at the Americana Hotel in New York, where he had been booked to play a benefit. Tirman told me that Carter's agent had come up with a $5,000 club date afterwards, but Jack had turned it down. Carter was pacing back and forth backstage, peering out behind the curtain at the waiting audience, muttering and cursing to himself.

"Jack," Tirman said, "it's only a lousy benefit, for God's sake! Not only are you not making a nickel on the deal, you're dropping five gees to boot. Stop aggravating yourself!"

Carter ignored him as he peered out from behind the curtain. "Looka that skinny bastard at the front table. He looks like a nonlaugher to me . . ."

Tirman was amused. "It's like talking to the wall to tell Jack to stop aggravating himself. That's his only pleasure in life."

We heard the master of ceremonies announce Carter's

name. A roar went up from the audience. Carter turned pale, then walked onstage, looking as though he were headed for the electric chair ...

A postscript which might also be a statement about the art of comedy: early in 1970 Jack Carter was divorced from his wife Paula and the event, celebrated in Earl Wilson's column, *It Happened Last Night,* made the comic-most out of what we are still inclined to take for a tragic circumstance. According to Earl Wilson, Jack said: "Your wife gets half, your wife's lawyer gets half, and the judge says, 'You can put me down for about $350 a week.'" Jack also said that the settlement provided that his wife get the swimming pool while he got the diving board. And that's "Divorce Western Style" with a made-in-California label. "I can use the diving board any time I want to as long as I don't use the pool," concluded Jack.

7. MILTON "THE MISERABLE" BERLE

Milton Berle's famed broad grin, with the beaver-like front teeth, had disappeared. There were no funny gestures, no sarcastic quips. Even the great man's favorite cigars—king-sized Havanas worth $2 each—lay untouched in their humidor beside his bed.

The comedian was sick.

Wrapped in woolen blankets, shivering, moaning and complaining about aches in his stomach and back, Berle was the most miserable man in Las Vegas. And that meant a lot of other people were miserable ... because when Milton Berle suffers, he doesn't like to suffer alone.

His wife was miserable because she had been forced to sit up with him, babying him during the long sleepless night, listening while he recited all his miseries, physical and mental. "Ruth," he had groaned, "something terrible is happening to me. I don't know what it is. All I know is that it's getting worse ..."

Berle's doctor was miserable because the illness of his celebrated patient—allegedly one of Hollywood's most notorious hypochondriacs—was difficult to diagnose. It appeared to be partly a virus attack, but Berle's temperature was almost normal, his lungs were clear and his pulse was strong. The doctors believed that Berle was suffering mostly from nervous exhaustion brought on by worry and overwork. But it was impossible to convince the comedian of this.

"Doc, do something!" Berle pleaded. "Get me back on my feet! I've got a show to do!"

Berle's manager was miserable because a $160,000 booking (four weeks at $40,000 per week) was in jeopardy at the Desert Inn. The inn's entertainment director was miserable because it was difficult to replace an artist of Berle's stature on such short notice. And two dozen members of Berle's cast were miserable, facing the probability of being thrown out of work

By noon of the second day, Berle's condition had worsened. He lay trembling and pale in his $100-a-day hotel suite, complaining that the aches and pains had shifted to his legs and neck. Aspirin and other medicines had not helped. His moans were so loud they could be heard in the outside corridor His wife, former actress Ruth Cosgrove, had become distraught. Berle was now running a genuine fever, and his face and pajamas were wet with perspiration. He looked like a dying man His chin was shadowed with dirty gray stubble, his long hair was unkempt, revealing his bald spot, and his blue eyes were glazed.

Most distressing of all was his despondency. He was convinced that he would never work again. The man who, for 20 years in succession, had earned $500,000 or more a year was certain his career was finished. Again and again he mumbled fears about a great doom that would soon crush him. But he did not make it clear whether he expected bankruptcy, pneumonia, death—or what.

Mrs. Berle (she is his second wife) had nursed him through similar emotional crises in the past. But none had ever been this critical. She felt that drastic action was needed and she knew who could supply it—Miss May Mehlinger, Milton's Christian Science practitioner. Ruth had been reluctant to summon Miss Mehlinger, an elderly woman who lived in Los Angeles and did not like to travel. But further delay was now out of the question.

Ruth telephoned her. The practitioner came to Las Vegas at once by plane, arriving at Berle's bedside that evening. She immediately began a session of prayer and meditation that was to last many hours. It was a remarkable scene, too melodramatic for even a daytime TV soap opera of a B movie. It was a scene that Uncle Miltie's millions of fans would never see—and wouldn't have understood if they had been able to see it.

The Jewish comedian, a devout Christian Scientist for more than two decades, clasped his hands and prayed for peace and serenity of mind. The elderly woman—white-haired and gentle-faced—prayed with him in a low, soothing voice.

Berle began to relax. Between prayers, Miss Mehlinger drew forth information about what was troubling him the most. Berle confessed that he had become obsessed with worry when one of the top acts in his show canceled out and he was unable to replace it with performers of equal talent. His manager and the inn's entertainment officials had argued that he could do his revue without replacing the act.

But Berle had insisted that the show would be a fiasco. An utter perfectionist who agonizes over every detail, he had fussed, fidgeted and fretted himself into total collapse.

"You must not close the show," Miss Mehlinger told him quietly but firmly. "You must be unselfish about it—and not throw all these people out of work."

"But I need another major act," Berle whispered hoarsely. I've tried, but I can't find one!"

"A better one will come along," said Miss Mehlinger serenely. "Now let us pray and read more verses to-gether . . ."

Around midnight Berle became calm enough to sleep. He awoke in the morning refreshed and alert, his temperature normal. He showered and shaved, had a small breakfast, and lit one of his elegantly long cigars. Then he went downstairs to the inn's cavernous lounge and began auditioning.

What Miss Mehlinger had predicted came to pass. He found another act. The act, and Berle's show was a hit.

Millions of TV viewers and night club audiences are familiar with *Milton the Glad*—the brassy, glib, sarcastic wit who strides on stage shouting one-line insults. The other Berle, is *Milton the Sad,* familiar to his family and such other intimates as the entertainers and staff employees who work closely with him as he suffers through the grueling preparations for each show.

Milton the Glad cavorts and mugs while performing, looking like the happiest man on God's green earth. He spouts gags like a pom-pom gun.

Pointing at a woman in the audience with a feather in her hat, he shouts: "That looks like the feather that signed the Declaration of Independence! (Pause.) And the guy with her looks like he signed it!" He glares at a bald man and exclaims: "That head has been shining in my face all night. I'd like to stick my finger in his ear and go bowling." To a woman trying to find her seat: "You can sit down, madam—we saw the dress." And to a drunk, trying to heckle him: "Look, I'm just a poor guy trying to make a living. I don't come down where you work and kick your shovel out from under you, do I?"

But it's all a front and Milton knows it. The real Milton Berle admits that he has an inferiority complex, that he is uncertain from day to day about his talent. This is a ridiculous fear, because Berle is acknowledged throughout the industry as one of the all-time geniuses of the performing arts. He is incredibly experienced as a writer, producer, composer, director and choreographer as well as a vocalist, actor and comedian.

And there's the rub. Milton Berle knows too much about show business. He knows everybody's job—and as a result he has a compulsion to tell each studio employee how to do his or her work, from lowly propmen, grips, script girls and cue card boys to top-talented directors and producers. Sometimes Milton keeps his mouth shut and endures their alleged mistakes in painful silence. But usually he interferes. His endless criticisms and corrections of others create tension and turmoil wherever he works.

Away from the job, at home or social affairs, Berle can be charming and erudite, a gifted conversationalist who can discuss politics (he is an ardent Democrat), religion or the Dow-Jones averages at a highly intelligent level. At such times he is never the boor or loudmouth he pretends to be on stage. Occasionally, for laughs, he indulges in insults and biting sarcasms. But he is basically a very likable man who enjoys being around people and values their friendship.

That's why he becomes Milton the Miserable whenever he's working. He detests criticism. He dreads being disliked by his co-workers. But, striving for perfection in each show, he is compelled to argue and quibble, to agitate and quarrel until finally the matter under consideration is done exactly *his* way. Berle is respected as a craftsman by all who work with him. But out of his earshot, they tear their hair, gnash their bicuspids and complain: "He's unreasonable! He's impossible! He's a holy terror!"

After years of banishment from television, except for guest appearances, Berle worked out a complicated financial deal in 1966 which enabled him to return with a series on the ABC network. Those selected to work with him hoped that Berle, now approaching his sixties, would be mellower and easier to please. Their hopes were dashed on the very first production day when Berle mounted the stage at the Hollywood Palace theater and promptly changed the positions of all the color TV cameras and sound booms.

In the weeks that followed the man who had once been Mr. Television acquired a new and unwanted title—Mr. Temperamental. He presided over the set like a grumpy grandpa. The experts he worked with were brilliant men in their twenties and thirties who were stunned by the number of technical and artistic roadblocks he strewed in their way. An assistant director who kept count reported that one day Berle shouted "Hold it!" 14 times in the morning and 10 times in the afternoon, halting production 24 times.

Only once during the day did Berle crack his celebrated beaver grin. That was for a studio photographer who needed some publicity pictures. Berle gave him one quick pose and sent him on his way. The rest of the time Berle pouted, sulked and fumed. He complained that the gold evening gowns worn by guest stars Martha Raye and Jayne Mansfield glittered so much that the audience wouldn't be able to see the star of the show.

"In case you've forgotten," he reminded the director, "that's me."

He complained that the stage lights were so blinding he couldn't read his lines on the cue cards. He complained because one sound boom was being used instead of two. He exploded with rage when the cameras ignored the star during a slow-motion skit, focusing for much of a minute on the graceful antics of former football star Jimmy Brown. "What about me?" whined Berle. "Is it too much to ask for a picture of *this* once in a while?" He pointed a finger dramatically at his own face.

When Martha Raye gave him a light love tap on the skull with a flimsy sign, he complained that it was such a vicious, hard blow he was in danger of suffering brain damage. He wasn't kidding, causing a camera assistant to comment soto voce: "What brain?" During a song-and-gag skit with Jayne and Martha, Berle stopped the action abruptly and complained: "I'm too darn tired. I just can't rehearse any more!"

He walked off the stage, letting the girls go it alone. He slouched in the theater's center aisle, hands clasped across his paunch, offering sour comments on how the rehearsal was progressing. Since no one paid any attention to his criticisms, he stopped pouting after a minute or two, rejoined the girls and went wearily on with the skit.

When the show was broadcast the following week, Berle looked like his youthful self of years past frolicking with apparently boundless energy, his paunch concealed by skillfully tailored clothes. Although the critics gave the series favorable reviews, it sank out of sight in the Nielsen ratings (ranking 80th among 92 shows), stirring predictions that it would be dropped by ABC. Berle, choking down his disappointment, declared that he wouldn't quit, no matter how bad things got.

Just before the show was axed, in mid-season, a studio spokesman, 20 years Berle's junior, declared "That's the trouble with these old-timers. They never know when they're finished."

Born in New York's Harlem section on July 12, 1908, Berle comes from the old school of performers who battled poverty and near-starvation to reach the top, and who insist on sticking in show business until the day they die. When Milton was born, his parents, Moe and Sarah Berlinger, lived on the sixth floor of a six-story walkup. He was the fourth of five children.

During Milton's baby years, the Berlingers were dispossessed six times for failure to pay the rent. Moe Berlinger was a loving father but totally ineffective as a job holder. Suffering chronic rheumatism, he worked a few days here, a few there, selling paint, mixing perfume, trying to invent household gadgets. Once he spent months on the development of an unbreakable umbrella. Like his other ideas, it was an impratical failure, so heavy and sturdy it wouldn't fold properly.

Milton recalls, still with bitterness, a dismal event which occured when he was about 4½ years old. The family had been on short rations for about a week, with both parents out looking for work. One morning Mama Berlinger fed her four small boys toast and water for breakfast, then left them a small amount of boiled codfish and three hard rolls for lunch. Long before noon, one of his older brothers (Milton declines to identify him) grew ravenous and secretly raided the icebox. He ate all the codfish. Still hungry he went to the tin breadbox and wolfed down the hard rolls.

"The rest of us got no lunch," Berle remembers sadly, "It was one of the worst days of my life. Also the longest. The three of us were so weak with hunger we just lay around the flat, waiting for Mom to come home. It got later and later. Finally, long after dark, Mom came in. Crying and hollering, we rushed her, demanding something to eat. All she had was four bagels which she'd gotten for two cents because they were leftovers at the bakery. We each got a bagel plus one third, carefully divided. The brother who'd stuffed himself didn't get any. Instead he got a whipping. Then we all went to bed and cried, because we were so hungry and miserable . . ."

A few days later the family fortunes improved. Mama landed a job as store detective at Altman's department store. Her salary was a lofty $30 a week. Sharp-eyed and curious, she was the best detective the store ever had. Often she took her whole brood along as a cover. Shoplifters were stunned when they realized—too late—that the friendly faced woman with four boys and a babe in arms (sister Rosemary) was a store cop whose charges could send them to jail.

Milton's show business career was launched the following year, quite by accident. On Halloween night, the five-year-old boy dressed himself in his father's suit, shoes and bowler. He cut a tiny square of black fur from his mother's muff and pasted it under his nose. Then he waddled down the street, twirling a bamboo cane and followed by an admiring group of youngsters. A passer-by corralled him and brought him back to Mama.

"Say, this kid is good," he said. "I want to enter him in a Charlie Chaplin contest up in Mount Vernon." Milton won the $5 first prize. Mama did some swift calculation and realized he had made as much in one hour as she earned in a day. A frustrated actress whose immigrant parents had forbidden her to work in the theater, Mama decided there and then that Milton would have the career denied to her.

"We'll be rich," she promised, "but you're going to have to work very hard." Taking time off from her store job, she took Milton by ferry the next morning across the Hudson to Fort Lee, New Jersey, where Biograph Films paid photogenic moppets $1.50 per walk-on. Soon he graduated to film parts, with Marie Dressler in *Tillie's Punctured Romance*, and Pearl White in *Perils of Pauline.*

The money was less than Mama hoped for—sometimes they wasted entire days waiting in producers' offices for jobs that didn't materialize. But she was sure on the right track. She quit her job at Altman's and became a full-time, super-aggressive stage mother.

Eddie Buzzell, an old-time vaudevillian recalls emerging from the door of the Palace, in New York, after a matinee nearly half a century ago. Waiting for him in the narrow alley was a woman clutching the hand of a small boy. Says Buzzell: "She grabbed me by the lapel. 'I just caught your act,' she said—I knew she was fibbing because I'd come off the stage that minute—'and my little boy does the most wonderful impersonation of you. Show him, Milton!' Little Milton let go of her hand and hopped into a perfect imitation of Eddie Cantor."

Unflattered, Buzzell shrugged and walked away. But mistakes like that didn't bother Mama. She was certain Milton could make the big time in a twinkling if he could be seen by somebody important. She tried again. She sneaked him backstage at the Winter Garden, where Al Jolson was appearing. She hid in the wings, prepared to propel Milton on stage the moment the great star walked off. Milton was to launch into one of Jolson's songs, *April Showers,* and make an unforgettable impact on Jolson and the audience.

But the crowd kept Jolson on for encore after encore. Mama waited, fuming. Suddenly, in the midst of a mighty burst of applause for Jolson, Milton jumped with a yelp of pain. For no reason at all, other than her burning frustration and envy of Jolson, Mama had smacked Milton furiously on the backside and yelled: "Now you will rehearse!"

The boy broke into tears. He was still crying when Jolson came off. Mama, aware that Milton couldn't perform in that emotional state, grabbed his arm and they fled from the theater. Outside, Mama broke into tears. Milton stared at her in silent wonder. It was the only time he ever saw her weep.

Mama refused to quit. While Papa Moe stayed home taking care of the other children, doing the cooking and washing, Mama kept hammering on producers' doors. When acting jobs weren't available, she got Milton small fees for singing and dancing in private clubs. By the time he was eight, Milton had missed so much schooling that the Gerry Society, a watchdog group which sought to keep children under 16 off the stage, cracked down on him. While Milton was entertaining one night at a club smoker, a society official made what was, in effect, a citizen's arrest. He strode onto the stage, stopped the show, seized Milton and dragged him off to a nearby precinct police station.

Mama was outraged. Like an express train, she roared into the station after her darling. But she didn't identify herself as Milton's mother. Instead, striding up to the juvenile authorities, she declared: "I'll handle this!" She flashed her defunct store detective badge, implied that she was a truant officer from another part of town—and whisked Milton home.

The following week Mama shortened his name from Berlinger to Berle and enrolled Milton in the Professional Children's School, where fellow students included Lillian Roth and Ruby Keeler. He was a bright student, able to memorize quickly whole pages of script, and he had a brash, toothy grin that made everything he said seem funny or smart, whether it was or not. The school helped him acquire work as a kid comic, singer and dancer with theatrical and silent movie companies.

By the time he was 11 years old, he was on the Keith-Albee vaudeville circuit, earning $95 a week, supporting his entire family. It was an incredible salary for even an adult in those days. But Mama, still thinking in terms of Really Big Money, was dissatisfied.

"We'll do better," she insisted. And they did.

The next year, she nailed down a spot for him in a Shubert revival of *Floradora*. Milton was one of 12 boys and girls chosen to perform a precision dance number. The job was the turning point of Berle's career and he still enjoys telling the story at parties or while chatting backstage.

"It was one of Mom's classical maneuvers," he says. "We had rehearsed for weeks all regimented to dance in exactly the same way. We opened in various cities and then came to New York for the big effort. On the way to the theater, Mom said, 'Milton, what foot do you start with when you walk on?' I told her—the left foot.

"She said, 'Tonight, at the opening performance, you start on the right!'

" 'But, Mama,' I argued, 'it'll knock me off for the wholenumber. I'll be out of step!'

"She glared at me with her stern blue eyes. 'That's right!' she said. 'And you'll do it—or I'll slap you silly!' "

When the number started, Milton braced himself and began with his right foot while the 11 others came on with the left. To his amazement, the audience howled with laughter and never stopped. When the curtain came down, the great man himself, J. J. Shubert, strolled backstage. "Where is that little boy who was out of step?" he asked.

Mama, holding a trembling Milton firmly by the hand, brought him forward.

"Young man," J. J., "what happened to you?"

Mama squeezed Milton's hand very hard, a warning for him to keep silent. Then she spoke: "Milton was very nervous. He forgot what foot to start on."

Since J. J. was unforgiving about mistakes, Berle expected to be fired on the spot. But J. J. looked down at him and said: "Can you do it the same way from now on?"

"That was our first great triumph," says Berle. "And it proved what a great showman my mother instinctively was ..."

When he was 17, Berle was a master of ceremonies, knitting together the various acts on the bill at Loew's State. By then he could also juggle, perform quick magic tricks, ride a unicycle, do acrobatics and act in dramatic sequences. During the next few years he developed the smart alec comedy style which was to earn him the acrid hatred of every established and powerful comic in the industry.

Other comedians started out as humble young fellows eager for the favor of their professional superiors. Berle started out by brazenly using the material of other comics, editing it to suit himself—and then insulting those same comics as he spouted their jokes on stage.

His style was the outgrowth of his conviction—which he still holds—that all jokes are public property, and that no matter who told the gag first he, Berle, can tell it better. While in his teens, Milton began a filing system which today includes 1,800,000 gags of all kinds, carefully catalogued alphabetically, some dating back to 1857. Berle claims that he has 50,000 of these jokes stored in his memory, along with key words that trigger them into action when needed.

In the Thirties, Berle's alleged joke thievery had all the comedians in New York screaming for their lawyers, demanding that legal action be taken to restrain him. Finally, in 1936, two comedians dragged Milton into court, accusing him of lifting their copyrighted comedy material without payment. Berle proved by witnesses, and his file records, that he had done the comedy bit a dozen years previously. "And furthermore," Berle told the judge loudly, "I did it funnier!"

His victory discouraged similar complaints and Berle

and his Mama went their merry way. Like the jokes about stolen jokes, Mom was soon the basis for Berle comedy routines, too. When some woman would laugh exceptionally loud at a Berle sally, he would pause and say, "Thank you, mother." Later, if a man laughed, he would repeat the line and then do a double-take.

Comedians who loathed Berle the most played foolishly into his hands. Cracks about "Milton Berle's mother" were soon part of almost every comic's routine. Sometimes the cracks were funny, sometimes merely cruel. All they accomplished was to give Berle and his Mom free publicity.

Frequently Milton invited his mother on stage for a bow. This was a useful device calculated to save his energy by eliminating one of his many encores. Mama loved it. Her pride in Milton was boundless. Once she waited in a busy hotel lobby for a phone call from him. The page boy found her and she hurried to the counter where a sizeable crowd was waiting to use the house phones. Mom picked up a phone.

"THIS IS MRS. SARAH BERLE," she said in a voice which could be heard on the fourth floor. "The MOTHER OF MILTON BERLE!"

With the money rolling in by the barrelful, the Berles could afford a few luxuries. Mama loved furs and jewels, and even changed her name from Sarah to Sandra to match her glamorous surroundings. Milton enjoyed fine cars and $275 suits. He spent $10,000 to have his prominent beak remodeled. The sum was a pittance compared to his bill for cigars, which eventually soared to $15,000 a year!

Although Mama discouraged his interest in girls, he dated frequently, usually show beauties whom he took to the best night clubs. Quite often he let Mom tag along. Some of the girls objected; most didn't, because it was to their advantage to be seen in public with a man of his stature.

In 1941—ignoring Mama's objections—he married Joyce Mathews, a gorgeous blonde show girl with bedroom eyes and a figure to match. She was 18; he was 33. The marriage was unsuccessful for two reasons: Mama's alleged interference and Milton's frantic new career in radio. Adding brothers Phil and Jack to his personal staff, Berle labored 16 and 18 hours a day, performing in radio and night clubs, a schedule which gave him little time for his cute bride. Added to this was the tension of smashing headlong into the stone wall of his first major defeat.

He was a bust in radio. After one sponsor fired him, he tried again with the same results. Then again—and still again. Every gimmick he had developed for his successful stage routines worked against him. Repeatedly he relied on visual tricks for visual laughs from the studio audience—all of which was wasted on the radio audience. He insisted upon being his own brash, overpowering self, regardless of what the script called for in characterization and story line.

Cracked a studio official: "The trouble with Berle on the radio is that his personality comes through!"

Milton returned to night club work, demanding—and getting—$12,000 a week, making him one of the nations's highest paid performers during the early Forties. Rejected by the draft (he was 4F), still stewing about his radio flops (did they portend more failures?), he grew increasingly nervous and insecure. Unlike many others in his profession who released their tensions with booze and dames, Berle was a highly moral man who didn't drink to excess, or chase after girls.

But he badly needed escape. Smoking to excess was one vice; he burned up from 15 to 25 long Cuban stogies a day. But that was hardly big league escape, so he turned with a passion to betting on horses. He used half a dozen bookies, phoning them wherever he happened to be— backstage, in the steam room or restaurants. During one frantic period of several months, he managed to be on 32 races daily between breakfast and bed, his wagers ranging from $50 to 150 each.

Asked "How'd you do today, Miltie?" his stock reply was: "Wonderful! I only lost $5,000!"

Sometimes he wasn't kidding. Other times he even had tumultuous winning days, picking up $5,000 or more. Inevitably he suffered an awesome losing streak. Trying to recoup, he bet $97,000 in two weeks—and was clobbered again. He never revealed, even to his closest friends, the full extent of his losses. They were so shockingly high, and he went so deeply into debt, that Berle decided to quit cold turkey. For several years he didn't bet at all. Later he relented, becoming a casual, gentleman bettor, seldom wagering more than $20 on a horse.

During his most frenzied gambling period, he contributed as usual to many charities. He established the

Milton Berle Foundation in Aid of Crippled Children, raising $2,000,000 through benefit entertainments and donations he collected from other performers and groups.

In 1946, long before the era of swollen show biz salaries, his total earnings were $710,000. But the money did not make him any happier. His marriage to Joyce Mathews was stumbling toward the divorce courts; often he couldn't sleep nights, despite being exhausted from his man-killing entertainment schedules; and he was developing into a full-fledged hypochondriac, worrying endlessly about drafts and colds, dosing himself with patent medicines, troubled with painful attacks of abdominal gas from nervous indigestion.

But what really bugged him were the assaults of newspaper and magazine writers. No matter what Berle did, no matter how successful he became, he was the butt of unceasing criticism which he considered underhanded and unjust. Insatiably curious, he read every word published about him, flying into antics of rage when he encountered a particularly galling insult. One Saturday night, noticing that Berle was downcast, his trumpet player, Leonard Sues, took him aside.

"Milton," he said, "why don't you take it easy? Why not come with me to church and get a little mental relaxation?"

They went to Sunday morning services at the Christian Science church in Camden, New Jersey. "It was an entirely new experience for me."

The following day Leonard introduced Milton to Miss Mehlinger, the woman who was later to move to California and become Berle's practitioner. They had a long, intense talk. Afterward Miss Mehlinger said: "I found Mr. Berle to be a most warm and decent human being. He was troubled. His main theme was that he was mentally and physically sound, but he feared some impending doom. I reasoned with him along the religious lines we are taught."

Commented Berle: "That woman is wonderful. Her voice is so reassuring. It's like the voice of God."

His new-found religion sustained Berle through the breakup of his marriage in 1947 and the mad but wonderful era of his success as "Mr. Television" on the Texaco Star Theater. For eight long years, starting in 1948, he dominated the then new entertainment medium. For an incredible five of those years, his was the No. 1 show on the air. He was so full of energy and optimism that he even remarried Joyce. Again they clashed, quickly divorcing. She married Billy Rose, after slashing her wrists during a fit of despondency in the apartment of the pint-sized showman.

During his heyday in TV, Berle did 366 live, one-hour weekly shows, a record still unchallenged by any other performer, causing him to comment proudly: "The longevity of that program will never be equaled. Week after wearying week, another show, more jokes—I'd say it was the equivalent of making 8,000 motion pictures. I finally went off the air in June, 1956. Why? I needed rest. I was overexposed and the ratings showed it. I was starting to get lousy. I'm a perfectionist and perfection is impossible on live TV. I have eyes to see and my ears are sensitive to sound and after a while I saw too many mistakes and heard too many. I'd had it, but good . . ."

After exiting from TV, Berle spent a few months resting, counting his money (the show had made him a multimillionaire) and enjoying a second honeymoon with his new wife.

Ruth Cosgrave, 15 years younger than Berle, was exactly the kind of woman he needed. She had helped him through the bad days in June, 1954, when his mother died suddenly at the age of 77. The loss of his greatest fan had knocked him into a mental funk which only the loving care of another woman could dissipate. Ruth had the ability to coddle him when he needed it, but—being a former WAC captain as well as an actress and ex-press agent—she could also restrain him and discipline him whenever necessary.

"She's a cool one," Berle once said. "She can stop me with a glance, or the lack of a glance. She has settled me down. I call her Rocky, because she's my Rock of Gibraltar."

From Ruth, Berle draws what he once drew from his mother—approval (most of the time), reassurance and sharp criticism when he gets out of line. "Being married to Milton is the hardest job I ever had," she says. "He can be very difficult. He's a worrier who's never content. In the beginning I found him childishly impossible. I had always been self-sufficient, accustomed to come and go as I pleased. Many times I resisted the urge to belt him one—and walk out."

Ruth discovered that Berle was a maniac while working

in TV, but a bigger maniac when he was out of TV and moping around the house with nothing to occupy his mind. She encouraged him to return to TV in 1958 with a new weekly series, *Milton Berle Starring in the Kraft Music Hall*. He lasted only 39 weeks. The old routines and the old wisecracks couldn't cut it with viewers spoiled by television's incessant experimentation with new ideas and new faces.

Again Berle moped around his $250,000 Regency mansion in Beverly Hills. He played golf, collected jokes, played benefits, read scripts, suffered chronic insomnia, complained about his ulcer and generally drove Ruth wild. She was delighted two years later when he returned to TV with—of all things—a weekly sports show. It was called *Jackpot Bowling Starring Milton Berle*. But he actually had second billing to a bowling ball.

It was a horrible mishmash which was mercifully put out of its misery after one season. It earned Berle nearly $600,000, but the money was meaningless. "Who needs it?" he commented sourly. "Uncle Miltie makes it, and Uncle Sam takes it. Hell, I even make dough when I'm just sitting around on my tail, doing nothing."

His reference was to his unusual NBC contract which, signed in 1951, assured him an income of $100,000 a year for 30 years, whether he worked or not. But it turned out to be a reeking albatross draped around his neck, preventing him from working for other networks which—eager for his services—offered him juicy deals. After the bowling fiasco, NBC ignored his pleas for a new series, keeping him on the shelf year after year.

Matters finally reached a stage where NBC's top brass wouldn't answer the phone when Berle called, and that was the deepest wound of all in his pride. He fended off the feeling of creeping uselessness by playing with his baby son Billy, adopted in 1962, making night club appearances, and acting in such films as *Mad, Mad, Mad World* and *The Oscar*. He also made one-shot appearances in TV dramas (a tragic role in *The Defenders* won extremely high praise from the critics) and dabbled in Democratic politics.

Attending a state dinner in 1964 at the White House, Berle, resplendent in white tie and tails, strolled up to the receiving line and stuck out his hand. Bearing his beaver teeth, he grinned up at the tall Texan and said: "Er, I didn't catch the name—" President Johnson broke into a guffaw that echoed throughout the room. Later, Berle danced with Lady Bird while Ruth waltzed with the President.

During an interview that same year with writer Gerold Frank, Ruth made it painfully clear that she opposed Berle's stubborn attempts to return to TV in a weekly series. "I couldn't go through that again," she said. "It was a nightmare. I wasn't his wife. I was just someone in his house who had to listen to the tirades when something went wrong. No time for pleasantries. It was the show, the show, the show. I began enjoying marriage to him only when he stopped having that damn weekly show. I don't want him to go back to one. I told him I'd leave him if he did."

Nevertheless, Berle kept negotiating for one. Finally he coaxed NBC into eliminating the exclusivity clause in his 30-year contract. He agreed to a 40 per cent pay cut, reducing his annual stipend to $60,000, but gained permission to work regularly for other networks. Commented an NBC spokesman a bit smugly: "It wasn't a difficult decision for us. Not really. We love Milton, of course. But we know he'll never be Mr. Big again. The other networks can have him—if they still want him."

ABC did. Once the deal was set, he still had another roadblock to remove: Ruth. He needed her permission— and she still refused. Berle coaxed. He sulked. He argued. He complained about his ulcer acting up. He paced through the house long after midnight, whining about how badly she was treating him. Sometimes his grumbling awakened his small son and made him cry.

Ruth capitulated. She was raising two children, one 4, the other 58. The big one was by far the most trouble, requiring constant babying. Sometimes his crying got on Ruth's nerves so badly that it was easier to give in to his demands than to listen to him wail.

Occasionally she went to great lengths to show him how ridiculous he was. But that didn't work either.

Like the time a few years ago when he awoke suddenly around 1 o'clock in the morning and announced loudly: "I want some corn flakes and bananas!"

Ruth shook her head sleepily and said: "But we don't have any bananas."

"What?" shouted Berle in utter disbelief. "No bananas!"

"That's right, Milton," said. "As long as I've known you, I've never seen you eat a banana."

This provoked a new storm of protest. "My God, Ruth, why aren't there bananas in the house in case I want some? Haven't I worked long enough to have bananas if I want them? Don't I provide well for you?"

And he was off on a harangue for many emotional minutes, carrying on about how long he'd worked and how much money he'd made.

"What am I working for?" he demanded. "Answer me, Ruth!"

When he came home the next night, Ruth had bananas for him. She had bought a whole truckful from a wholesaler. There were bananas hanging from the front door of their mansion, draped over the crystal chandeliers, decorating the picture windows and piled high in the bathtubs. She put peeled bananas in Berle's bedroom slippers and hung others in his closets. She lined his side of the bed sheets with a dozen banana skins.

Berle was delighted. But he had the last laugh.

The top banana didn't eat even one.

8. HOLLYWOOD'S BIGGEST LOSERS

For years they'd been washed up in show business. Hollywood—never having regarded them as more than B-type clowns—had kicked them out in 1945 after they made their last comedy, *The Bullfighters.*

It was a stinkeroo. At the preview even Laurel & Hardy held their noses, agreeing with the audience that it was terrible. They'd been eager then to try again. But the powerful studio chiefs shunned them like dandruff, refusing to talk to them on the phone and ignoring their letters.

Ten years of rebuffs and idleness followed. In 1955, they were a couple of jobless old duffers in their mid-sixties. Stan, a frisky flyweight during their heyday, had developed a little potbelly and a double chin.

Ollie had changed some too. Dieting on doctor's orders, he had reduced to 280 pounds but still resembled a jolly elephant.

For most of a long, frustrating decade they'd sat around twiddling thumbs, hoping and praying for a chance to make some more films. Then, at last, came what seemed to be a good break. Hal Roach, Jr., son of the man who'd first teamed them back in the Twenties, phoned Laurel one morning and said, "Stan, do you realize you and Hardy are the hottest thing on TV right now?"

"Well, I don't know how hot we are," Stan replied, "but I know we're on nearly every night."

"On stations all over the country," declared the youthful producer enthusiastically. "So here's my proposition. How would you and Ollie like to go back to work, making new comedies?"

"Are you serious?" asked Stan. He'd heard such deals before, many times, but nothing had ever come of them.

Within a fortnight, Laurel, Hardy and young Roach began laboring 12 and 14 hours a day, assembling gags and other ideas for the first of four comedies planned as hour-long TV shows. L&H were delighted to learn that the filming would be done at the old Roach Studios in Culver City where they'd been so successful in the past. They grinned like eager teenagers as Roach explained that everything would be done in the "old way," with L&H having the freedom to create once again all the funny trivia which had endeared them to generations of theatergoers throughout the world.

"This time, however," warned Roach, "there's going to be one big, important difference."

"What do you mean?" chorused the pair nervously, fearing he intended to exercise the close supervision which had wrecked the subtlety of their work at MGM and 20th Century.

"Relax, boys," said Roach. "All I mean is that this time you'll own a share of the films. Eventually, we'll do a series, a dozen or more comedies. With any luck at all, you two will finally start making the kind of money you should have had all these years."

It didn't happen. The long losing streak of Laurel & Hardy was to drag on and on. During most of their career, they had been poorly paid studio employees. For an all-too-brief period in the Thirties they'd received $3,500 a week each, and it had been dissipated by bad investments, forcing them to eke out their old age on meager savings. It was bad enough that they weren't getting a cent of the millions their old comedies were earning on TV. But fate—as tricky and foul as the villains in their films—had more heartbreak in store for them.

Ten days before shooting was to start, Stan, who was 65, suffered a stroke which affected one leg. His doctor predicted he would make a good recovery but refused to say how long it would take. Although the paralysis was slight, the doctor's verdict was stern: "Mr. Laurel, you've been working much too hard for a man of your age. It's not just the effects of the stroke. There's your high blood pressure to consider—and your diabetes. You've got to settle down and take a long, long rest."

"But I just had a rest," Stan argued. "For God's sake, I rested for practically 10 years!"

"You're going to do as I say, Mr. Laurel, or you're a dead man. Do you understand?"

Stan nodded glumly.

Then came an even worse break. Hardy, called Babe

by his friends, suffered a much more critical stroke. A year before—when his weight ballooned to 350 pounds—his physician warned that his overworked heart could not stand the strain. Sixty-three-year-old Babe dieted strenuously, and kept on dieting after hearing the bad news about Stan's stroke. It was the most difficult ordeal Hardy had ever gone through, because he loved to gorge on starches and rich foods. Worried about Stan, eager to return to his beloved comedy routines, he overdid it, shrinking himself to 180 pounds, weakening his constitution dangerously. He no longer resembled the happy fatty of old. He became a gaunt scarecrow, the flesh hanging from his huge-boned frame in weird wrinkles and folds.

Babe's stroke was massive. He was unable to speak or walk. His left arm hung uselessly. When they brought him home from the hospital, he was a shrunken wreck. He lay without moving, able to communicate only with his expressive eyes which stared sadly from his pillow.

One afternoon Mrs. Laurel phoned and said she would drive Stan over to Hardy's home for a visit. They didn't make it. Shortly after the Laurels left their small Malibu apartment, Stan became dizzy and nauseous and they were forced to turn back.

Neither man realized the significance of that afternoon. It marked the beginning of the end for them—and they would never meet again. Still, they refused to give up. Each kept alive an ember of hope. Each believed that somehow they would defeat their infirmities and return in triumph to the sound stages at Roach Studios.

Meanwhile, they had their memories of the golden pioneer age of slapstick comedy, when both were young and brimming with energetic ideas. Never, during those early days, did they dream that half a century later the world would honor their derbies, bumbling escapades and dignified sad-funny faces as classics of cinema art . . .

The fat one, Oliver Norvell Hardy, was born in Harlem, Georgia, in 1892, the youngest of five children. His father was a lawyer who died when Norvell, as he was known in those days, was 10. He missed his Dad so much that he became a compulsive eater and swelled up like a porker. When he was 13½ years old he was six feet tall and weighed 250 pounds.

No one else in the Hardy family cared about show business. Norvell became fascinated with the idea when he was in the third grade and developed a clear, beautiful boy soprano voice which won praise from his teachers. He promptly ran away from the Baldwin Hotel operated by his mother, and joined a traveling minstrel show. He loved singing on the makeshift stage, but was frightened and lonely the rest of the time.

One night while the boy was sleeping in a tent, a horse poked its head through the flimsy canvas and went *"N-n-n-neigh!"* In panic, the little fattie bolted through the darkness into a nearby tent of another entertainer and his wife. Norvell's screams of terror scared them out of their wits. They tried to flee, but became trapped in the tent when it fell down. The man, his wife and little Norvell rolled over and over in the tangle of poles and canvas, arousing the entire minstrel camp.

The next day Norvell went back to his family in Milledgeville, Georgia. He didn't run away again until he was 14. This time he decided to go to Atlanta and sing with a vaudeville show. He chose the worst possible day to arrive—April 17, 1906, when Atlanta was embroiled in a skull-bashing, shack-burning race riot. While Norvell watched innocently from the sidelines, he was swept up in a mob of battlers, kicked, punched and knocked down. He got up and was quickly knocked down again.

Dazed, he lay there listening to the sounds of combat roaring above him. Then he escaped by rolling over the ground through a forest of struggling legs. But he went too far. His barrel-like body rolled down a slope into a pond that was mostly red mud. Hours later, he found refuge at the train depot. A kindly telegrapher scraped the caked mud off his cheeks and sent a message to his mother. When Mrs. Hardy arrived to take him home, Norvell refused to go.

"Mother," he said, "I will *not* return to school. Do you understand?"

"But why, Norvell?" she asked.

The boy elevated his plump chin, trying to look proud and dignified despite the red mud that streaked his nose and mouth. "Because of the other students," he said. "Mother, I can't stand the way they make fun of me because I'm so fat. Do I have to go back?"

Mrs. Hardy agreed to let him stay in Atlanta and take voice lessons. When she returned two months later to check on him, she was told by his music teacher that Norvell hadn't shown up for a lesson for two weeks. She found him in a theater singing the accompaniment for illustrated slides at a salary of 50 cents day.

Dragging him back home, Mrs. Hardy enrolled him in a military school. Life there soon became a torment of jokes and taunts about his weight. He complained to his mother that the school didn't feed him enough. Once he marched off the drill field and kept walking till he was back at his mother's hotel. He refused to return to the academy until she baked him 20 biscuits which he ate one after the other.

In 1913, when he was 18, Norvell left home again. He had heard that a film company was making comedies in Jacksonville, Florida, and he thought it would be exciting to do that kind of work. For a week he hung around watching the actors and cameramen. Because he was polite and cooperative, the crews let him work as a non-paid helper, lugging equipment from one set to another.

One day the director suddenly needed a fat boy for a comedy sequence. As Norvell walked by carrying two chairs, the director shouted, "Hey, you there. Fatty. Put this on." He tossed Norvell a torn coat, mussed up his hair and told him what to do in front of the camera. The boy did so well he was hired as a regular actor for $5 a day and guaranteed three days work a week.

For the next five years Norvell worked in Florida for the Lubin and Vim movie companies. He was now 6-foot-2, extremely large boned and unusually muscular for a fat man. His weight, 280 pounds, made him perfect for comedy roles and his height made him ideal for villainous parts.

On their days off, the film companies organized football teams composed of actors, grips and cameramen. Amazingly light on his feet for a fat man, Norvell was the Lubin company's best player, even though he lacked the killer instinct. He refused to tackle his opponents, all of whom were smaller than he. Instead he clasped opposing ball carriers in his arms like a huge bear and lifted them off the ground.

It was during this period that he acquired his first nickname. He and the other members of the film company visited an Italian barber who liked to pat Norvell's soft, plump cheeks and call him "Baby." His pals shortened it to Babe. He liked the name so much that he dropped Norvell entirely. For a time he was listed as Babe Hardy in his comedy credits. Then he changed his billing to Oliver Babe Hardy in memory of his father, Oliver Hardy.

When America entered World War I in 1917, Babe patriotically tried to enlist. The sergeant at the recruiting station glanced up at his enormous bulk, blinked with astonishment and then yelled to his assistant, "My God, Corporal, look what wants to join the Army!" The sergeant and corporal didn't bother to determine whether there was any muscle under Babe's fat. For five cruel minutes they ridiculed him, laughing so hard that he fled from the station in tears. He was so hurt and ashamed that he hid in his hotel room and refused to do any work for two days.

Hearing about the film boom in Hollywood, Babe went to California the following year. He had no trouble finding work. Many of his Florida cronies had migrated there before him and helped him line up jobs at the King Bee and Vitagraph studios. He was popular with directors because he worked hard and was well-behaved. Except when clowning around, Babe had the courtly manners of a Southern gentleman. If ladies were present, he refused to swear or listen to off-color stories.

Shortly after arriving in California Babe was given a bit part in a quickie two-reeler called *Lucky Dog*. Its featured comic was a small, natty English actor named Stan Laurel. Although no one realized it at the time, the film—the first comedy ever made with both Laurel and Hardy—was historic. Artistically it was a mediocre silent comedy which disappeared into oblivion after being cranked out by the studio.

L&H were on the set together two days. They nodded and spoke politely but didn't become well acquainted. During the next half-dozen years they met occasionally on other sets. Each became fairly successful on his own; neither imagined that some day they would be one of the funniest teams in movie history.

The full name of the skinny little English comic was Arthur Stanley Jefferson. Born in Ulverston, England, in 1890, he came from a family steeped in the theater. His mother, beautiful actress Madge Metcalf, was the Theda Bara of her day in northern England. His father, Arthur Jefferson, called A.J. by his friends, was a versatile impresario who managed theaters and wrote, produced and acted in plays. Young Stanley had a haphazard education, sometimes attending school in cities where his father was employed, on other occasions attending boarding schools which separated him from the family.

He despised school and played hookey whenever possible, using a variety of schemes. One of his most ingenious began when the family was living together in Glasgow, Scotland. Because of illness, he was kept out of school for a few days. His father sent a note to his teacher, enclosing a few complimentary tickets to the Metropole Theater. Half a dozen times after that, Stanley played hookey, sending his teacher notes bearing A.J.'s forged initials, craftily enclosing tickets which he manufactured with his father's "complimentary" stamp.

One afternoon, A.J. came home unexpectedly and caught his truant son playing with a kite. The rubber stamp was locked away permanently in a desk. Then A.J. stared grimly at the little boy who had inherited his flaming red hair, and gave him the tongue-lashing of his life: "Stanley, I'm so ashamed of you I could die. How do you expect to amount to anything if you don't go to school?"

"I don't care if I never amount to anything," the boy replied innocently. "I just want to grow up like you and have fun on the stage."

Young Stanley's burning zeal to be a baggy pants music hall comic reached its climax when he was 16 years old. He persuaded Albert E. Pickens, a friend of his father, to give him a secret tryout in a revue at Pickens' music hall in Glasgow. Stanley's costume consisted of a black derby (standard headwear for English comics), a tight coat and a pair of magnificent checkered trousers which were three sizes too large. The trousers were part of his father's favorite suit. Stanley not only borrowed them without permission, but also committed the crime of hacking several inches off the legs to make them fit.

Suddenly he heard his cue. "Hop it, Jefferson! You're on!"

The boy scampered out from the wings and began a peculiar jig. He was so nervous he couldn't control his feet. They skipped about like a pair of squirrels. *I'm awful,* he thought desperately. *Thank God, A.J. isn't here to see me make a fool of myself!*

He spun around, faced the audience and opened his mouth to tell his first joke. His oversized jaw fell like an anchor. The first person he spied across the footlights was his father. A.J. and Pickens stood together at the rear of the center aisle, watching the show with amused smiles.

Stan finished ·the joke lamely. He told two more that were better. Then he did another eccentric little jig, imitating the performances of comics he'd been watching and studying for years in his father's theaters. He finished energetically, sliding off amid tumultuous applause. Later he guessed, correctly, that the audience had clapped out of sympathy for his pitiful efforts.

Realizing he could not avoid facing his father, he trudged up the stairs to his father's office at the Metropole, wondering how many weeks of chores would pay for the ruined trousers. He knocked cautiously on the door.

"Come in," thundered his father.

As the boy approached his desk, A.J. gave him a long, sharp look. Then he smiled and said, "Congratulations, son. Care for a whiskey and soda?"

Stanley's jaw dropped farther than it had on stage. As he sipped from the small glass, his eyes filled with tears, partly from the bite of the liquor, more from the knowledge that A.J. for the first time had indicated that he would not stand in the way of his son's theatrical hopes. A.J. gave Stanley permission to quit school and helped him develop the gags, skits and outrageous costumes that enabled him to become a musichall standout despite his youth.

When he was 20, Stan toured the United States with Fred Karno's *Mumming Birds* troupe, England's most famous and funniest music-hall show. Its star comic was Charlie Chaplin, already a brilliant, selfish egotist although only a year older than Stan, who was his understudy. Stan and Charlie became pals, rooming together during the tour.

While walking to the theater in New York one night, both suddenly felt an urgent call of nature. Being strangers in town, they didn't know where to find a men's room. They approached a policeman and Stan said, "Good evening, sir. Could you direct us to the nearest public convenience?"

"What did you say?" demanded the cop. Stan repeated the question. The officer still didn't understand. He stared suspiciously at the two skinny youths, wondering why they were dressed so peculiarly. Both wore the modish clothes of London dandies—derbies, tight coats, fancy vests, gloves and black and white high button shoes. They also carried canes.

"Please, my good man," said Charlie imperiously. "Where's the nearest lavatory?"

Thinking they were playing some kind of silly game, the cop grew angry and threatened to arrest them. Stan went up on tiptoe and whispered in his ear . . .

"Ya wanna go to the can?" roared the policeman. "Whyn't ya say so?"

He directed them to a saloon across the street. Extremely uncomfortable by this time, Stan and Charlie hurried in. Their proper English manners wouldn't permit them to use the facilities without first purchasing something. Squirming as if with ants in their pants, they stood at the bar for a few minutes, sipping beer which didn't improve their condition. Then they made a mad dash to the toilet.

Stan's pay was $30 a week. Charlie, the star, got $50. When Mack Sennett offered Charlie $125 a week to make comedies in California, he quit the troupe immediately. His decision was a disaster for the others in the cast. Within a month the show folded.

During the next few years, Stan was a vaudeville headliner gaining modest attention for his imitations of Chaplin, who had shot to instantaneous fame in Hollywood. One day Stan realized that his stage name, Stan Jefferson, had 13 unlucky letters. Hoping to improve his foundering career, he tested several new last names, choosing Laurel because he liked the sound of it.

In 1917, Stan performed his Chaplin routine at the Hippodrome in Los Angeles. The theater's owner, Adolph Ramish, was so impressed he said: "Stan, you're a hell of a lot funnier than Chaplin. How would you like to make some comedies with me?"

"Are you pulling my leg?" asked Stan.

Ramish wasn't. He rented a small studio, hired a top crew and let Stan dream up a story about a man escaping from an insane asylum wearing a business suit and a Napoleon hat. Titled *Nut in May*, Stan's first film attempt was very funny and so successful that he quickly made several more.

Stan, then 27 years old, employed an entirely different comedy style than the shy, slow, dumb technique which was to bring him fame with Hardy. In his first films he was a swift, deft pantomimist with brash, volatile movements resembling Chaplin's. His offstage personality was much the same. He was a dapper dresser, a fast talker and fancied himself quite a lady's man.

Much to his surprise and distress, his next four comedies were flops because of poor ideas and casting. Stan returned unhappily to vaudeville. During the early Twenties he vacillated between stage work and comedies, paid poorly by both. He appeared in 58 comedies before joining Oliver Hardy as a member of Hal Roach's Comedy All Stars. Although they appeared together in many of Roach's early pictures, they were not a team. They were supporting players filling a variety of straight and comic roles.

Roach's decision to co-star them in a comedy of their own was not reached suddenly. He did not slap his hand against his forehead and shout: "By God, I've got it. We'll make them a team—Laurel & Hardy!" The idea came about more naturally. Roach had long known that L&H worked well together. Gradually he gave them more important parts, increased their pay to $140 a week each and encouraged them to originate funny bits which were not in the scripts.

Putting Pants on Phillip was the first of 89 two-reelers and feature films that Stan and Babe were to make during their career. *Phillip* was not L&H at their best by any means. But it convinced Roach that Laurel & Hardy were destined to become a major comedy team.

Wise as he was, however, Roach never fully realized how great the pair would become. He did not guess that their comedy would blossom into art which would live on for generations. Because of his mistake, Roach also failed to share in the millions of dollars earned by the release of their films. Long before they became popular on TV, Roach disposed of the films for a pittance, then watched with dismay as the distributing corporations earned a 10,000% profit on their investment.

In 1927 Stan and Babe made their second co-starring comedy, *The Battle of the Century*. When they sat down to work out the basic pie-throwing idea, they didn't dream it would some day be ranked as one of the all-time slapstick masterpieces. "Look here," argued Stan, "If we're going to toss pies, we might as well do it right. There's nothing new any more about someone getting squished in the face. Sennett does it, Chaplin does it, everybody does it."

"That's right, Stan," said Babe. "So what shall we do that's different?"

"We overdo it," Laurel replied triumphantly. "We make

the pie picture to end all pie pictures. We toss more pies than anybody has ever seen before."

Roach, who had supplied the original story, agreed to purchase 4,000 fresh pies from the L.A. Pie Company—its total output for one day. The film started slowly. Hardy took Laurel for a leisurely stroll around town, planning to collect secretly on an insurance policy by involving him in an accident. Laurel had several narrow escapes. Then Hardy ate a banana and threw the peel carefully on the sidewalk. Laurel innocently stepped over it, but a pieman wasn't so fortunate. He slipped, tossing a tray of pies which came down on his head, covering him with magnificent goo.

Hardy laughed. The angry pieman shoved a pie into his fat kisser. Laurel, resentful, promptly pushed a pie into the pieman's face. A stranger passing by tried to stop the argument and caught a pie in the eyes. Gradually other people joined the donnybrook until the entire city block was beserk with flying chocolate, custard and cream pies. The cameraman shot down from the roof of a building, showing a panoramic view of the entire battling mob. Then came quick, ingenious closeups of innocent bystanders getting theirs. A dental patient, mouth wide open, was clobbered with a pie that sailed in through a window. A bored dowager, staring through her lorgnette, got plastered. The scene ended with a neat touch. A pie-covered cop arrested Laurel & Hardy, and as he led them away, the cop slipped on the banana peel, then plunged gloriously through an open manhole.

Two decades later, while the film gathered dust in Hal Roach's vault, critic and writer Henry Miller recalled it fondly: "This, in my opinion, is the greatest comic film ever made. It is the ultimate burlesque . . . the *chef d'oeuvre* of pie-throwing festivals."

In most of their subsequent films L&H used their own first names. Hardy became known as Ollie in the comedies, but continued to be called Babe by his offstage pals. Bit by bit the pair perfected and coordinated the tricks which became their trademarks of genius. Some of their stunts, such as Ollie's perplexed tie-twiddle and Stan's wrinkled-faced whimper, had been originated by them before they teamed up. Later they added Ollie's exasperated slow burn and his spit curls plus Stan's nervous hair-scratching and flip-floppy walk. The latter was created by cutting the soles out of his shoes.

In their early movies L&H were simply dumbbells. In the Thirties they developed their characterizations, making themselves more believable, refining their stupidity into something profound, delightful and even rational. Analyzing this process one day, Babe told an interviewer: "These two fellows we created, well, they are very nice people. They are very polite to one another, much of the time. They never get anywhere because they're both so dumb they don't even know they're dumb. They're also very dignified—and there's nothing funnier than a guy being dignified *and* dumb. Another of the reasons people like us, I guess, is because they feel so superior to us. Even an eight-year-old kid can feel superior to us and that makes him laugh."

As the years passed, Babe let Stan take on more of the responsibility of supplying the basic gag ideas. Stan also took a greater interest in editing and cutting their films, spending weekends and nights at the studio in order to make certain this vital work was properly done. Babe spent most of his free time on the golf course. Despite his great size, he was one of Hollywood's top golfers, shooting in the low seventies.

Although their pictures were invariably financial successes, Hollywood snubbed them year after year, rating them as secondary talents. They were given no massive publicity build-ups and most of the country's major critics ignored their work. From the Twenties through the Fifties not one important national magazine was willing to devote space to them. Their films were considered banal, of interest mainly to children.

Stan and Babe stayed out of the limelight, living quietly in Los Angeles, attending no parties, socializing together only occasionally. They worked very hard, scarcely catching their breaths between films. After finishing *Pack Up Your Troubles* in 1932, they decided to take a nice long vacation, their first in seven years.

They planned a sojourn in England, with Stan anticipating a quiet reunion with his family and Babe looking forward eagerly to weeks of golf on the plush greens of Scotland. Their train trip across America was uneventful until they reached Chicago. Then pandemonium erupted around them in the station. Hundreds of fans tried to shake their hands at once, nearly suffocating them in a bellowing crush of humanity.

The same thing happened in New York. Laurel & Hardy

were stunned, having never realized how famous they were. Wherever they went in Manhattan, they were chased by mobs of fans. When they got on their ship, the *Aquitania,* matters grew even worse. They were dogged by so many rude, persistent autograph seekers and gawkers that they were forced to hide in their staterooms for most of the trip.

Stan had assured Babe that no one in England would bother them. "They won't even know who we are," he said, "and if anybody does recognize us we'll be treated with fine British respect." Stan's eyes all but popped like corks from his head when the ship docked in Southampton and he was told that the swarms of people on the wharves had been waiting for hours to see him and Babe.

As they came down the gangplank, the throng whistled their theme, *The Cuckoo Song,* in unison, then cheered, clapped and screamed.

Their arrival at Waterloo train station was like a battle scene in World War I. Both men were seized by a shrieking mob and dragged back and forth.

The frenzy continued throughout their stay in England. Babe had no opportunity to swing a golf club. Stan had no chance for a little casual trout fishing with his family and was intrigued by the conversations of strange women who phoned his London hotel room and offered to make love to him.

When they returned to Hollywood, L&H began work on a new feature. But their attitude had changed. They asked Hal Roach for more money and he agreed on substantial, regular increases. They discussed acquiring an agent to obtain even better terms, then changed their minds. "Hal's always treated us fine," Stan commented. "Why should we give away 10% of what we've been obtaining for ourselves?"

Hardy nodded. Whenever the subject came up again, they made the same bad decision. Not until it was too late did they realize that a good agent would have trebled and quadrupled their incomes by insisting they acquire certain basic rights to their films, enabling them to reap TV and foreign distribution residuals in their declining years.

After their European trip, L&H also insisted on more freedom to develop their own story ideas. Roach agreed, but he had misgivings, particularly about Stan. Discussing this many years later with a magazine writer, Roach declared: "Stan came back from England with a swelled head. He developed a Chaplin complex. He wanted to do everything—write, direct and produce. And somewhere over there he picked up the idea that he was a real devil with the ladies."

Stan's multitudes of fans were stunned the following year when they discovered that the funny little man who was usually so meek and shy on the screen was in real life a snappy, even debonaire Don Juan whose bedroom escapades were the talk of Hollywood. When his wife Lois filed for divorce after seven years of marriage, she ripped him from derby to shoe tops, charging scathingly that he often left home for one to three days at a time.

"He did this on 20 or 30 occasions," she testified tearfully. "Night after night, I wouldn't know where to find him. When he came home, I'd ask him if he'd been seeing another woman. But he wouldn't talk to me. He wouldn't say where he'd been or what he'd been doing."

Mrs. Laurel was awarded a generous property settlement and the custody of their five-year-old daughter, Stan's only child. Before the divorce was final, Stan dashed off to Mexico and married a voluptuous young blonde, Virginia Ruth Rogers. To quiet gossip about the legality of their marriage, he wed her again a few weeks later. Their romantic bliss was brief. When Virginia dragged Stan's name through the mire of the divorce courts, she made shocking revelations, claiming he was a Jekyll-Hyde personality—comic on the screen but definitely unfunny at home.

"He is a cruel little man," she declared.

Virginia's testimony was corroborated by their chauffeur and maid, and she was awarded support of $1,235 a month. While that case was being heard in one court, Stan became involved simultaneously in another legal mess. A woman who listed herself as Mrs. Mae Laurel sued him for separate maintenance, demanding payment of $1,000 a month on the grounds that she was his common-law wife.

The judge ruled in Stan's favor. When a reporter broke the news to other correspondents in the Los Angeles courthouse press room, he said waggishly: "Well, Lothario Laurel finally won a round. I hear that he likes a good fight so much that his next bride will be Mrs. Jack Dempsey."

The reporter's exaggerated remark came closer to the truth than anyone, least of all Stan, expected. For his third bride he chose Russian entertainer Illiana, a buxom and beautiful soprano and dancer with a fiery, emotional nature. She was 28 years old; he was 48. Their off-on relationship, a tumultuous series of fights followed by lovey-dovey billing and cooing, resulted in Stan wedding her three times.

In 1946 he wed for the eighth and last time. His fourth wife was another young Russian, blonde Ida Kitaeva Raphael, even-tempered and cooperative. He settled down, mellowing so much that he even became willing—after years of hiding from the press—to laugh and joke about his marital troubles. When a writer asked him to describe his favorite hobby, Stan replied with a grin: "Oh, come now, you know what it was. But I want you to know I married them all!"

Babe remained a bachelor until he was 48. Because of his immense bulk, he had always been somewhat reserved around women, certain he'd never find one who could truly love a person as gross as himself. Then he met Lucille Jones, a script clerk on the set of *Flying Deuces*. She disliked him at first, mistaking his Southern courtliness for the mannerisms of a pompous, conceited oaf. When she understood him better, they became great friends. They were married in 1940, had no children, but it was a happy marriage.

Babe loved to sit at their kitchen table, stuffing biscuits into his mouth, commenting: "Bring another platter, Lucille. I've only had 15. *(Chomp, chomp.)* Can't stop till I've had 20 or maybe a few more. *(Chomp, chomp.)*"

No doubt it was only coincidence, but the year of Babe's marriage also marked the beginning of Laurel & Hardy's decline. Their last two pictures for Hal Roach, *Swiss Miss* and *Blockheads*, were made under conditions of bickering and dissension. Stan battled with Roach, insisted on being the producer of *Blockheads*. It was a good comedy, but far from their best, with a weak ending that was blamed on Stan. "He was having too much woman trouble then," Roach explained. "I don't think he had his mind on his work."

Blockheads was the final effort of the Roach-Laurel-Hardy partnership. Stan and Babe formed their own company, Laurel & Hardy Productions, but never made a film, lacking finances. After going jobless for two years, they signed with MGM and then 20th Century, making eight pictures which were mostly failures. After the fiasco of *The*

Bullfighters, Stan and Babe went into their long period of enforced idleness. It was a time of disgrace and heartbreak. No producer would hire them. Theater owners preferred to run the more modern slapstick of Abbott & Costello.

Then came an opportunity which temporarily interrupted their monotony. L&H films were still so popular in France that a French producer invited them to make a movie in his country. Their high hopes were soon dashed. The film, *Atoll K* (retitled *Utopia*) was a calamity, the worst picture Stan and Babe ever made and also their last. Budgeted for 12 weeks of shooting, it stretched out through 12 weary months, largely because of a diabetes-related illness which struck Stan. He dwindled to 114 pounds, but forced himself to work, though barely able to stand.

It was a dismal finale to two magnificent careers. After that L&H were two old men robbed of their strength and confidence. They never fully recovered from the strokes which wrecked their comeback plans in the mid-Fifties, when they hoped to star in new TV comedies for Hal Roach's son.

Babe's condition was the most pitiful. For a time after returning home from the hospital, he was able to sit in a wheelchair. One night when a Laurel & Hardy comedy, *Two Tars,* was on TV, his wife rolled his wasted body into the living room to watch. It was one of their most hilarious misadventures. Lucille laughed at their antics, hoping her husband would do the same.

"Look, Babe!" she cried. "Look at what you and Stan did to that poor touring car. The whole top is falling off!"

Her efforts were in vain. Babe slumped in the wheelchair like a sack of clay, staring at the TV screen without the least comprehension of what was going on. Nor was he capable of showing any interest when Lucille rolled him into the dining room to let him see the enormous heap of letters forwarded from TV stations throughout the nation. Stan had a similar pile at his home. The news of their illnesses had caused thousands of fans to send them get-well cards and letters of sympathy and encouragement. Some of the envelopes contained dollar bills, quarters and dimes from people who had heard that the two were destitute.

Although the doctors told her Babe's mental condition would never improve, Lucille kept trying to revive sparks of intelligence in him, even during the long final bedridden months. But it was hopeless. Babe died in 1957 at the age of 65. Stan was so weak from his own stroke that he could not attend the funeral.

Partially paralyzed, trembling and pale, Stan clung to life for nearly eight more years, living with his fourth wife Ida, in a tiny beachfront apartment. When diabetes hospitalized him in 1964, officials of West Valley Baptist Hospital tried to keep his presence a secret, but word leaked out. After that 1,000 letters a day arrived at the hospital from his fans.

Unable to afford a secretary, he could not reply to them and he was pained by the sight of the cash many contained. "I'm not ready for the poorhouse," he complained to his doctor. "Not quite yet. I've got a little bit of money tucked away."

He remained mentally sharp, often noticing little happenings around him that could have been the basis for a gag in a Laurel & Hardy comedy. One day a nurse almost tripped as she brought in his luncheon tray. She dropped the tray on his bed, but it landed so squarely that nothing spilled.

"Amazing!" commented Stan. "It gives me an idea. Ollie and me are patients in a hospital. We have a mean and cranky doctor. We're very scared and want to go home. So we glue all the dishes onto our trays. When the doctor comes in we do crazy balancing tricks with our trays, never spilling a thing. The mean and cranky doctor is fascinated. He wants to try it. He takes a tray and tries to balance it. The glue comes lose and all the dishes crash down on his head. In the confusion, Ollie and me make our escape from the hospital on our hands and knees. . . ."

The old man in the bed erupted with uproarious laughter, slapping his pillow with his trembling hand. Then, abruptly, he stopped laughing. He turned his head and gazed at the wall, his eyes sad and moist with tears.

He was 74 years old when he died the next year. He left a modest estate which was reduced greatly by debts and taxes. The amount which remained was peanuts compared to the fortunes of the men who became millionaires through distribution of the L&H films.

Not long before his death, Stan told his wife: "Ida, that's the one thing I regret. That I have so little to leave you."

In the eyes of the money-grabbers, he and Babe were losers. But today in a hut in Afghanistan natives squat on a dirt floor and laugh at the funny bungling of the fat one and the skinny one on a flickering screen. The same phenomenon occurs in India and Argentina. In a remote village in China's interior, a picture of L&H enjoys a place of esteem in the same prayer room where peasants worship Buddha.

Throughout the United States, members of the *Sons of the Desert* film cult, named for an L&H comedy, meet regularly to praise them and laugh it up during special showings of their films.

Laurel & Hardy pictures have played to more people in more places of the world than any other comedy figures in history. It is a legacy of far greater magnitude than mere money.

9. JACKIE MASON'S WAR WITH FRANK SINATRA'S "PALS"

Threatening phone calls came at all hours. Sometimes at 3 or 4 o'clock in the morning. At first Jackie Mason thought they were the usual crackpot calls, the harmless verbal blasts every big time comedian gets from night club customers complaining bitterly about certain jokes.

But then the phone calls grew more vicious. One afternoon the phone rang while Jackie, a former rabbi, was quietly studying a book of Greek philosophy in his suite at Las Vegas' Aladdin Hotel. Again it was a man's voice, tough and harsh.

After cursing Mason roundly, the voice rasped: "You don't listen good, Jackie. We told you before. You wanta keep on breathin', you lay off the Sinatra cracks!"

The next day, a Sunday, the phone rang about the same time. Again there were obscenities followed by threats: "We heard you last night, baby! We heard that Frankie crud you dished out. Now you're gonna get it, baby!"

The phone was slammed down with a crash that echoed in Mason's ear. A small, gentle man who had avoided violence all his life, he still refused to believe that the warnings were serious. Why should anyone want to do him harm? He had never hurt anyone. It was true that he spoofed Frank Sinatra occasionally during his monologues in the Aladdin's Baghdad Theatre. But those jokes, discussing Sinatra's love life, were mild and funny, no more insulting than those he used in satirizing such other public figures as Ed Sullivan, Alfred Hitchcock, Bing Crosby and President Johnson.

That night, however, an act of violence occurred which radically changed Mason's thinking, introducing him to a unique ordeal of terror.

It happened while he was chatting with a friend, Eddie Kirk, in his ground-level living room at the hotel. There was a sharp rap at the door followed by a voice saying, "Room service!"

"Come in," Jackie said.

Just as the waiter stepped through the door, three loud explosions erupted in the adjacent bedroom.

"My God!" exclaimed Kirk. "What was that? A gun?"

Jackie, stunned and surprised, did not reply. It was one of the rare times when the $350,000-a-year comedian—noted for his ability to talk swiftly at length on any subject—had nothing to say.

All three men stared tensely for a few moments at the bedroom doorway. Then Jackie and Kirk jumped up from their chairs and went into the bedroom, followed by the waiter. At first they didn't see anything unusual.

Then Jackie gestured at the window, exclaiming: "Look at that!"

In the window were three holes. Each was neat, small and circular, surrounded by a web of tiny cracks. Splinters of glass glistened on the window sill and on the orange-hued rug below. It was obvious that the holes had been drilled by bullets and the three explosions they'd heard was gunfire.

Suddenly Jackie remembered the phoned warnings. Realizing the gunman could be lurking in the shadows outdoors, ready to fire again, he herded Kirk and the waiter back into the living room. Then he dialed the hotel's operator and told her to call the police.

After that the comedian flopped down on a chair and pressed a trembling hand against his forehead. His whole body was shaking and his face was pasty. "I can't believe!" he said. "What have I done? Why would anybody be out to get me?"

Within a few minutes his suite was a bedlam of voices. First to arrive were hotel officials, followed by sheriff's deputies in suntan uniforms, reporters, photographers and a couple of curious tourists from rooms across the corridor. The deputies let the press interview Jackie briefly and take a few pictures. Then they ordered everybody out, except Mason, his friend Eddie Kirk and the waiter. During the next hour, the officers made a meticulous search of the suite.

Three hardly noticeable holes in the bedspread revealed where the bullets had gone. The deputies found all three slugs in the mattress. Going outdoors, they hunted for footprints beneath the window, but found none because the ground was covered with a plush lawn. They also failed to find a gun or cartridges which might have been ejected from one.

The officers dismissed the waiter, deciding it was mere coincidence that he had entered at the time of the shots. Then they began an intense questioning of Jackie and his friend, studying both men suspiciously.

"Where did you hide the gun?" the officer in charge asked Mason suddenly.

The comedian looked at him with amazement. "Are you kidding?" he asked.

The officer's expression, grim and stony, indicated he was deadly serious. He asked more questions along the same line, each showing that he doubted Mason's story, implying that Jackie had arranged to have a gun fired into the mattress as a publicity stunt.

"I had nothing to do with it," Jackie insisted. "I'm telling you the truth!"

The officer shrugged. A few minutes later he and the other deputies finished their investigation and departed. The next day Lieutenant Glenn Simmons, Las Vegas chief of detectives, asked the comic to take a lie detector test. Mason indignantly refused. Shortly after that, the sheriff's department dropped its investigation.

Jackie Mason was still angry and edgy about the matter when I interviewed him not long afterward. During our question-and-answer session in his rooms at Vegas' Caesar's Palace, where he planned to appear later in the year, Mason paced nervously up and down, lambasting the Nevada authorities' investigation of the shooting.

"It was a whitewash!" he charged, speaking in quick bursts of words. "Somebody shoots up my room! I could have been killed! My friend could've been killed, or the waiter. I ask the cops to investigate. So who turns out to be the chief suspect? Me, that's who! They think I'm a nut with a gun. They think I'm a cowboy rabbi!"

As he talked, slurring his staccato words in an accent that ranged from Bronx Yiddish to tough lower East Side, Jackie cocked his finger and thumb like a make-believe pistol, a gesture familiar to millions of TV viewers.

For a moment I marveled at the unique contradictions of the sallow-cheeked, thick-lipped little man. At times he looked and talked like a real eastern gangster (which perhaps accounted for why the Vegas officers had doubted his story of the shooting.) He was not acting, however; he acquired that part of his personality while being raised in poverty in a rough-and-tumble "dese, dem and dose" neighborhood of New York.

From studying his family and educational background I also knew that his upbringing had been basically scholarly. His father was a rabbi, his three brothers are rabbis and Jackie—a college graduate, intellectual and comic genius—had been an ordained rabbi for several years before exchanging his pulpit for the entertainment stage.

Continuing his attack on the Las Vegas police officials, Mason said resentfully:

"They got trouble in this town. Everybody knows the big casinos are owned by the syndicates, the ex-mob guys. So they're always soft-pedaling the crime angle. The cops try to make you believe Vegas is a clean town, the Lux, Rinso, detergent capital of the world. They don't want to scare away the tourists, the nice little mamas and papas who come to gamble. Are there gangsters in Las Vegas? Of course not! Did a dirty gangster shoot holes in my window? Of course not! The cops want us to think Jackie Mason did it because his bedroom was getting stuffy and he wanted fresh air. Bang! Bang! Bang!"

Jackie pointed his finger at the window of his room and squeezed off a few imaginary shots. When I asked him if he thought his suite had been shot up by some of Frank Sinatra's hoodlum pals, he shrugged expressively. "How should I know?" he said. "How can anybody know for sure? But I can manage to add two and two. Sometimes I even get four. I get phone calls from tough guys telling me to quit making jokes about Sinatra. I'm told to quit—or else something will happen. So something happens. Bang, bang! So what am I supposed to believe?"

Asked for an explanation of how his feud with Sinatra began, Mason plopped nervously onto a safe. He pushed his fingers through short curly dark hair which is graying at the temples. Then he smiled, somewhat grimly.

"Would you believe?" he asked, "that I have never spoken one word to Frank Sinatra—not even hello? I have never had any business dealing with him. I have never had anything to do with him, period. But still he has this venom for me, this hatred that just keeps spilling over."

Jackie said his trouble with Sinatra began one night

when the multi-millionaire crooner—notorious for his quick temper and combative nature—came into the Aladdin, while Jackie was performing. "It's true he was drinking," Jackie pointed out, "but that's no explanation for what he did. Suddenly he began abusing my reputation in a very loud tone of voice. He was insulting. He called me a lousy comedian and other things. I was amazed. I simply couldn't believe it."

The little comedian (he's 5 feet 5, weighs 145 pounds and is 37 years old) insisted that his jokes about Sinatra were mild as milk and water, offering little incentive for the singer's savage insults. "Other comedians tear him up far more than I do," he said. "I talk a little about his love life, but I underplay it. Like this. I say Frank always seems to have many girl friends, so many that psychiatrists say he must be suffering terrible agonies of guilt. The psychiatrists also say that Frank's real trouble is that he doesn't even know he's suffering. In fact he's so happy with all those girl friends that he makes the psychiatrists suffer terribly."

The abusive phone calls, purportedly from Sinatra's cronies, began a day or so after the singer's shouting attack on Mason at the Aladdin. When I asked Jackie if he'd had more calls after the shooting episode, he nodded, saying he still received them at odd hours of the day and night.

He admitted that the harassment was hard on his nerves, causing him to worry so much he lost sleep and his appetite. "But I needed to lose a little weight anyway," he quipped.

He said he hired a part-time bodyguard to accompany him to and from his club jobs, but then he quickly pooh-poohed the suggestion that Vegas hoodlums were responsible for a traffic collision which occurred two weeks after the shooting incident.

News reports on November 21, 1966, stated that Jackie was injured when a hit-run car suddenly veered across the double line, deliberately ramming the car he was in, forcing it off the road. The accident occurred on a highway south of Las Vegas, with the other car reportedly speeding away after the collision.

Mason shook his head, labeling the early reports erroneous and over-dramatic. "Some of the reporters got carried away," he said. "They built it up like in one of those movies where the gangsters try to rub somebody out with a car. There was an accident all right. I got sore knees out of it and a couple of little cuts on the forehead. But there was nothing deliberate. The other driver was a dumb broad who lost control of her car. She wasn't hurt and kept right on going."

Like the shooting accident, the traffic collision produced radio bulletins and news headlines across the nation—publicity which didn't hurt Jackie's career a bit. Two years previously he had received similar amounts of eyebrow-raising publicity when he feuded at length with Ed Sullivan about an allegedly obscene finger gesture which Jackie had used on Sullivan's TV show.

The incident had occurred near the end of Mason's first appearance on the program. His monologue had been interrupted for a foreign policy message by President Johnson. Then Jackie had come on again. Sullivan, who was off-camera, signaled to him, pointing upward with his index finger to indicate that the comedian had one minute to finish his act.

Jackie reacted with a flurry of ad-lib finger gestures which were seen by 50,000,000 viewers. These included pointing and thumbing his nose, followed by the fleeting gesture which stirred up the verbal hornets' nest. Moments after the show went off the air, Sullivan—ashenfaced and quivering with rage—fired Mason, charging that the gesture was the most flagrant violation of good taste ever seen on TV.

"He was vulgar!" Sullivan shouted. "And contemptuous! I've always had a homey show, watched by millions of children. How a man can do a thing like that—right after a speech by the President—is absolutely beyond me!"

Mason's response was equally angry as he denied Sullivan's accusations. "I'll sue!" he cried. "It's out-and-out libel! At no time was I trying to be vulgar or obscene!"

"It's all on the tape!" countered Sullivan. "The proof is there and all the king's horses and all the king's men can't change it!"

"I am not a dirty comedian!" insisted Jackie. "I have always used such gestures. I have always been considered a very clean performer, but now my reputation is being dirtied!"

Sullivan canceled Mason's $35,000 contract, which called for five more appearances on the show. The comedian immediately filed a $3,000,000 libel and slander suit, listing numerous grievances, including an accusation that right after the show Sullivan had shouted, in the presence of witnesses: "Jackie, you're all through! I'm going to destroy you in show business!"

While the suit was awaiting its court decision, Jackie Mason enjoyed lucrative benefits from the publicity, including an unprecedented demand for night club appearances at higher fees than he previously commanded. "Isn't America wonderful?" he said. "I haven't changed my act. It's Rinso clean like always, but now people think I'm dirty and I'm making a fortune!"

When New York Supreme Court Justice Harry B. Frank handed down his verdict 15 months later, he declared—after studying the tape—that he found nothing offensive or obscene in Jackie's gestures, including the finger bit which had caused Sullivan such consternation.

The furor concluded peacefully a few months later when Jackie reappeared on Sullivan's show. The two shook hands, acting like a pair of small boys promising not to sling any more mudballs at one another. It was obvious that Sullivan was the loser and was trying to make amends. He had made a mistake in judgment, firing Jackie in haste and anger without checking into all the facts.

If Sullivan had investigated the comedian's background he would have realized that Jackie Mason, of all people, was the least likely to abuse the nation's TV screens with smut and filth. From the day he was born, June 9, 1930, in Sheboygan, Wisconsin, he lived in an atmosphere of religion, education and meditation. Jackie's real name is Yacov Moshe Maza. His father was Rabbi Eliahu Maza, descendant of a long, unbroken line of Russian rabbis. The rabbi, his wife Meila and their first three children emigrated to the United States in 1927. Later they had four more children, Jackie being the first to be born in America.

While Jackie was still a small boy, the family moved from Wisconsin to a tiny three-room apartment on New York's lower East Side. His father became the rabbi of the Pike Street Synagogue, receiving a salary too small for a single penny-pinching aunt to live on, let alone a couple with seven children. What money there was went for food and the grim necessities of life; there was rarely any change left over for candy, gum or other small amusements.

Jackie, always frail and small for his age, had few

contacts with the young toughs who ran wild in his neighborhood. Like his older brothers, he spent most of his free time in devout study. No one in the family ever dreamed that some day young Yacov would be a fast-lip comedian earning $10,000 for six minutes on stage, making up jokes which claimed he had a colorful and dangerous hoodlum childhood:

"Were the kids tough on our street? You better believe it. When we played cops and robbers we used real cops. And we played hopscotch with real Scotch."

Rigidly following the doctrines of his faith, Jackie's father taught his sons to avoid all forms of violence. He stressed that as rabbinical scholars they were also expected to refrain from all forms of physical labor. Once, when he was a teen-ager, Jackie violated the code in order to earn enough money for a pair of shoes to replace his old ones, which were falling apart. Without telling his father, he obtained a job in a kosher winery, earning $6 for his first day's work.

His father, however, had intelligence pipelines throughout the neighborhood, keeping track of the activities of all members of his synagogue. When young Yacov came home that night, his back aching, he was met at the front door by Rabbi Maza, who was boiling over with fatherly anger.

"My son," he demanded in Yiddish, "how did you spend your day?"

"In honest toil," replied Jackie.

"Did you lift?" the rabbi demanded.

Realizing his father knew everything, Jackie bowed his head and confessed that he had indeed spent the entire day lifting heavy cases of wine. His father gave him a tongue-lashing, ordered him to spend the night reading the Talmud (Hebrew law) and forbad him from ever returning to the winery.

Jackie obtained a B.A. degree from City College, and studied for the rabbinate at the Yeshiva Tifereth Jerusalem on East Broadway. When he was 25 years old, he became the spiritual leader of a Conservative congregation of 100 families in Weldon, North Carolina. At first the young rabbi delivered his sermons in the traditional way. Then after a few weeks he began to relax, spicing his preachments with a few jokes.

The Congregation was so delighted that Jackie's sermons became immensely popular. His fame spread to the non-Jewish segment of the population and he was invited to speak at school and fraternal functions. His original jokes and dead-pan, machine gun style—emphasized with finger gestures similar to those used in the pulpit by his father and brothers—convulsed his audiences.

One night an Atlantic City night club impressario heard Jackie address a veterans meeting and spoke to him enthusiastically afterward. "Rabbi," he said, still chuckling, "you were sensational. Where in heaven do you get your material?" When Jackie admitted that he wrote his own jokes, the impresario was more impressed, adding: "You could make a fortune on the circuit. Did you ever think of becoming a professional comedian?"

Jackie nodded, then explained: "I wouldn't dare. My father would never forgive me."

After his father died in 1957, Mason began to feel inadequate and uneasy in the pulpit, as if it were not his true calling after all. More and more he felt that humor was his forte; if he enjoyed making people laugh and they got pleasure from hearing him, would it be so utterly wrong to try for a career as a comedian? After consulting with his brothers, he made up his mind. He would try it—and give it everything he had.

Adopting the name of Jackie Mason, he got a $35-a-week job as social director for a small resort hotel in the Catskills. His duties included planning daytime game activities for the guests and producing a stage show for their entertainment at night. The other performers were guests, amateurs like himself. They were so untalented it was easy for Jackie to cast himself as the star of the show. He spent hours composing jokes based on people and incidents at the hotel. When he stepped before the mike the first night, he was so nervous he knocked it over and then dropped it twice as he tried to pick it up.

He needn't have worried. He was sensational, his jokes and dry style so unexpectedly original and devastating that audience clapped until their hands hurt. He was equally sensational on the second and third nights. On the fourth night, however, he was a failure. The audience hardly snickered, causing the hotel manager to issue a stern warning: "Jackie, you better be a hit tomorrow night or you're all washed up."

On the fifth night the audience yawned—and Jackie was fired. But he learned a lesson he never forgot. No matter how great you are, audiences won't laugh at jokes they've heard before. He failed because he'd run out of fresh material.

That summer he worked at nine different hotels on the Borscht Circuit. He toiled frantically, writing new jokes, but never had enough. As soon as his routines dulled, he quit or was fired, moving on to the next hotel and a fresh audience. When the season ended, he was convinced he had the ability to be a big-time comic. All he needed was material and a few decent breaks .

The breaks didn't come. For the next few years Mason spent his winters working as a salesman at Gimbel's, Macy's and Sak's, and his summers on the Catskill resort circuit. Now he was nagged by doubts about himself. At times he deeply regretted quitting the pulpit. He wondered if his failures were God's way of punishing him for turning away from the work of his father and forefathers. He was not comforted by the thought that he could never return to the rabbinate; to do so would be sacrilegious.

Outwardly, he maintained the self-confident attitude of a brash young comedian. One day Perry Como walked up to Jackie's counter at Sak's. Jackie sold him six pairs of silk pajamas, then introduced himself.

"Mr. Como," he said, "my name is Jackie Mason. Have you ever heard of me?"

"No," said Como.

"I'm a comedian," added Jackie, "and I'm very, very good."

"Is that so?" said Como politely.

"Yes," said Jackie. "So remember my name—Jackie Mason. Because I'm going to be on *your* show!"

Como, constantly beseiged by would-be performers, mumbled a reply, grabbed up his package and fled from the store. He promptly forgot the incident. Mason didn't.

A few years later—when he was the hottest, fastest-rising comic in show business—Jackie appeared on all the top TV shows, Jack Paar's, Garry Moore's, Steve Allen's—and Perry Como's. The Como signing was a particularly sweet victory. Approaching the crooner at their first rehearsal, Jackie said casually, "Hi, Perry. Remember me?" Como didn't. Jackie whipped out an imaginary sales book and pretended to write up an order for some pajamas. Recognition dawned, they both laughed and Jackie commented: "When you walked out on me that day, I felt so bad I hoped all six pairs would be so small they choked you!"

Mason's big break had occured the previous year, 1960, when he obtained a booking at the Slate Brothers Club in Hollywood. Steve Allen dropped in one night and listened as Jackie, looking shy and wistful, discussed his personal problems. "I used to be so self-conscious," Jackie confided, "that when I attended a football game, every time the players went into a huddle I thought they were talking about me." To overcome this, he went to a psychoanalyst and was told the fee was $25 a visit. Jackie, glaring in disbelief at his audience, declared: "For $25, I don't visit. I move in!"

Allen, recognizing the fresh style and the deft sophistication of Mason's material, signed him immediately. Jackie appeared several times in succession on Allen's show, using it as a springboard to other major TV programs and lucrative contracts with top night clubs throughout the country. Overnight his salary exploded from $350 and $500 a week to $3,000 and then $5,000. At first some night club owners—dubious that his style of comedy could hold blasé audiences used to off-color routines— urged him to use suggestive "blue" gags involving sex deviates. Jackie refused, saying: "I don't have to be dirty. I've got better things to offer."

He was right. Gazing around slowly with his heavy-lidded, sleepy-looking eyes, he took audiences by surprise with his rapid delivery, sly digs and satires of public figures and social problems. Punch lines came by the score, some based on self-deprecation, with Jackie taking the role of the bewildered underdog, while others tackled situations so ludicrous that only Jackie's timing and droll comments made them worthwhile. If a bit of wit failed (perhaps it was too intellectual), Jackie got a laugh anyway by scowling through the tobacco haze at nearby tables and cracking: "Amazing! Did you know you are the first dead people I ever saw smoke?"

During our interview, I asked Mason if his insults ever provoked any of the guests, especially heavy drinkers, into angry attacks on him. He said this happened occasionally, explaining that he usually cooled them off with more jokes. "A few have taken socks at me," he said, adding that—adhering to his religious beliefs—he never traded blows with them. "If they look really mean, I just duck and run off the stage."

While working in a Detroit supper club, he aimed a few inoffensive barbs at a beefy-cheeked man seated at a ringside table. The man puffed up with anger and shouted back in a heavy German accent, calling Jackie a "Jewish son of a bitch!" The remark was so uncalled for that Jackie asked: "How did you ever get into this country? I thought there was an ocean between us and you Nazis."

The man's round face turned firecracker red and he thundered: "Wait till after the show. I'll get you and all your Yid pals!" As soon as Jackie finished his act, the man jumped up on the stage. He was well over six feet tall, looked as strong as a drayhorse and doubtlessly could have crushed the diminutive comedian between his thumb and forefinger. Jackie scampered off the stage, picked out the biggest man he could find in the audience and ran over to him.

"I had been watching this second big man from the stage," Jackie recalled. "I knew he was a fan and liked my jokes. So I asked him to help me. When the beefy guy came over, still cursing me, my friend stood up. He was just as big as the beefy guy and just as tough. He said 'Where ya goin', fella?' and the other guy said, very nasty, 'I'm gonna get me a kike rat!' Meaning me, of course. So my friend hit him in the nose. Not very hard, either. The beefy guy turned pale and shaky. He grabbed his nose and ran off hollering, 'Where's the men's room?' "

Jackie's career went along nicely in 1962 and 1963, but didn't really accelerate until after the "obscene gesture" donnybrook with Ed Sullivan. The headlines brought him show offers of $10,000 and $12,000 a week. Suddenly he was a full-fledged, diamond-studded celebrity, recognized wherever he went by head waiters and the man in the street. His publicity aides advised him to display the trappings of success which would keep his name continually in the newspapers.

"Jackie," they said, "you've got to live it up. Buy a big house with a couple of swimming pools. Drive snazzy cars. Throw big parties. Get married—maybe even have a juicy divorce scandal!"

But Mason refused to change his way of living. He has never owned a car, preferring taxis. He lives in a comfortable but modest-sized Manhattan apartment where he spends his off-stage hours reading scholarly works or patiently writing and rewriting material for his monologues. (A perfectionist, he devotes approximately 300 hours of preparation to each six-minute TV stint.)

Jackie seldom socializes with other entertainers, leading the life of an Orthodox Jew. He never uses profanity, never eats pork or shell fish and never performs on major Jewish holidays. Remembering the poverty of his youth, he hoards his money in banks, investing some in stocks, motels and insurance companies. He is a generous spender only with members of his family, giving his rabbi brothers large gifts to help them stretch out their low salaries.

As for marriage, Jackie's attitude is: "No thanks. I wouldn't dare ask any woman to share the upside-down life I lead, with all this traveling, staying up all night and sleeping till noon." He admits, however, that he never lacks girl friends, pretending to be amazed that pretty dolls like to be seen in the company of a "drab little guy like me." Then he adds with wry smile: "I guess they can't help if it they've got good taste."

I asked Mason if there weren't times when he felt compelled to quit the entertainment racket. He nodded, saying that the Sullivan obscene-gesture period was specially difficult because of the effect it had on his brothers and their families. "They knew it was all a misunderstanding" he said, "but still it was very hard on them. They hated to see my reputation besmirched. And I hated to see them drawn into it, even remotely, because I knew it was inevitable that a few of the people in their congregations would have criticism for me. They would make little comments, like what a shame it was for a former rabbi to be mixed up in something like that. All very well-meaning and harmless, of course. But hurtful, too."

Jackie acknowledged that the publicity from the Vegas shooting, although a valuable aid to his career, was also very hard on his family. "They didn't like that lie detector business with the police," he said. "They hate seeing me involved in any way with the Vegas hoodlum and gang elements. My brothers keep telling me to stay away from Vegas. They worry about me. They're afraid somebody may try to beat up on me again."

His reference was to an episode which occured last winter in Miami. It was by far the most violent and vicious of all the incidents in this incredible story. Like the Nevada shooting, it began with anonymous phone calls from tough guys, warning Mason to quit using jokes about Sinatra at Miami's Saxony Club.

The attack came in the early morning darkness after

Jackie's last show. He'd been out on a date with a pretty TV receptionist, Myrna Falk. At 5 A.M. they were sitting in her car, parked in front of an apartment building where Jackie was staying.

Suddenly the car door was yanked open on Jackie's side. A fist slammed against his face. As the girl screamed in terror and Jackie tried to dodge, the fist struck again with terrific force, smashing his nose, spattering him with blood, knocking him sprawling across the seat.

A man's harsh voice cursed him, adding: "We warned you to stop using the Sinatra stuff in your act!"

Jackie never saw his attacker. Stunned, half-blind with pain, he heard the man run away. Vaguely he remembers sounds which could have been a car racing from the scene. Blood streaming from his nose, he staggered into the apartment building. The police were summoned, they questioned him and Miss Falk briefly and then Jackie was taken to a hospital for emergency treatment. X-rays revealed that his nose although swollen like a sausage, was not broken.

When I asked Jackie what the police investigation turned up, he shrugged and said: "Nothing. Whoever planned it was careful to leave no clues."

Asked whether he thought Sinatra himself had anything to do with the Vegas and Miami attacks, Jackie replied: "I doubt it. Sinatra knows my jokes are harmless. Even though I intensely dislike the man and everything he stands for, I don't think he himself would stoop so low. It's the tough guys who hang around Sinatra that are responsible. I think it's the sort of thing that gives them a thrill."

Jackie offered a theory—obviously the product of much careful thought—that the hoodlums have no intention of killing him. "If they really wanted to," he said, "they could finish me off any time with a gun, like when I'm out walking or riding. But that's not their purpose. It's a game with them. They want to scare me into stopping my Sinatra jokes. They're trying to run me out of town. They're trying to make me so frightened and nervous I fly out of my mind."

"Why don't you stop the Sinatra jokes?" I said. "Wouldn't that end it?"

"Maybe," he said. "But I'm not going to quit. It's a matter of principle. Of what's right and what's wrong. I am not going to quit because some musclemen with the minds of insects want me to. The only thing you can do is be as tough as they are, because that's all they understand. So let them make their stupid phone calls and their threats. I can take it."

I noticed that his small hands were clasped together so tightly that the knuckles were white. Jackie glanced down, then quickly unclasped them.

He grinned at me. It was the grin of a man trying to be casual about his fright, like a boy whistling past a graveyard.

"I'm not going to quit," he said. He grinned again. "Maybe I'll take up karate."

10. SCARRED COMIC

It hit him gently, like a hammer wrapped in velvet. It was a stroke, but Joe E. Lewis wasn't aware of it.

The first sensation was a fluttering dizziness. Joe E., the most popular night club comedian in America, thought it was simply light-headness from the Scotch he'd been drinking. Sitting down on the bed, he leaned over to tie his shoelace—and kept right on going.

The next thing he knew he was lying flat on the floor in his plush suite at Las Vegas' Aladdin Hotel, staring up at the gleaming light fixture on the ceiling. It hurt his eyes.

Lewis still didn't realize he was suffering a stroke, that a small artery had burst in his brain. The rest of his brain, perhaps the most brilliant joke machine in the world, kept working perfectly. A gag occured to him: *Christ, I only had one Scotch. I don't particularly like drinking, it's just something I do while I'm getting drunk . . .*

He couldn't understand how one lousy drink could knock him over like that. Why, there had been times, only a few years ago, when he'd been able to drink all night and all day with little effect. And that made him think of another one-liner: *If you drink like a fish, don't drive—swim!*

As Joe E. got up from the floor, he noticed that his right leg was numb. Also, there was a funny feeling in his right hand . . . sort of an electric tingling, as if he'd touched a hot wire.

He started at his hand, puzzled, as another wave of dizziness passed over him. His vision became blurry. He began to topple sideways. He fell on the bed, then slid off and found himself on the floor again.

"Hey!" he said.

It was the last word he spoke, because the stroke had hit the speech center in his brain, paralyzing it. The word was a strangled shout heard by two of Joe's gambling-drinking cronies, in the sitting room, watching TV. Curious, half-expecting one of Joe's zany practical jokes, they went warily into the bedroom.

They knew at once it wasn't a gag. The 64-year-old comic lay flat on his back, gasping for breath. His flabby cheeks—usually an alcoholic pink—were the color of oatmeal. As they picked him up and put him on the bed, they asked quick, anxious questions, demanding to know what had happened, whether he was in any pain and why he couldn't breathe.

Joe tried to answer, but only a dry croak came from his throat. The man who'd hobnobbed with presidents and crime czars, lay across the blankets like a gaffed fish, unable to move. He recognized what was happening now, because he'd been through it many years before. There were no funny lines for this, no grins, no sly put-ons. Because this was the way death came. And no matter who you were—gangster, president or comic—it came with dread and terror.

His pals phoned for a doctor. Within minutes, the hotel's resident physician was at Joe's side, taking his pulse, examing his eye pupils with the beam of a small flashlight. The doctor summoned an ambulance and Joe was taken to Vegas' Sunrise Hospital.

There, on the night of November 7, 1966, Joe E. Lewis began a monumental struggle. The neurosurgeons who examined him discovered with dismay that he was a 64-year-old man living in a 94-year-old body. Four decades of excessive drinking—perhaps the most prodigious liquor intake ever attempted by one man—had weakened him dangerously with diabetes, high blood pressure and liver disease. Most of his stomach, burned out by booze, had been removed by surgery 12 years previously. The stroke had occurred on the left side of his brain, damaging the same area crippled many years before when Joe was brutally attacked by hoodlums who left him for dead.

As they compiled those medical facts, the physicians shook their heads. "Another stroke like this," one commented, "and he's finished. It's amazing that he isn't dead right now."

Cooperating with Joe's business managers, who feared wholesale cancellation of half a million dollars worth of future night club bookings, the physicians agreed to withhold certain facts about the comic's condition. In their first statements to the press, no mention was made of the paralysis of his right leg, right hand and speech center. Joe was described as "resting comfortably," sitting up and watching TV in his hospital room. The strategy worked. The scores of worried phone calls from Joe's celebrity friends in Chicago, New York, Hollywood and Miami fell off to a trickle.

The next evening Joe was visited by a young brain specialist, the top consultant of his case. "I think I know your biggest worry," he said. "You want to know when you'll be able to walk and talk—right?"

Joe's brown eyes, usually lit with roguish humor, looked up at the doctor dully, as if he didn't understand. But he nodded slowly.

"I'll level with you, Joe," said the doctor. "You may walk in a few days. Or it may take months. As for when you'll speak again—well, it's impossible to say. You didn't have an ordinary stroke, you know. The blood vessel burst in a part of your brain that was already badly wrecked and scarred."

The doctor hesitated, then looked down sternly at his patient. "Joe, your drinking days are done. It's not a matter of whether you'll ever talk again. It's a matter of whether you want to live or die."

For a moment Joe made no response. Then his left hand picked up a pencil and scrawled awkwardly on the pad that was his only means of communication. *"I already cut my drinking in half,"* he wrote. *"I don't take chasers no more."*

It was an oldie he'd used on countless stages, but under the circumstances, it wasn't funny. It was pathetic. The doctor smiled politely and said he would return in the morning. He opened the door and went out.

Joe E. slumped against his pillow. It was bad enough not to be able to walk. It was bad enough to have a right hand that felt like a dead piece of lumber. But why did his voice have to be affected? He could probably get by with a bum leg and a bum hand. But what good was a $400,000-a-year comic who couldn't talk? He was finished. Washed up. The dice had crapped out for good.

He thought about the irony of it. Machine Gun McGurn and his boys were having the last laugh after all. The beating and knifing they'd given him 39 years ago had finally done him in. Oh, it was funny, all right. Funny as an abscessed tooth.

His mind drifted back to Chicago and the year 1927. *"Chicago, Chicago . . . that toddling town . . ."* That was his theme song, the way he opened each show. That was the year he first hit the top. He was 25 years old then, full of fire and wisecracks, a tough little guy unafraid of the hoodlums and gangsters who thronged the joints where he worked.

He was earning $650 a week at the Green Mill, a hell of a salary for a Jewish kid born in a tenement on New York's East Side. Raised in poverty with seven brothers and sisters, he looked and talked like a mug. He'd knocked around the clubs ever since he was a teen-ager, performing for dimes and nickels, learning songs and little comedy bits, changing his name from Joe Klewan to Joe E. Lewis because it sounded more professional. It had been a long, agonizing climb. But he'd made it.

Now he was gangland's favorite jester, the biggest name in Chicago showbiz. When bootlegger John Fogarty offered him $1,000 a week to work at the New Rendezvous Club, Joe accepted eagerly. It was more dough than he'd ever dreamed of, worth any risks which might be involved. Danny Cohen, owner of the Green Mill, didn't like it one bit. When he heard Joe was quitting to work for the competition at the nearby New Rendezvous, Cohen immediately got in touch with Machine Gun Jack.

Jack McGun was a debonair, black-haired mobster who owned a part of the Green Mill. The next day he strode up beside Joe E. as the little comic walked along Diversey Parkway. "Hi, Joe," he said, grinning pleasantly. "What's the beef with Danny?"

"No beef," replied Joe E. "My contract's up. I'm not renewin'."

"You gotta be foolin'," said Jack. "You wouldn't quit us, would you, kid?"

Joe shook his head. "I ain't foolin', Jack. I open at the Rendezvous November 2."

McGurn stopped walking. He grabbed the sleeve of Joe's coat and dragged him to a halt.

"Get this, Joe," he hissed. "You'll never live to open!"

Joe E. refused to be frightened. He brushed Jack's hand off his sleeve. "I'll not only open," he said brashly, "but I'll even reserve a table for you, Jack."

Joe turned his back on McGurn and walked away. He knew McGurn carried a gun, but doubted that he'd use it. Not in daylight on a crowded street. He kept on walking.

When he arrived at the New Rendezvous, its owner, Fogarty, was waiting for him, a worried expression on his heavy Irish face.

"Joe," he said, "it ain't good. I hear Machine Gun Jack's out lookin' for you. I don't want that kind of trouble, Joe. What d'you say we call the deal off?"

"The deal's on," said Joe grimly. "To hell with McGurn!"

It was the only code he knew. *Never back away from a fight. If you do, you're finished.* He'd learned that back on the streets of New York, where he'd fought proudly with the kid gangs, starting at the age of 10 when his father died.

Word spread through the underworld that Joe E. was on McGurn's death list. No one knew exactly how many men McGurn had killed with his Thompson submachine gun. But there was no doubt in any one's mind that he intended to add one more. (And two years later McGurn would add seven more, as triggerman during the St. Valentine's Day Massacre that rubbed out Bugs Moran's gang.) Even Captain Joseph Goldberg, of the Chicago police, heard the rumors and tried to persuade Joe E. to go into hiding.

Joe refused. But he did accept a bodyguard, Big Sam, a hoodlum and ex-heavyweight fighter hired by the owner of the New Rendezvous. Big Sam carried two pistols, one inside his belt, the other in a shoulder holster. He accompanied Joe wherever he went.

On opening night the New Rendezvous was jammed wall-to-wall, with more customers waiting outside in a long line. The chorus gals, a dozen cuties who displayed more skin than talent, pranced off the stage. The house lights dimmed and then Joe E. Lewis was introduced to tumultuous applause.

He stood alone in the glaring spotlight, wearing a white suit. *Jesus,* he thought, *what a target I am.* His eyes searched the smoke-filled room, focusing on the ringside table he'd reserved for Jack McGurn. It was unoccupied.

Midway through his second song, there was a crashing report a few feet from the stage. Joe's voice broke, his face paled and his hand shot to the .22 pistol in his pocket. Captain Goldberg and four plainclothesmen sprang from the shadows and converged on the unoccupied table, followed by Fogarty and Big Sam holding drawn guns.

But Joe was safe. The noise had been caused by a

nervous bus boy who'd dropped a wooden tray on the plank floor.

No one tried to kill Joe E. Lewis that night. But he killed business every night at McGurn's Green Mill. Joe's fast patter and risque song parodies kept the New Rendezvous' cash registers ringing like fire bells.

In his biography, *The Joker Is Wild,* written by Art Cohn, Joe revealed what happened one week later when he returned to his room at the Commonwealth Hotel, accompanied by Big Sam. They went in quietly to keep from waking Captain Goldberg, who'd insisted on sleeping in Joe's room ever since McGurn's threats had started. Big Sam took one of the cots that had been set up, Joe took the other. As he undressed, he spread his first week's pay on the dresser top. Ten green bills, each a hundred. They were beautiful.

At 10:30 A.M. there was a knock on the door. For Joe it was the middle of the night. He sat up slowly, still half-asleep. He looked at the other beds. Captain Goldberg's was empty—he'd gone to work. Big Sam was deep in dreamland.

Without thinking, Joe went to the door and unlocked it. He stood there in his pajamas and watched three strangers walk in. He didn't snap out of his drowsiness until he saw the first man draw out a huge .45 pistol. By then it was too late.

"Easy does it, Joe," said the man, who looked seven feet tall and was ugly as a Brahma bull. "Don't yell, understand?"

Joe braced for the bullets, but they didn't come. Instead the tall man leaned over Big Sam's cot and bashed his skull with the heavy pistol butt, sending him deeper into dreamland. At almost the same moment, a tremendous blow came down on the back of Joe's head. He turned and saw the second man standing with arm upraised, ready to clout him again with his gun.

As Joe fell, he saw the third man draw a long-bladed hunting knife from inside his coat.

The pain was incredible, exploding and blinding, engulfing him totally. As Joe writhed on the floor, the men with the guns took turns hammering his skull with the butt of their weapons. They continued pounding long after he was unconscious.

Then the knifeman did his bloody work. He sank the blade deeply into the flesh beneath the left side of Joe's jaw, and he slashed Joe's throat from ear to Adam's apple. Then he ripped Joe's face open, carving up, down and sideways like a butcher.

Then the three strangers departed as quietly as they came, leaving what they thought was a corpse on the floor. But the knifeman had made a mistake. His blade has missed Joe's jugular vein by a sixteenth of an inch.

Many minutes later Joe battled back to partial consciousness. At first he thought he was in deep water somewhere, drowning. He coughed and sputtered, trying to get the fluid from his throat. Then he forced his eyes open and saw that he was lying in a lake of blood. Slowly he realized it was his own and he was choking in it. He didn't remember what had happened to him, but instinct told him he was dying, bleeding to death.

He did not remember finding the strength to crawl from the room into the hotel corridor. He lay panting on the rug for a long time before he was able to crawl to the elevator doors. Many more minutes passed before the elevator finally stopped at that floor and the operator saw him.

A police car took Joe to Columbia Memorial Hospital, three blocks from the hotel. An ambulance brought Big Sam, whose injuries were not serious. Joe was in surgery for seven hours. During the ordeal his surgeon, Dr. Daniel Orth, twice gave him up for dead, but Joe's remarkable constitution—inherited from his mother, who lived to be nearly 100—pulled him through.

His injuries included 12 knife slashes, a fractured skull and brain damage which paralyzed his right arm and speech center. Dr. Orth removed a dollar-sized piece of jagged bone from the top of his skull. The throat and face slashes required 70 stitches. When Dr. Orth finished, he had changed Joe's expression radically, sewing his mouth into a perpetual pixie grin.

During the following weeks, Joe's hospital room was guarded 24 hours a day by two Chicago killers, brothers Pete and Frank Gusenberg, members of Bugs Moran's North Chicago gang. They were under orders to make sure Machine Gun Jack McGurn and his boys had no opportunity to strike at Joe again. Other members of Moran's mob hunted through the city for McGurn with orders to execute him and his three henchmen.

"We'll get 'em," said Frank Gusenberg, seated beside Joe's bed with a sawed-off shotgun across his knees. "Those sons-a-bitches are gonna die, Joe, for what they tried to do to you."

Unable to speak, his face and throat wrapped in bandages, Joe nodded his head.

Three days later, the mob trapped Machine Gun Jack in a phone booth. A dozen bullets slammed into the booth. Ten missed, but two pierced Jack's belly. He was taken to the same hospital Joe was in and placed under heavy police guard. His condition was salisfactory.

The next week, Joe's three visitors got theirs: The knifeman was found shot to death in an alley, and not long afterward Machine Gun Jack's other two hoods were rubbed out.

Joe meanwhile was battling another kind of terror— his brain was haywire. His inability to speak was only part of the trouble. There were great gaps in his memory. He could remember the lyrics of *Macushla,* but could not recall the names of the simplest objects in his room— the hospital bed, chair and mirror. He tried to write with a pencil, using his left hand, but didn't know how to form the letters.

He held a newspaper in front of his face, but couldn't read it. The letters and words meant nothing to him. They were merely peculiar marks on the paper. The thought that he was both a mental and physical cripple was so overwhelming that he turned his face to the wall and wept.

His gangland pals came to his rescue. They contacted a Catholic priest, Father Heister, an English teacher at Notre Dame known for his ability to correct the speech defects of mentally disabled persons. Every Sunday for five weeks, he spent hours at Joe's bedside, patiently teaching him to talk and read again. Like a child learning the alphabet, Joe began haltingly with the letter A. At first his vocal chords, slashed by the knifeman, produced unrecognizable, gutteral sounds. Gradually, he improved, progressing slowly to B, C, D and, eventually, X, Y and Z.

Eleven weeks after the attack, Joe insisted on attempting another performance at the New Rendezvous. His pals begged him not to, saying: "Not now, Joe. For Christ's sakes, can't you wait till you're stronger?" But on the night of January 28, he strode on the stage, his right arm still partly paralysed, his head bandaged, the scars on his mouth and cheeks red and ugly.

The place was jammed with well-wishers and curiosity

seekers who stared in awe and respect at the man who had defied Machine Gun Jack McGurn and lived. They clapped and shouted his name: "Joe! Joe! Joe!" After emcee Ted Healy waved frantically for silence, the crowd quieted down and waited for Joe's first words.

He tried to speak but couldn't. The orchestra played another chorus of his opening song. "Hi," croaked Joe, with great effort. Then he launched into his first gag, attempting to explain casually how McGurn's men had worked him over. "It was like this," he said. "Three of the boys came up to my room to talk over old times. They told a few jokes and I laughed so much I thought I'd die!"

It was macabre but funny. The trouble was, no one understood it, because Joe's delivery was uncertain and some of the words were gibberish. The crowd applauded anyway. He went on for a faltering half-hour until his voice faded completely. Then he ran off the stage while the club resounded with applause and laughter.

He slumped at his dressing table, burying his face in his arms. The club owner, John Fogarty, came in and shouted enthusiastically, "Joe, you were absolutely great!"

"You're a lousy liar," Joe croaked.

"Hell, no," said Fogarty. "They tore the place apart. What more do you want?"

"I'm finished," Joe whispered hoarsely. "They didn't understand a damn word I said. They clapped out of pity."

He stayed at the New Rendezvous for three more weeks and then quit. On his last night, only four tables were occupied and the applause was as weak as his voice.

A few weeks later such stars as Al Jolson, Sophie Tucker, Tom Mix and Hoot Gibson held a benefit performance for Joe, raising $14,000 which was supposed to buy him a men's clothing store where he could retire in peace. Joe, drinking heavily to forget his woes, squandered most of the money, then went to California to rest and recuperate.

For most of a year he was inactive. Then he tried a couple of guest spots in Hollywood niteries, found that his voice had improved slightly, and accepted a four-week job at the Parody Club in New York City.

The engagement was a disaster because few of the customers could understand him; but the owner, Johnny Hodges, an old friend, kept him on anyway. Then came a surprise offer from the Green Mill back in Chicago. It was under new management who wanted him to return for $1,000 a week. Joe went, happy to be back among his Chicago pals. His voice was not as pitiful as it had been the year before, but his brain and tongue still lacked full coordination. Business was rotten. Most of the customers came out of curiosity; few returned.

One night in February, 1929, Frank and Pete Gusenberg stumbled into the Green Mill. The brothers were roaring drunk, loaded with dough and insisting that Joe drink with them. They laughed about old times, recalling how they had enjoyed pinching the pretty nurses while guarding Joe's hospital room.

"You're all right, Joey," said Frank, slapping him on the back. "Here, take this!"

Peeling $150 off his roll, the gunman jammed the bills into Joe's coat pocket. Joe protested that he didn't need the money. Frank squinted at him angrily and insisted he keep it. Joe nodded. It didn't pay to argue with Pete and Frank when they were drunk. Both men were armed and when they were in this kind of a mood they would just as soon shoot you as look at you.

The next morning Joe got up earlier than usual, intending to return the $150 to Frank. It was a cold windy day and he looked around for a cab. The fact that he couldn't find one undoubtedly saved his life. Had he gone by taxi to a certain garage at 2122 North Clark Street, he would have arrived early enough to be lined up against the wall with the seven victims of the St. Valentine's Day massacre.

By walking to the garage, a bootlegging headquarters of the Bugs Moran gang, Joe arrived there at 11:50 A.M., just in time to see Frank Gusenberg being carried out on a stretcher. Frank, his brother Pete and five others had been riddled with machine-gun and shotgun slugs.

That night Joe's old nemesis—Machine Gun Jack McGurn—was arrested, having been identified by witnesses as one of the men who had been seen leaving the garage after the slaughter. McGurn beat the rap. It was common knowledge that he'd been hired for the job by Al Capone, but no one could prove it. Seven years later McGurn finally got his. He was sprayed with 14 machine-gun bullets while bowling in a Chicago recreation center.

A few months after the St. Valentine's Day murders, Joe—out of work and with no prospects—was tapped on the shoulder while drinking double whiskies at the Four Deuces. As he glanced around he was greeted by a tense, hard-eyed messenger from Al Capone. "The Big Guy wants to see you," he said. "Better get your ass over to the hotel right now."

The hotel was the Lexington, where Capone's sprawling headquarters occupied the fifth, sixth and seventh floors. Joe, escorted to Capone's executive suite, found the fat syndicate overlord seated behind a walnut desk as big as the Super Chief.

"Hi, Joe," said Capone. "How're things?"

"Swell."

Capone scowled. "Joe, you're a stinking liar. You're washed up and you know it. You got no voice. No place in town wants you."

Joe shrugged. Capone opened a drawer in his desk and drew out a thick Manila envelope. He handed it to Joe, who looked inside and saw that it was crammed with bills. All were thousands.

"Fifty grand," said Capone. "It's all yours Joe."

Bewildered, Joe shook his head. "What's it for? What's the gag?"

"No gag," explained Capone. "You open your own joint. With your brains and my contacts, you'll do all right, Joe. In five years you'll be worth a million. I'll see to it."

It was a staggering proposition. But it stank to high heaven. With Capone as his partner, his joint would be connected with all the crime and vice in Chicago. He didn't want any part of it. But he pretended to think it over because he didn't want to make Capone sore at him.

"Sorry, Al." He put the envelope on the desk. "I ain't cut to be a boss. I'm an entertainer. And that's what I'll always be."

"Don't be a sap, Joe."

Capone came around the desk and tried to jam the envelope into Joe's pocket. But Joe turned away, a gesture that made the crime boss explode angrily.

"You asshole!" Capone roared. "What makes you so God damned high and mighty?"

He slapped the envelope onto the desk, spilling out layers of green. Then he pointed to the door.

"Beat it!" he commanded. "And keep your trap shut, understand? You don't mention this to nobody!"

Joe went. That night he packed his suitcase and left Chicago, staying away for three years . . .

Many more years passed. Young, tough Joe E. Lewis

became old, tough Joe E. Lewis. Even after three long decades, he was still the greatest wit on America's club circuit. Until that night in Vegas when the stroke hit. It was the sheerest kind of irony. His bad luck had made a full circle. Once he'd been the weakest-voiced comic in Chicago. But he'd overcome it. Now he was Vegas' voiceless wonder. The question was—could he overcome the odds again?

The flabby-chinned old man slumped back in the hospital bed. It was a hell of a lot easier to lick the impossible when you were young. Like that decision he'd made in Capone's office. That had been the crossroads. He could have become a hoodlum like many of his Chicago pals. Instead he'd taken his slashed vocal chords and scarred face and made *more* than the million Capone had promised him. A hell of a lot more. And he'd had just as much fun losing it.

The old man in the bed shook his head and laughed silently. God, what years those had been. He'd worked for peanuts and handouts in the worst dives in Boston and New York. He'd tried everything. Jewish dialect routines. Imitations of celebrities and movie stars. Nothing worked. His speaking voice was O.K. . . . fully recovered, although scratchy at times. But he was always a second-rater. Until that night in 1933 when he met a song writer named Fred Whitehouse.

Fred had a song he wanted to sell for $25. At first Joe wasn't interested. The tune was a parody of a hymn, *Lord, You Made the Night Too Long.* There was no percentage in satirizing religious songs; people resented it. But, listening as Fred read the lyrics, he had to admit the song was whimsical. It was called *Sam, You Made the Pants Too Long,* and it had lines such as the following:

> *"I get the damnedest breeze*
> *Through my BVDs.*
> *My fly is where my tie belongs.*
> *Sam, you made the pants too long."*

Although he couldn't afford the 25 bucks, Joe bought the song. It was the beginning of a complete change in his comedy style. It wasn't the flat, toneless way he sang that the customers liked. It was the whimsy. It took him a long time to make the transition. Gradually the noisy buffoon with the crude Yiddish ditties disappeared, replaced by a droll, sophisticated wit. A lot of his jokes were risque, even dirty. But he delivered them with the deft touch of a pixie, a style so refreshing that he was welcomed in the finest supper clubs.

At Chicago's High Hat he got $1,200 a week. At New York's Riviera he drew $2,000 and not long after rose to $3,500 a week, then $4,000 and $5,000, salaries which continued week after week and year after year. All he did was wobble around a stage, sipping good Scotch, offering such quiet little lines as: "I only drink to be sociable. I'm the biggest Socialist in town . . . I learned dancing from Arthur Murray. Later I found it was more fun with a girl . . ."

The jokes themselves were far from hilarious. What put them over was his sly delivery and ad-lib ability which always enabled him to say or do the right thing at the right time. One night at the Copacabana in New York he was annoyed by a foul-mouthed heckler who became excessively vulgar. Joe glared at him, saying: "You can go home now. Your cage is clean."

The heckler continued to recite all the four-letter words in his vocabulary, upsetting a number of well-dressed women in the audience.

"Perhaps, sir," said Joe, "you would like the microphone?"

"Yeah," bellowed the heckler. "You're f- - - - - - well right I would!"

Joe took his portable mike to the man's table. "Here!" he said and slammed the mike into his mouth. No four-letter words came out. Just teeth, because Joe had shattered his upper plate.

The audience, aware it wasn't a gag, applauded Joe thunderously. The following day the heckler threatened him with a damage suit. Joe got off easily by arranging to pay him $100 through a lawyer. "What an idiot," the comic commented. "To get rid of a creep like that I would've been glad to pay 10 grand!"

Money meant very little to Lewis. His personal needs were modest. All he wanted was a fresh bottle of Scotch every day, a hotel room where he could sleep undisturbed until noon and an occasional girl friend. He never lacked feminine companionship. During his early Chicago days, he had his choice of brunettes and blondes, usually showgirls attracted by the glamour of his association with the city's top hoods. Later, when he was a high-salaried star, he was the target of hordes of lovelies, each hoping to marry him and force him to settle down. He didn't succumb until he was 44 years old.

He married shapely actress Martha Stewart in 1946 after being her steady boy friend for two years. She was 16 years younger than he, a strong-minded girl who knew exactly what she wanted. The marriage lasted longer than anyone predicted, all of 27 months, foundering because Joe gave up none of his bachelor habits. He insisted on living in hotels, refused to have a family, refused to quit drinking and refused to quit staying out all night with the boys.

"But what really burned me up," Martha wept to her friends, "was the way Joe gambled. One morning in New Orleans I watched him lose $56,500 at cards and dice. At Hialeah he lost $22,000 one day and all he could say was 'Hell, honey, I just go to the track for exercise. That's how I work off my extra cash.' I didn't think it was a bit funny. That $22,000 would have bought us a very nice house!"

Joe didn't become a chronic gambler until the late Thirties. Prior to that time he considered himself merely a "modest" bettor, confining his top wagers to $250 or $500. He was nearly always a loser. His worst streak involved Joe Louis, whom Joe E. resented—not because he was a Negro but because, in the comic's words: "He borrowed my name and doesn't even spell it right." During Louis' heyday in the ring, Joe bet against him 27 times in a row—and lost every time.

For years Joe E. was a loyal Cubs fan, betting on all their games. When Charles Grimm was ousted as manager in 1939, Joe became so disgusted he gave up baseball completely and turned to horse racing. It was the worst decision of his life. His track losses in the last 25 years are estimated at somewhere between $1½ and $2 million.

"The trouble with Joe," said his old pal Swifty Morgan, 'is that he doesn't give a damn about dough. He makes a lot of his bets when he's so bagged he doesn't even know what track's open. But his bookies always know."

It was the boozing, not the betting, that finally did him in. But he refused to mend his bad habits. Three days after his Vegas stroke, he wrote his physician a note, asking: "When can I start drinking?"

"Never!" was the reply. But Joe coaxed and wheedled

until his doctors said: "All right, starting next week you can have one drink a day."

Joe conspired with his cronies at the Aladdin. They brought him a giant Martini glass used in one of the hotel's shows. Its capacity was a quart. Joe filled it to the brim with Old Belly Burner. He'd downed a third of it before a nurse intervened, confiscating it and reporting his transgression to the doctor. "He was just following orders. One drink a day."

After that Joe's liquor allotment was zero and visits by his cronies were banned. Meanwhile, he was faithfully abiding by the doctor's other rules. Within him was a burning desire to overcome his handicaps and return to the stage the way he'd done at the New Rendezvous after his slashing in '27.

Every day he exercised, leaning against a pretty nurse as he forced himself to walk on his bum right leg. Instead of holding a glass, he exercised his right arm by raising and lowering a heavy book. A speech therapist advised him that he would be able to talk again as soon as a new portion of his brain could be taught to perform the duties of the damaged area.

For the third time in his life, Joe began haltingly with the first letters of the alphabet, spending an hour on the letter A, progressing slowly to B and C. Then came an unexpected break. Drugs administered by his physicians caused a partial easing of the pressure inside his head.

"Hey, I can talk," he said one day, laughing at his young nurse. "Listen, you beautiful doll! I can talk!"

On February 8, 1967—only three months after his stroke—Joe E. Lewis stood in the wings at Miami Beach Auditorium, waiting to go on in a charity show. The old man was nervous and trembling as he listened to the applause the other performers were getting from the audience of 3,000.

Could he do it? Would his tongue and his brain work together—or would he go out there and make a fool of himself?

There was only one way to find out. The band struck up his theme, *Chicago* and he ran onto the stage. Not as briskly as in past years because of his limp, but nevertheless he ran.

His hand shook as he adjusted the mike. Sweat poured down his gray, flabby cheeks. Then he said his first words:

"Post time!" raising his cocktail glass and sipping delicately.

The crowd roared and kept on roaring as he delivered his whimsical one-liners: "My doctor says not to drink, it cuts down your years. Maybe . . . But looking around I see more old drunks than old doctors . . ." He flexed his biceps. "I'm in great shape, folks, really great. Every artery is hard as a rock . . . I guess you know I was in the hospital. I was doing lousy until I took a turn for the nurse . . ."

He swayed around the stage, pretending to be drunk, an easy task because some of his muscles still lacked coordination. After 10 minutes he limped off to tremendous applause.

He slumped onto a chair, grinning as he listened to the continued clapping and shouts of "More!" But he didn't return. "That's enough for the first time," he told a stagehand. "Christ, what an audience! They thought I was really plastered!"

He set the glass down carefully on the floor, gazing at it with repugnance because it contained only tea.

Later that night he celebrated his comeback by partying at a nightclub with his pals and their good-looking girl friends. Against doctor's orders he had a couple of small drinks, followed by a couple more.

"So maybe some day the stuff will kill me," he commented wryly, using one of his show lines. " I guess it's what I deserve. Anyway, when they lay me out on that cold slab I'll have something inside to keep me warm . . ."

11. MARTHA RAYE—UNFUNNY GIRL

It began with explosions, fires and threatening phone calls. Before it ended, Martha Raye was so distraught she nearly killed herself.

Not a skit from one of her wacky television shows, it was real and frightening . . . a chain of bad luck and blunders, calamity and catastrophe. It happened at the height of her career when she was lolling in luxury, earning more than $150,000 a year.

Across the land 30,000,000 fans regarded Martha Raye as the queen of slapstick, a carefree clown who made people laugh every time she opened her auditorium-sized mouth. But the public did not know the truth about her.

Off-camera, she was an unfunny girl, one of the most tormented and mixed-up women in America. Her personal life was a disaster area. Five times she had married. And five times she had displayed a unique talent for picking out the wrong guy. Each marriage was more miserable than its predecessor.

When Martha returned to her Miami Beach town house that night in mid-August, 1956, she was desperate. For months she had been involved in the ugliest of court battles. She was accused of stealing another woman's husband, a strapping, handsome policeman 12 years younger than she. Martha was accused of luring him with costly gifts, seducing him and breaking up his happy home.

Earlier in the evening Martha had been out with friends who tried to cheer her. But she shunned their efforts. She arrived home at 2:30 A.M., tired and shaky, dreading the thought of another night of lying alone in her bed, hour after restless hour.

She went into the bathroom and took her bottle of sleeping capsules from the medicine cabinet. Their color— dark blue—matched her mood.

She took two pills. Then she examined her drawn, ex-

hausted face in the cabinet mirror. It was a peculiar face.
Viewed from some angles it was quite beautiful, the face
of a voluptuous, sexy woman. From other angles it was
the mask of a buffoon. The difference was in her rubbery
mouth. If she wished, it could be average size, lovely,
feminine and soft. Just as easily it stretched to a gar-
gantuan shape, the mouth of an ape or cow, the trademark which had earned her millions of dollars during
the 30-plus years of her up-and-down career.

She swallowed three more sleeping pills, praying that
they would bring the relief she needed, knowing from
experience that they would help very little. "Oh, God,"
she asked bitterly, "what's wrong with me?"

She continued to stare at the face in the mirror, her
thoughts badly disorganized. She no longer understood
herself. She wasn't even sure any more what the name
Martha Raye stood for. Once everything had been so
simple. She had been one of the most respected girls in
show business, never too tired to give another charity
performance or visit a veterans hospital. During World
War II, she'd been an eager-beaver, a female Bob Hope,
traveling continually overseas from base to base, spending
her energy unselfishly and recklessly until she'd caught
the blood disease which had knocked her for a loop. Its
effects had weakened her for years afterward.

Now she was much older—in a few days she'd be
40—but not wiser. If anything, she was more foolish. She
was still a scatterbrained schoolgirl searching for love,
hoping that every boy she met would be the big adventure
of her life.

That was how she'd met Bob. It had started 10 months
ago with those threatening phone calls back in Connecticut.
Her 10-room mansion was in Westport, a muckamuck
social town she'd grown to detest. She called her 3½-acre
estate Shangri La. Some joke. It was anything but a
paradise.

There had been only a few phone calls, but they'd been
terrifying. They came at odd hours. They were quick,
lasting less than half a minute to prevent identification.
The man's voice was menacing and crude, threatening
physical harm, implying that her face and bosom would
be disfigured.

"Start gathering up some dough," he'd said once. "Keep
it handy, Maggie. For the ransom . . . because you're
gonna be kidnapped . . ."

The fact that he knew her nickname, used only by relatives and close friends, gave the police a clue. They decided the man knew her very well and might possibly be one of her ex-husbands, disgruntled and trying to make trouble. The investigation went on for days, but uncovered no suspects or other clues.

One night the kitchen range blew up when Martha tried to light it, singeing her hair and scaring the hell out of her. It could have been an accident, an accumulation of gas from a leak. Or it could have been allied with the threats on her life.

"It was more than just a little *whoosh*," Martha told the detectives, wringing her hands nervously. "It was a real blast, an explosion with force. It knocked me away from the stove and nearly off my feet!"

The incident left her tense and fearful. Separated from husband No. 5, Ed Begley, she lacked masculine protection, living with two maids, a cook and her 11-year-old daughter Melodye. She insisted that the Westport Police Department post officers around her house 24 hours a day. This was impossible, because of a manpower shortage, so the comedienne agreed to pay for the guards herself, hiring policemen to work as her protectors during their off-duty hours.

One of the officers was Patrolman Bob O'Shea, 6 feet, 2 inches tall, lithe and muscular. He was also 28 years old, blond and had a shy smile. Martha was the first celebrity he'd ever worked for and he treated her with respect and courtesy, opening and closing doors for her, saying "Yes, ma'am" or "No, ma'am" as he carried out her orders. He was far different from the conceited, egotistical show-business husbands who had tried to dominate her life for so many years. She liked Bob O'Shea from the moment they met.

Bob wasn't on duty when the next explosion occured. Worse than the first one, it rocked the house like thunder, frightening Martha out of her wits· She and the servants ran screaming from the house as flames roared up from the rear of the structure and spread to the adjoining garage. Her huge boxer dog (also named Maggie) whimpered and cried, running in crazed circles. Martha picked up the 60-pound animal and comforted her, then sat cuddling her on the lawn while the fire trucks roared to the scene.

The damage, amounting to $5,000, was confined to the

kitchen and garage. Arson investigators decided the cause was two tanks of butane gas, used for cooking and heating. Located outdoors near the kitchen, they had exploded in a geyser of flame and flying metal fragments.

Was the blast an accident? Or could someone have sabotaged the tanks and then tossed a match into the leaking gas?

"That's what we're checking," the investigators told Martha. "We're looking at very piece of evidence and every possible angle."

While police guarded the mansion night and day, Martha remained indoors in seclusion. There were no more threatening phone calls. When the probe ended a fortnight later, it was inconclusive. The tanks were so badly torn up it was impossible to tell whether they'd been tampered with . . .

Exactly what happened at Shangri La during the next three weeks was never revealed. From subsequent events it can be assumed that Martha—who had always fallen in love easily and impetuously—became infatuated with the tall, handsome patrolman she'd hired to protect her. In her fear and worry, she turned to Officer O'Shea for comfort and assurance.

The lid was blown off their relationship late in April by the policeman's angry young wife. Mrs. Barbara Ann O'Shea, 20 years old, filed a court suit only a few days after she gave birth to her first child. Her suit was a blockbuster. She charged that while she was in the latter stages of her pregnancy, her husband had spent his nights at Shangri La doing far more than merely guarding the mansion and its mistress.

Mrs. O'Shea's suit called Martha a "ruthless" homewrecker who had used "arch blandishment and seduction" to steal O'Shea's love. She filed a writ of attachment against Martha's property, demanding $50,000 damages.

While Martha went into hiding, her attorney, Shirley Woolf, issued a flock of statements designed to shore up the comedienne's reputation. She denied all of the young housewife's accusations. She proclaimed Martha "completely innocent," adding that "Miss Raye is shocked by this totally unexpected action because she has never had any romantic alliance with Mr. O'Shea."

Patrolman O'Shea also denied his wife's charges. Called on the carpet by Westport's police chief, the pale-faced young officer insisted that his relationship with Martha was a simple and sinless business arrangement. The chief placed the policeman on suspension.

A few days later the situation grew stickier. Martha's hubby No. 5, dancer Ed Begley—to whom she'd been married only briefly—pirouetted into the act, announcing that he was suing her for divorce. His suit was filed in New York, where adultery is the only legal ground. Begley's attorney declined to name the corespondent.

Noting that 30-year-old Begley, like O'Shea was far younger than Martha, a wag at NBC's television studios commented: "Well, why shouldn't she have a new model every year—as long as she can make the payments?"

Tongues waggled again the following month when still another fire broke out in Martha's mansion. This time in her bedroom. The first person to respond to her excited call for help was Patrolman O'Shea, recently reinstated to the force. He quickly located her bedroom and helped douse the blaze, which was minor. Its cause was presumed to have been a smoldering cigarette.

After that incident, Martha couldn't wait to get out of town. As soon as she finished her last TV show for the season, she booked a flight from New York to Miami. For the first time since the scandal erupted, reporters managed to collar her. Quizzed at the airport, she refused to discuss her future plans regarding Policeman O'Shea, saying only that she was leaving Connecticut for good.

"I'm never coming back," she said, her mouth turning down like a broken umbrella. "Three fires in six months are three more than I need. I'm going to Florida to cool off. Down there when the heat's on you know it's just the damn weather."

In Miami, her attorneys reached an accord with Begley. He agreed to withdraw his divorce suit, allowing Martha to file instead, charging him with desertion. This ploy eliminated the untidy adultery implication in New York.

It appeared that Martha's luck was finally improving, but looks were deceiving. Early in August, she was clobbered again. A Florida judge tossed out her divorce action, ruling she had failed to meet the state's residency requirements.

After that her morale deteriorated rapidly. In New York and Westport, her hectic 60-hour work week had kept her too busy to mope about her troubles. In Florida she had little to do except sit around the house and cry. Every way she turned she was frustrated. Even though her friends and family were strongly opposed, she wanted to marry Bob—tomorrow, if possible—and put an end to all the "living in sin" gossip. But now she couldn't even do that.

Her suffering reached a bitter climax the night she stood alone in her bathroom, staring at her woebegone mirror image, clutching the bottle of blue sleeping pills. She was at the end of her rope, tired beyond all understanding, so tense her body was one huge writhing nerve. She put more pills into her mouth. And then some more.

Vaguely she realized what she was doing. She knew it was wrong. But she kept stuffing the blue capsules into her mouth and washing them down with gulps of cold water. She didn't stop until the bottle was nearly empty.

She turned away from the mirror. She went into the bedroom and stood by the bed. Except for a sense of sadness, she felt no reaction.

She moved a step closer to the bed. Then everything hit her at once. Dizziness. Nausea. The sensation of floating weightlessly. She was certain she could at least make it to the bed, but she didn't. She went down like a felled tree, thumping heavily onto the rug, her arm knocking a lamp over with a shattering crash.

The noise awakened her maid. She took one frightened look at Martha's silent form and flew to a phone, summoning a physician. Doctor Ralph Robbins and an ambulance crew arrived about the same time.

They found Martha in a coma, her pulse weak, her breathing forced. On the way to the hospital, they began pumping out her stomach, an emergency action which saved her life. Her condition remained critical for hours afterward. In his report to the police, Doctor Robbins said: "She took about 20 sleeping pills. She's a very lucky woman. If the maid hadn't found her, the pills would have been fatal."

Martha's recovery was speeded by an outpouring of sympathy and affection from her show business friends who sent telegrams, letters and flowers and made long-distance calls to the hospital. Throughout the ordeal, ex-husband No. 4, Nick Condos, and Melodye, their daughter, stayed near her beside, offering love and encouragement which helped lift her spirits.

Condos, who'd continued as Martha's business manager after their divorce, had always been available to her in times of crisis. As man and wife, they had been battling enemies; as business partners they got along amazingly well. Martha regarded Nick as one of her closest, most trusted friends.

When she was thinking clearly again, she made some resolute decisions about her future. "I'm willing to face the music," she told Nick. "And the truth about myself. I made a mess of everything. Now I'll try to do right. I'll do my best to straighten everything out."

As soon as she could find a buyer with the cash, she sold Shangri La for $50,000. Then she agreed to an out-of-court settlement with Mrs. O'Shea, paying her $20,000. This was $30,000 less than the policeman's wife had demanded. It was, in the eyes of many, a belated admission on Martha's part that Mrs. O'Shea's accusations of "love theft" and "ruthless seduction" had some basis.

On one subject Martha could not be persuaded to change her mind. Despite all of Nick's arguments, she insisted on pushing ahead with her plans to marry O'Shea, who had resigned from the police force and was operating a private detective agency in New York.

"I love Bob," she declared, "and I know he loves me. If people will just give us a chance, I know the marriage will succeed."

She had to wait nearly two years, until all the assorted legal snarls could be untangled. On November 7, 1958, she and O'Shea were married in Teaneck, N.J. Martha had hoped the ceremony would be quiet and dignified. It was exactly the opposite. Performed by Mayor August Hannibal in his Teaneck home, impressive glamour was supplied by Martha's good friend, Joan Crawford, matron of honor.

Midway through the ceremony, 35 news photographers —angry because they'd been ordered to remain outdoors— shattered the lock on the mayor's front door. They burst in like a stampede of Texas longhorns, cursing and jostling as they vied for the best camera positions.

"Gentlemen, gentlemen!" pleaded the mayor. "Please!"

He was nearly trampled in the rush. A flood of tears smeared the bride's makeup as one lensman crowded in so enthusiastically he nearly bowled her over. The mayor shrugged and got on with the ceremony.

While the couple climbed into their honeymoon sedan, the photographers made rude wisecracks, wagering on how long the union would last; six months was the figure mentioned most frequently. Their estimate fell short by four months.

The marriage came unglued for the same reasons as Martha's five others—incompatibility, arguments and flare-ups of temperament. During the divorce proceedings, ex-cop O'Shea, displaying what some construe as lack of gallantry, dealt Martha another blow. Claiming the marriage was her idea entirely, the man who had abandoned his wife and child in order to pursue her, declared that Martha had promised him a $100,000 gift if he would become spouse No. 6. Charging she had reneged, he filed suit, demanding as proper compensation title to her new Long Island home and its furnishings. His claim was quickly denied by the court.

From the very beginning, four decades previously, it was evident that Margie Reed (Martha's real name) would have an exciting but grossly abnormal life. Her parents were second-rate troupers billed as Reed and Hooper. Her father was Pete Reed, her mother Peggy Hooper. Martha was born backstage amid a jumble of trunks and props in a theater in Butte, Montana, on August 27, 1916. Less than 48 hours later her mother was back on stage, singing and dancing and hoping no-one in the audience would notice how she winced on the fast turns.

Martha grew up in the back seat of the family Stude-baker, traveling from town to town with a tab show, a miniature revue which sometimes paid her parents $35 a week, but usually less. The little girl had one doll, with a cracked head, and few other toys. Her schooling was haphazard and she had little playtime with kids her own age. As soon as she could toddle, she joined Reed and Hooper in front of the footlights, jigging and mugging. When she was four years old, her mouth was already as big as a pie plate, easily stretchable into clown shapes that won laughs and applause.

"I thought I was having a wonderful life," Martha told a Los Angeles press conference many years later. "I never realized I was being culturally deprived, that I was having a lousy upbringing. We were too busy making a living to worry about stuff like that. So I guess I grew up insecure, with no home ties. And maybe that's why I'll always be insecure and worried about finding happiness. But I do remember those as happy years, even when we didn't have enough to eat."

One of the most memorable events of her childhood was the birth of her brother Bud, who also arrived backstage. "It happened without any warning." she recalled. "The show had folded in Grand Rapids, Michigan. We were in the theater, feeling low, packing our costumes. Suddenly Mama put her hand on her stomach and fainted. Papa carried her to a broken cot that was used in one of the acts. The theater manager came running up all excited, shouting 'Call a doctor!' But Papa told him to forget it. The manager kept insisting, so finally Papa just grabbed him by the belt and threw him out the door."

Papa Reed's behavior was based on logic and experience. The family could not afford a doctor. Four nervous chorus girls delivered the baby, protesting throughout that they didn't have the slightest idea what they were doing. They dashed about with basins of hot water. They got in each other's way. They swore like cavalrymen, but somehow did everything right, even tieing the cord.

"Afterward," said Martha, "Papa got a bottle out of his trunk and gave all the girls a drink to celebrate. He told me it was ginger beer and I believed him. If it was, it was the most powerful ginger beer ever brewed because pretty soon those chorus girls were kicking their legs and jumping around like bugs on a hot stove. The party ended when Mindy, the tall pretty one, fell into the orchestra pit and broke her kneecap."

When Bud was old enough, he joined the act. Soon the children, especially Martha, displayed more talent than their parents and it was decided to change the name of the act to Bud and Margie. The kids caught on with vaudeville audiences in the Midwest and East, dancing, singing, doing mimicry and comic bits. Their salary went to $100 a week, then $200. When it reached a fabulous $400 a week, the ecstatic Reeds went on a buying spree, dining in the finest restaurants, staying in plush hotels and stuffing their battered suitcases with flossy new clothes.

That was the top and their stay was brief. "We never knew why," said Martha, "but we began slipping. We were just as good as we'd ever been, but nobody wanted us. Pretty soon we were only working one week out of three. Then we were down to club work, one-night stands. We'd drive 60 miles for a $15 date at an Elks club or a Saturday night binge put on by the machinists union."

They sold their fancy duds and extra shoes. The only thing they kept was their rusty old sedan because their lives depended on it. It took them from job to job, also serving as kitchen and bedroom. They ate and slept in the car. Mama Reed and the two kids bedded down on a wooden platform laid across the back seat. Papa curled up in front.

That kind of living took its toll. Papa developed lumbago from cold air seeping in through the broken windshield. The kids—now in their teens—had chronic coughs which often broke up their singing numbers. They hit bottom one Depression winter in Cleveland. It was too cold to sleep in the car so they spent their last dollar for a room in a slum hotel. Then came the shocker. The family had been promised a whole week of work in a theater, but it fell through due to a schedule mixup.

It was the week before Christmas. Too proud to ask for help, the Reeds rationed their meager groceries while Papa looked vainly for any kind of work. Finally they were down to their last box of soda crackers. Recalling the incident some 20 years later, while dining with friends in a Long Island restaurant, Martha said:

"People today don't believe things like that ever happened. But they did and it was horrible. I remember going for a walk that afternoon with Bud. We were so hungry and tired we could hardly talk. We watched a truck unload some supplies in front of a dingy little cafe. Pickles. Mustard. Loaves of bread. The sight of all that food was just too much. Then the truck drove away and we saw a big jar sitting on the curb. We kept looking at it. Nobody seemed to want it. Nobody else even noticed it. So after a while I went over and picked it up."

It was a half-gallon of strawberry jam. Martha and Bud ran back to the hotel with it, and the family feasted on jam, crackers and water for the next two days. "It looked like our luck might be turning," said Martha. "So I put on my best dress, a red one with sequins, and I went downtown and looked up Paul Ash."

Ash, a band leader playing in one of Cleveland's better hotels, remembered Martha from shows they had done together on the Midwest circuit. He not only agreed to give her a job singing with the band, but came through with a week's salary in advance. It was salvation for the Reeds, but it also marked the breakup of the family troupe. After that, Martha—only 15 but mature for her years—worked and traveled on her own. She sang with Ash for 11 months in Chicago, then went to New York as a vocalist with the Borris Morros Orchestra at the Paramount Theater.

For years afterward she sent money to her parents and Bud, who kept struggling with the old act. Her progress was steady if not spectacular. Noticing the success of Ethel Merman and other belters, she changed from straight singing to a loud, lusty style, practicing with a phonograph or radio blaring at full volume. She also changed her name. After appearing at New York's Riviera and Chez Paree clubs, she latched onto a $100-a-week booking at the Century Club in Hollywood. She was only mildy successful. For a time she sang in smaller clubs, her salaries so unmentionably low that she was forced to work days as a nurse's aide at Cedars of Lebanon Hospital.

Then she began using a technique which had helped her career back in New York. She offered to sing for nothing, merely to be heard. It worked. She did guest spots with Louis Prima at the Famous Door and with other bands at the Casanova and Clover clubs. Her big break came unexpectedly on what she thought would be a dull Sunday night at the Trocadero. It was her first appearence there.

She didn't do things any differently that night in 1936. Until she started to sing, she looked like any other young band vocalist. She was 20 years old and quite pretty, wearing an evening gown which emphasized her shapely figure. She opened her mouth and hit the first note of *I've Got You Under My Skin*. She opened wider and hit another note, louder. Then she unhinged her jaws all the way and loosed a blast which could be heard in Pasadena and the mountains.

Not until she finished, to loud applause, did she discover that it was the habit of Hollywood's biggest names to gather at the Troc on Sunday nights. Then all the obstacles in her path crumbled. Talent agents got up from ringside tables and swarmed toward her. Others seemed to come out of the woodwork. Each wanted to be the first to sign her.

Their fast chatter left her giddy with joy and shock. But more was to come. Studio mogul Adolf Zukor sent his card; Darryl Zanuck sent his No. I assistant, and director Norman Taurog came over in person. After that night, everything was incredibly easy. All her wildest dreams came true. She accepted Paramount's offer because it was the most generous, $1,300 a week, and because the studio was willing to write a comedy part for her into *Rhythm on the Range*, which was already under production, starring Bing Crosby.

She signed for a series of pictures, including *Waikiki Wedding*. She signed for radio and night club appearances. She endorsed a beauty cream and lipstick, for fat fees. Within six months she was a full-fledged celebrity. The handsomest men in Hollywood dated her, maitre d's recognized her at once and saw to it that she was seated at the best table in the house.

She began spinning on an emotional merry-go-round which didn't slow down for years. A typical day included energetic mugging before the cameras at Paramount from 9 to 6, followed by a radio rehearsal or broadcast and then sessions at her favorite night clubs where she sang until 1 or 2 A.M. simply for the love of it.

Before she was 21 years old, she eloped with makeup man Buddy Westmore. The marriage lasted three months. The following year she ran off with band leader David Rose. That lasted slightly longer. In 1941 she tried for the third time marrying hotel executive Neal Lang.

All her husbands were dark-haired and extremely good-looking. All discovered within a few months that Martha Raye was impossible to live with. Watching her clown around at a 3 A.M. party in Beverly Hills one of her ex-mates confided to columnist Hedda Hopper: "I loved Maggie, I really did. But she wore me out. She's a bundle of nerves wrapped up in a ball of fire."

Each of her divorces left her more neurotic and confused about herself. Then came the biggest blow. Her brother Bud died of tuberculosis, doubtlessly related to the hardships and malnutrition the family suffered on the road during their impoverished years. Martha wrongly blamed herself for his death, feeling she hadn't done enough for him. The difficulty was that Bud wouldn't ask for help, nor had he let her know how badly off he was. While she was living it up in Hollywood, he had been quietly starving in New York on a musician's pittance of $22 a week.

When she married Nick Condos, the handsome Greek, in 1944, Martha vowed to be a better wife, to cook for him and raise a big family. Her fine intentions scattered like dust in the wind. Although her movie and radio schedules were more frantic than ever, she was convinced she could find the time for trips to the war zones, entertaining the troops. She overspent her energy.

One morning in North Africa she couldn't budge from her bed. The woman who'd had more bounce to the ounce than a wallaby was suddenly listless, pale and shivering. The blood infection she'd contracted resulted in anemia and kidney impairment.

Her convalescence was lengthy, requiring many blood transfusions. She returned to Hollywood and made more films, but things were different. She tired more quickly now. And her slapstick pictures were not successful. Then one of the brass at the studio got a brilliant idea.

"Martha's really quite good-looking," he toll his associates. "In fact, from some camera angles she's damned sexy. What's the report on her chest size?"

"Over 38," replied a consultant. "Practically a 39."

"See what I mean!" said the boss triumphantly. "Hell, she's practically another Jane Russell!"

They de-emphasized her mouth, glamorized her dark hair and shot publicity pictures emphasizing sleekness, cleavage and curves. In her next two pictures they offered Martha Raye as the nation's newest sex-symbol.

The ticket-buying public took one look and said no, most emphatically. Martha Raye bombed in theaters from Cucamonga to Cape Cod. The studio promptly decided she was washed up, but no one had the nerve to tell her. They took the coward's way out and broke her heart.

"They did it this morning with a yellow slip," she wept to her friends. "They stuck it under my dressing room door. I picked it up and read that I was fired. There were no goodby's and not one little bitty thank you. I packed my things and left."

She lingered in Hollywood for a year, trying to find work. Nobody wanted her. Then she returned East and went on the night-club circuit.

When TV came along she was reluctant to try it. Having lost her confidence once, she didn't want to be burned twice. Finally Nick persuaded her to accept a few guest shots. She was a hit from the start, her funny-mouth antics and pratfalls being perfect for the new medium. Along with Milton Berle, she pioneered the technique of embarrassing or roughing up her guest stars. On one show, she belted singer Ezio Pinza in the stomach, did a swift turn and downed ex-boxer Rocky Graziano with a looping right to the chops. NBC was so delighted it upped her salary to $5,000 a week.

Somehow her marriage to Nick Condos survived for nine years. When she sought her divorce in 1953, she charged that he "beat me and mistreated me terribly."

She indicated he would remain as her business manager, however, because "we don't fight over money—just everything else."

The following year she wed young Ed Begley, one of the dancers on her TV show. The marriage lasted not quite 11 months and was soon followed by the series of explosions, fires and romantic misadventures which led to her reported suicide attempt, marriage No. 6 and still another divorce.

After the humiliation of those defeats, and the unsavory press notices they generated, Martha charted a new course for herself. Swearing off marriage for good, she hurled her energy against new challenges. Like other stars of her stature, she made generous financial gifts to charity. But she also gave more. She performed tirelessly in orphanages, hospitals and old people's homes, usually without publicity.

When the Vietnam War worsened, Martha sailed into battle with the devotion and know-how of a veteran. It was her third war, counting the Korean conflict, and she spent more time with the troops than any other entertainer. During 1965 and 1966, she endured the combat perils, the insects, mud and heat for 14 months.

Garbed in a jaunty Special Forces green beret, combat boots and a camouflage suit, she staged over 600 performances, going by copter to the front line jungles and rice paddies. Sometimes she performed for as few as two soldiers at a remote post. The troops were so delighted with her they called her "Boondock Maggie."

In the fall of 1965, she was at Plei Me outpost when the Viet Cong began a bloody attack. A copter lifted her to safety just 29 minutes before the Reds surrounded the position, starting a seige that lasted eight days and cost scores of Allied dead.

Her most heroic service occurred the following year at Soc Trang on the Mekong delta. She showed up at an Army dispensary prepared to sing and dance, but quietly changed her mind as she saw bullet-riddled copters dart in with dead and wounded from a battle that was continuing nearby.

Martha's eyes filled with tears of sympathy as stretchers went past bearing teen-aged boys with ugly red bandages on their torn limbs and torsos. She dashed up to an Army doctor, crying: "Oh, my God—those poor kids. You've got to let me help!"

"But, Martha," protested the doctor, "what can you do? You're no nurse."

"The hell I ain't!" she replied proudly. "I was the best scrubber Cedars of Lebanon ever had!"

The dispensary had no nurses, only the one doctor and eight overworked corpsmen. Although it was 30 years since Martha worked at the Hollywood hospital, she hadn't forgotten how it was done. And she displayed astonishing energy and strength. Hour after hour, she scrubbed the wounded, preparing them for surgery. Then she helped the doctor, handing him his instruments. Later she labored patiently in the ward, changing bedsheets and scores of bandages.

She worked the first day from eight in the morning until nine at night. She also donated a pint of blood to a dying sergeant. The following dawn she returned for six more hours of hard work. When it came time for her to continue her entertainment tour, the soldiers cheered her departure until they were hoarse.

She made two visits to Vietnam in 1965, two more in 1966 and her fifth trip in 1967. Between journeys she rested up in her Bel Aire, California, home, sallying forth for a Broadway run in *Hello Dolly,* frequent $7,500 guest appearances on TV and work on the Vegas-Reno casino circuit.

Although she's met scads of eligible men since the late Fifties, Margie Maggie Martha Raye Reed Westmore Rose Lang Condos Begley O'Shea hasn't changed her mind about the pitfalls of marriage. When she swore No. 6 would be her last, she wasn't kidding. Although a decade has passed since her last divorce, the subject is still painful to her and she rarely discusses it even with her closest friends.

Occasionally, if the timing is right, she makes an oblique reference to her marriages during a show. One night at the Sahara in Las Vegas, a heckler shouted from the audience: "Hey, Martha, when are you going to try for Number Seven?"

Casting a glance at the nearby crap tables, she shrugged and replied: "Ask those fellas over there. They'll tell you I sometimes roll an eight or a nine. But a Number Seven? Never, pal. Absolutely NEVER!"

The audience roared with laughter. But Martha—who doesn't think the subject is that funny—didn't even crack a smile.

12. THE GREAT GLUTTON

Few people watching the great glutton on TV today would ever suspect that Jackie Gleason—plump as a pregnant hippopotamus—was once so starved and skinny he had trouble keeping his pants up.

In the Thirties, when he was a brassy Brooklyn loud-mouth trying to break into show business, Gleason was gaunt from malnutrition. Unable to finance three meals a day on a honkytonk emcee's salary of $8 a week, and hoping to eat more regularly, he took a job as a carnival barker, working with the International Congress of Dare-devils.

He signed up without realizing that his new pay scale, a grandiose $12 a week, required *him* to be one of the Daredevils.

On his first afternoon, Gleason was told to report to the Helldrivers, a carefree group of lunatics who crashed cars head-on or rammed them deliberately through brick walls and flaming buildings. As Jackie entered the speed-way, he was met by a steel-nerved driver named Nifty Fargo.

"You the new barker?" asked Nifty.

Jack nodded. He was led to a locker and given a pair of grimy coveralls and a leather helmet with goggles. "What's this stuff for?" Jackie asked.

"Put 'em on," said Nifty.

Jackie shrugged. After donning the outfit, he followed Nifty to a stripped-down, beat-up car with a huge yellow "13" painted on its black hood. Nifty gave Gleason a megaphone and told him to get in. Jackie hesitated, looking dubiously at the car, an ancient Studebaker which had been wrecked and repaired many times.

"Scared?" said Nifty.

"Hell, no," replied Gleason. "I'm only shaking like this because it's July and I'm freezing to death."

He got in and listened while Nifty explained what they were going to do. At one end of the speedway was a wooden railing where the yokels were allowed to watch a small part of the show without paying. "Our job," said Nifty, "is to force 'em inside where they gotta pay."

Nifty revved up the engine. They tore around the track, Jackie turning pale as their speed increased. Raising the megaphone, he shouted at the yokels, warning them that they were in mortal danger. He wasn't lying. Pecan-sized gravel had been deliberately spread near the railing. As the car approached, Nifty made a sharp turn. The old Studebaker went up on two wheels, nearly overturning, and the tires shot gravel at the spectators like a fusillade from a machinegun.

"Look out!" bellowed Jackie. "Stand back, or you'll all be killed! That gravel has the velocity of bullets!"

There was only one way for the yokels to escape. They fled through a gate past a ticket seller who charged them 35 cents a head for safe seats on the inside.

Recalling the incident many years later during a party at Toots Shor's, Gleason said, "Sure, I exaggerated a little. The pebbles didn't really fly as fast as bullets. Just fast enough to take an eye out!"

During the next performance, Jackie pleaded with Nifty, saying, "Hey, pal, couldn't you slow this thing down a little?" Nifty grinned and drove faster and more daringly. As they made the turn, the right front tire blew. The car swerved crazily. It struck the railing, panicking the spectators with flying splinters as well as gravel. Then the car bounced back onto the runway, spinning like a top.

Jackie hung on with both hands, but—lacking a seat belt —was tossed out anyway. He landed on the gravel, his chin scraping the pebbles, but was unhurt, except for scratches.

Although only 20 years old, Gleason was wise enough— and scared enough—to realize there was no future as a daredevil. He went to the show manager and pointed out that he could do a much better barking job from a platform near the railing. The manager agreed.

The following week, Nifty miscalculated on the two-wheel turn. The Studebaker rolled over and over, demolishing itself and its driver. Had Gleason been sitting beside him, he would also have been killed—and the country would have lost a great comic.

After a month of carnival ballyhooing, Jackie was intrigued by a group of elephants who performed in a tent near the auto speedway. As part of their act, they staged a ponderous baseball game. Jackie noticed that each elephant was trained to play a certain position and wore a huge number so the trainer would know at a glance where to spot them on the playing field.

One morning, when the carnival was in Centreville, Michigan, Jackie crept into the elephant tent and rearranged all the numbers. The next performance was bedlam. Apparently, an elephant trained to play short-stop will have a nervous breakdown if converted into a catcher overnight. The elephants trumpeted wildly, bumped into one another like five-ton drunks and nearly trampled their trainer into the dust.

A water boy told the management that he'd seen Gleason hanging suspiciously around the tent. Jackie was fired. He hitchhiked back to New York and got a job as barker at Coney Island. His salary: a few bucks a week and all the hot dogs he could eat. He gorged. After a few days just the sight of mustard made him ill. He quit.

He drifted over to a resort at Budd Lake, New Jersey, working as a bus boy and part-time comic. His jokes were lousy, and he ate so much food while working in the kitchen that the chef fired him. Piqued, Jackie went down to the lake and cranked up the motor on a speedboat. He aimed the boat at a ramp and then jumped out. Gleefully he watched as the boat shot up the ramp, roared across a brick patio and bounced into the grand ballroom.

"I had only one regret," he said later. "It was 10 o'clock in the morning and the ballroom was empty· But *wowee,* you should have heard the racket as the prop chewed up that hardwood floor!"

Returning to Brooklyn, he slept three-in-a-bed with Sammy Birch and Walter Wayne, who were also struggling comedians and emcees. They stayed in the sack until noon, eliminating the need for breakfast, which they could not afford. Lunch was usually cheese, bread and a glass of water downed in their flea-bag hotel room. Dinner, the high-light of their day, was a blueplate special at Kellogg's Cafeteria. One special for the three of them. It cost 59 cents, including soup, entree, rolls and butter, dessert and coffee. The guy who dug up the 59 cents got the entree. The other two tossed a coin. The winner got the vegetable soup and rolls; the loser got the small triangle of cherry pie and coffee.

Finally Jackie got a chance to try out for a comedy

spot at the Tiny Chateau, a night club in Reading, Pennsylvania. Just before going on, he was a trembling, gaunt wreck. Weeks of skimpy meals had reduced him to 140 pounds.

Billed as Jumping Jack Gleason, he started out bouncing around the stage, doing cartwheels, laughing at himself and the band. Then he began his comedy patter. Instead of using his Brooklyn routine, which consisted of trading profane insults with the customers, he made the mistake of thinking people in Pennsylvania wanted clean comedy. The customers didn't laugh. They stared at him and watched him sweat.

When Gleason left the stage, the manager told him he was through after the second show unless he could do better.

Jackie went to the bar and asked for a drink on credit. He gulped it and ordered another. When he went on for the second show, he knew it would be his last. He didn't care what happened; as a result he was relaxed in the spotlight. He began to *think* funny. He impersonated famous people, satirizing them mercilessly. He kidded the customers, traded verbal darts with waiters, sang a dirty song, and then insulted the manager by making him the butt of an offcolor story. When he left the stage, the applause was riotous.

Gleason stayed for the season. Quick to catch on, he began to understand why one joke made people shrug and another broke them up. He learned that a little bird-like flutter of the fingers or a frisky two-bar step made the difference between happy or dour faces in the audience. A slowly elaborate "double-take," one of the hoariest strategies in show biz, could still be a sure-fire giggle producer, if done right. At 2 A.M., a sentimental song, delivered with more emotion than talent, could reach deep into a listener's heart.

He got other bookings. Sometimes he earned $25 a week, sometimes $17.50. Wherever he worked, he stowed away as much chow as the chef would permit. Between engagements, he lived with Sammy and Walter in cheap hotels. Sometimes they had enough for three 59-cent blue-plate specials.

Then Jackie got a good break at Newark's Club Miami, a tough joint run by two ex-cabbies. Gleason was in his element there. His brash, flip, take-it-or-leave-it style was lustily enjoyed by the customers, mostly working men.

Sometimes he went too far. One night he made the mistake of implying that a guy at a ringside table was a cuckold. The customer, a longshoreman, barreled up to the stage with blood in his eye, both knobby fists raised. Gleason rushed at him and they began wrestling. They tumbled down the stage steps to the floor, where the longshoreman began butting Jackie's jaw with his skull, which was as solid as concrete.

A woman sitting nearby screamed "Here, Jackie, use this!" She handed him her large purse, which contained a bottle of whiskey. Jackie swung it, the longshoreman's head rang like a gong and the fight was over.

One night a pot-bellied, balding Italian began to heckle Gleason from the audience. He was coarse and tough, but no match for Gleason's sharp wit. While the audience guffawed, Jackie hacked him to ribbons with insults. The paunchy patron growled and invited Jackie to settle the matter out in the alley.

One of the club owners, George Sossin, took Gleason aside. "Don't fight him," he warned. "This guy is dynamite"

"With that big belly?" grinned Jackie. "Hell, pal, watch me go!"

In the alley, Gleason took one swing and missed. Then something hit him. A soft, velvety blackness closed in around him. When he opened his eyes, he lay flat on his back on the pavement, looking up at a circle of anxious faces.

He gasped as Sossin forced whiskey down his throat. "Who the hell was that guy?" Jackie muttered.

"Tony Galento," Sossin replied.

Two-Ton Tony was a brawler who later gave heavyweight champion Joe Louis some anxious moments in the ring.

After work at the Club Miami, Gleason—still underweight—would go into the kitchen and put away a brick-sized chunk of roast beef, half a chicken, a dozen slices of bread and whatever pies and cakes were handy. The chef always listened to the applause. When it wasn't heavy, he'd say, "You didn't do a good show tonight, Jackie. No eats."

Years later when he was TV's top banana, earning $300,000 a year Gleason got even for years of deprivation by developing incredible habits of gluttony. His weight soared to 265, then 285 elephantine pounds. When he became too heavy he dieted strenuously, causing his bulk to fluctuate like a beachball being blown up and deflated. After discarding many expensive suits because they wouldn't fit, he wised up. Now he maintains three complete wardrobes, each costing thousands of dollars and each designed for different poundage (225, 250 and 285).

Gleason's hog-like gourmandizing flabbergasts people who see him in action for the first time. He has been known to down five stuffed lobsters at one sitting, drinking a small bottle of wine with each. "Just a snack," he'll comment. While Gleason was making the movie *Gigot,* in which he portrayed a lovable deaf-mute French bum, he turned the set into a pantry-with-cameras, keeping thick sandwiches, baskets of fruit and foot-long bolognas within reach for between-meal appetizers.

"Snacking didn't slow him down a bit," commented dancer Gene Kelly, who directed the picture. "At dinnertime I just ordered Jackie what I thought would be a decent meal for three men."

Gleason once wrote and starred in a CBS Special called *The Million Dollar Incident.* One scene called for him to be shown eating spaghetti with a group of men. Jackie sent out to his favorite Italian restaurant for the spaghetti. As they shot the scene, Jackie devoured a plateful. The director wasn't satisfied so they shot the scene over. This happened four times and each time Gleason ate a heaping plate of spaghetti. Finally the director called for a fifth take.

"Let's get it right this time," quipped Jackie. "If this keeps up, it will cut into my lunch!"

Gleason gluttony is not glandular. He simply loves to eat. One of his doctors says, "I don't think he'll ever return to a normal weight. Overeating is a form of aggression for him—getting back at the world. Besides, if a thin man does a tap dance, who cares? If a fat man does it, we marvel. Gleason can get away with more as a fat character than as a thin one. He'll stay fat."

When Gleason begins to worry about his flabbiness, he moves into Doctors' Hospital in New York, where he lieves in solitude and sourly counts calories. He has taken off 25 pounds in two weeks. Except for rehearsals and performances, he does not leave the hospital. A week or 10 days of dieting leaves him ravenous and irritable. When he can't stand it any more, he bribes orderlies with

$50 tips and sends them out late at night to buy great quantities of frankfurters and sauerkraut. He has eaten 12 extra-large franks in less than 10 minutes.

Asked what his stringent hospital diet is like, Jackie once replied, "For breakfast, one cracker. Wait. Faint. Eat another cracker . . ."

One night, after a week of solitude in the hospital, he staged a party in his room, inviting a dozen friends who turned it into a boozy bedlam.

Gluttony and dieting are only two of Gleason's monumental personal problems. The others involve chronic insomnia, booze, women and religion (he is a Catholic, tormented by his sins). All his problems are interrelated, and it doesn't take a psychiatrist to see that all come from the same basic source—the insecurity and tragedy of his childhood.

Herbert John Gleason was born February 26, 1916, in Brooklyn. His parents were Irish. His mother, Mae Kelly, sought gaiety in life; instead she found bitterness and illness. His father, Herb Gleason, was a failure who earned $25 a week as a clerk for the Mutual Life Insurance Company. The Gleason's moved from tenement to tenement, always in and around the Bushwick section, looking for cheaper rents and sunnier rooms. The parents argued constantly about money.

When Jackie was three, his brother Clemence—a frail, sickly boy of 14—died. When Jackie was nine, his hard-drinking father put on his hat and coat one cold wintry day, left their flat and never returned.

From that time, young Jackie's life was more nervous and erratic. To support them, his mother worked as a subway changer. Her salary was so low there were times—usually the day before payday—when they didn't have enough to eat. Jackie wolfed his meals, eating at irregular hours, gaining no weight. He had a sickly, pimply complexion. His mother was ill most of the time. Working in the winter made her legs and teeth ache. Often when she came home from work she had a pint of gin in her purse; she sipped it to keep warm and to soothe her pains.

Jackie slept on a cot in her room, hearing her moan and toss all night. Their misery and loneliness brought mother and son closer. They went regularly to Our Lady of Lourdes Church. Mrs. Gleason was zealous about Catholicism, telling Jackie endless stories of God, saints, heaven and hell. She was also superstitious. When the newspapers featured articles about a man who predicted that the end of the world was near—specifying the day and hour—she was certain he spoke God's truth.

When "doomsday" arrived, Jackie's mother huddled with him on the floor of their bedroom. It was a scene out of the Dark Ages. Mother and son wept and prayed. Jackie was terrified, unsure whether he would die by lightning, fire, flood—or all three. Once, at the appointed hour, the sky grew dark and a cold wind beat at the windows.

"Here it comes!" cried Mrs. Gleason. They cowered for hours on the floor. Nothing more happened, but the experience was so unnerving that Jackie stayed home from school for three days to recover. The incident marked him deeply. When he grew up, he was assailed by religious doubts. He read scores of volumes on the churches of the world and psychic phenomena. His readings convinced him that Catholicism was right for him.

When he was 14, Jackie graduated from Brooklyn's Public School 73. He was in the class play, a comedy, and had a wonderful time on stage. Instead of being nervous like the other kids, he was full of fire and fun. He upset the cast with ad libs and made his role seem more important than it was. Deliberately he knocked a floor lamp off the stage. When the principal picked it up, Jackie knocked it off again. The audience roared with laughter.

"Mom," he said afterwards, "I think I was great. In fact, I was so great I've decided to be an actor."

He wasn't fooling. He attended Bushwick High for a few weeks, working nights as an entertainer at smokers and social clubs. Often he received no pay; other times he made as little as 50 cents. Brashly convinced that he could earn more, he decided to quit school.

Jackie entered an amateur night contest at the neighborhood Halsey Theater and was so good, wisecracking and singing, that he won first *and* second prize. He also won the job of amateur night emcee, earning $2 per performance. Branching out, he found emcee jobs at other theaters and fraternal halls. His pay was always low, but he didn't care. He was driven by a deep, relentless compulsion to make people laugh. Nothing else mattered. When people laughed at his jokes, he felt good and forgot his troubles at home.

In April, 1935, when Jackie was 19, his mother became so ill she stayed home from work for longer periods. She was anemic, tired, nervous and afraid of people. An enormous red carbuncle formed on her neck, and developed into erysipelas, an acute skin inflammation. Her pain was intense and she moaned morning and night. Her cries frightened Jackie, although he remained outwardly cocky and relaxed.

"Mom," he said, "how would it be if I asked old Doc O'Connor to come over and take a look at you?"

His suggestion made her almost hysterical. All her life Mrs. Gleason had feared doctors. She feared only one thing more—death. Afraid to go to bed ("That's where people die . . ."), she stayed day and night on a couch in the living room.

The carbuncle grew larger, making her neck and face swell. Jackie tried to lance the red monster, but his mother's screams made him drop the darning needle.

One night Mrs· Gleason was so bad Jackie didn't dare go to work. He watched the couch nervously. Whenever she moved, he asked, "You all right, Mom?"

"I'm all right," she whispered, eyes closed.

A half-hour after midnight, he heard a loud sigh, then a little gasp of breath. He knelt beside her, touched her shoulder and knew she was dead. He sat on the floor beside her, staring at the wall, tears streaming from his eyes. She was only 50 years old and all her life she had known grinding poverty. He vowed then and there to break out of that trap. *Never again,* he told himself, *will anybody in my family die like this . . .*

But he remained stuck in the trap six more years, working for beer and peanuts in second-rate joints. He knew he was good; the audiences knew he was good. But he couldn't get ahead.

For solace he often turned to booze. It was always good for him, dispersing his blue moods, making him buoyant and funny. At the comparatively tender age of 20, he was a two-fisted drinker who rarely paid for his whiskey and gin. He mooched vast quantities by betting other drinkers that he could outdrink them and remain sober. He seldom lost.

A year after his mother died, Jackie married Genevieve Halford, a blonde dancer with beautiful legs whom he met at an amateur night competition. From the very beginning the marriage was an explosive mistake. Doubtlessly, Jackie was attracted to her because she reminded him of his mother. Genevieve, who he called Gen, was a devout

Catholic. He worshiped her, kept her on a pedestal and insisted that she get out of show business.

When she argued that they needed the money she could earn, he roared, "No wife of mine is going to work in the crummy joints I work in! I've seen what happens to nice girls who work in those joints . . ."

Gen gave in. She stayed home with their babies, Geraldine, born in 1939 and Linda, born two years later. From then on the patterns of the Gleason lives were in total opposition. Gen became a homemaker who despised parties and drunks. She wanted her husband to get out of the entertainment racket and become a respected salesman or executive. Jackie, doing better now as a comic, was becoming a playboy-type, a big spender (when he had it), a carouser who enjoyed showing up at bashes with a different blonde on his arm every night.

The gold rush stage of Gleason's career began in 1940 when he was invited into New York's Club 18, a swinging saloon dedicated to the principle that every customer was a creep who should be insulted. It was suited perfectly to Jackie's acid-tongued, rowdy ad libs. Any woman who rose from a table was promptly and publicly questioned about her obvious destination. When she returned from the ladies' room, Jackie would ask sweetly, "Could you hear us in there?" If she said no, he broke up the audience by cracking, "Well, we could certainly hear you!"

Jackie turned a spotlight on baldhead patrons and presented them with bedraggled wigs. When skater Sonja Henie dropped in, Gleason handed her an ice cube and sneered, "Do something!"

One night Hollywood's Jack Warner laughed noisily at Jackie's capers and offered him a $250-a-week movie contract. Gleason went eagerly to the Coast, certain that his career had finally turned the corner. He also was glad to leave New York because his marriage was a shambles. Naturally, since he was an up-and-coming comedian, the brains at Warner Brothers cast him as gangster.

For two years he shot his way through films with Humphrey Bogart and other toughies. He became disgusted when his pleas for comedy roles were ignored.

Finally, acknowledging defeat, Jackie sneaked out of Hollywood and returned to New York, where he appeared in such musical comedies as *Follow the Girls* and *Keep Off the Grass*. He called at the home of his wife and two small daughters, receiving such an affectionate welcome that he pleaded with Gen to give him another chance. They restated their marriage vows before a priest, lived happily for a few months and then saw the marriage start to unravel again.

It was the old trouble. Jackie couldn't stay home. He had to be out with the boozers, partying with the glib set, exchanging wisecracks with pretty girls, making new show biz contacts. Although his musical salaries were as high as $750 a week, he overspent so consistently he was always broke. He idled away his free time at places like Toots Shor's, cultivating a reputation as the big town's funniest scrounger of lucre and liquor.

When Jackie's bill at Toots' went over $800, he felt ashamed and told Shor that he wouldn't sign any more tabs. "Why, you crazy creep," said Toots, "who's asking you for any dough? If you're tired of signing your own name, sign mine."

"Okay," said Jackie brightly. He invited a gang of pals in for dinner. He studied the check, which amounted to $175, and marked down a $10 tip for the waiter. "I'd make it more, my boy," he said, "but you know how cheap Toots is."

In 1943, rejected by the Army because he was 100 pounds overweight, Jackie obtained his first starring job. He bounced onto the Roxy stage at $3,000 a week.

Two weeks later he was out of work. But he continued to live high, wide and to hell with tomorrow. His capacity for booze became the talk of the town. One day, feeling thirsty but unwilling to sign for more drinks, he devised a tactic. He challenged Toots to a drinking bout, shouting, "You bum, I can drink you under the table in less than an hour!"

Toots accepted. On hour later, almost on the dot, Gleason reached for a drink. He missed. He got to his feet, made a slow, 360-degree turn and fell flat on his back on the rug. Toots had won the bout, but Gleason had imbibed all the hooch he could swallow.

Jackie's drinking game became so popular it was known in his social circles as "The Challenge." At a party one Saturday night at the Astor Hotel, a well-known lady singer made this rash comment: "Male drinkers are bums. A talented lady drinker can out-drink any of 'em." Jackie immediately issued "The Challenge." The songstress accepted, agreeing to abide by the rule that the contestant who kept his eyes open the longest would be declared the winner.

The singer was famed as a lady whom alcohol did not affect. She chose brandy as the drinking weapon. A crowd of actors, comics and girls formed a circle around the duelists, who sat on the rug to minimize injuries which might be caused by a fall· Each contestant was given a bottle.

At 1 A.M. both competitors were bright-eyed, regaling the crowd with funny stories. Two more bottles of brandy were brought in. By 2 A.M. some of the non-contestants had passed out. Jackie was drinking from a prone position and perspiring heavily. The odds on the match had shifted heavily in favor of the lady, who was frisky as a parakeet. Two more bottles were brought in.

By 4:15 A.M., the lady's complexion changed from cheerful pink to sickly olive drab. Moaning softly, she crawled toward the bathroom on all fours. She didn't make it.

With a masterful effort, Gleason rose to his feet. He lurched into the hall, then fell. At breakfast-time, he was still snoring there, looking like the hulk of a great wrecked ship.

Meanwhile his career was also foundering. Hoping to change his luck, he went back to Hollywood and landed his first TV job, substituting for William Bendix in *The Life of Riley*. He was a flop. Again he went back to New York in disgrace.

Then came a new proposal. The Du Mont television network needed a fresh personality for its *Cavalcade of Stars. Cavalcade's* producers were dubious, but made an offer to Gleason. Having already failed on TV, he was dubious too, but needed the money.

Not until opening night did Gleason realize the full potential of *Cavalcade*. Unlike *Riley,* which was filmed, *Cavalcade* was live and wide open for ad libs, mugging and any funny business he cared to invent.

He was so funny on the first show, the cameramen laughed. When the show ended, people in the audience turned to one another and asked, "Who was that fat guy? He's terrific!" Du Mont's officials, equally ecstatic, wondered if Gleason could possibly be as good the following week.

Amazingly, he was better. On the second show, Gleason teamed in one skit with an unknown actor named Art

Carney, whom he'd met for the first time during rehearsal a few days earlier. Jackie portrayed top-hatted, square-mustached Reggie van Gleason III, posing in formal attire for a Man of Distinction whiskey ad. Carney had the role of a sissified, nitwit photographer. Since Reggie was unable to drink the whiskey properly, Carney kept showing him how to do it. Both ended up hilariously plastered.

Recognizing Carney's improvisation abilities, Gleason quickly signed him to a long-term contract.

When *Cavalcade* started, his audience popularity rating was 9 and he was up against the then fearsome competition of TV prize fights. In no time at all he zoomed to 28 and switched to CBS for a whopping salary of $10,000 a week. His show appeared opposite NBC's *All Star Revue*, Saturday night's top-rated program. Jackie and his gang knocked *Revue* into the dust even after NBC rushed up such prized reinforcements as Jimmy Durante and Tallulah Bankhead.

Jackie became known as Mr. Saturday Night. He seized production control and ran the whole shebang, including directing. He revealed a phenomenal mind, often memorizing 25 pages of script in an hour, while attending to scores of other show details. He disdained rehearsals for himself and drove his colleagues crazy by revising entire scenes only minutes before showtime. Sometimes he deliberately dropped many pages of script in the middle of a show, launching into ad lib scenes which panicked the other actors as they tried to keep up.

No show decision was too important or too small for his personal attention. He even determined what shade of nail polish would be worn by the gorgeous line-up of June Taylor dancers. He insisted on gigantic budgets and elegant production numbers. He hired eight writers who beat their brains out creating material for his endless list of characters, including the celebrated Honeymooners (with Carney and Audrey Meadows), the Bartender, the Poor Soul, Rudy the Repairman, the Bachelor, and Stanley R. Soog, the announcer for Mother Fletcher's products. Many of the characters were based on people Gleason actually had grown up with in Brooklyn.

Three months after he signed with CBS, Jackie and his wife parted for good, having seen their umpteenth reconciliation attempt go down the drain. A few weeks before the final blow-up, Jackie—unable to stand the constant arguing at home—had moved into the Park

Sheraton Hotel, leasing a swank penthouse for $25,000 a year, using it as a combination apartment-office. The penthouse made Gen steaming mad and she seared him with such questions as: "Why won't you come home like other men? Who are those blonde women you're seen with? What's going on at the Park Sheraton? Is it an office or a hideout?"

At that time there was no other woman as such in Jackie's life. He made dates with theatrical beauties, enjoying the way they flattered his ego. But all the women he dated were also seen regularly with other escorts. Aware of his bad habits, he took full blame for the failure of his marriage and arranged for a legal separation. He agreed to give his wife 12½ per cent of his gross earnings, plus 1 per cent to each of his daughters for their educations.

After signing the separation papers, Jackie threw up his hands and exclaimed: "Boy, am I glad that's over. If there's one thing I can't understand it's dames. So help me, I'll never get mixed up with another one!"

His promise lasted a few weeks. Then he fell hopelessly in love with dancer Marilyn Taylor. She was 27, 10 years younger than he. The younger sister of June, the choreographer for his shows, Marilyn wasn't attracted to Jackie at first. She knew his casual ways with women. Also, she had met Mrs. Gleason and the two daughters. A Catholic herself, Marilyn knew the Gleasons could never be divorced.

Among the boys who made it their business to know, Marilyn was considered a very good girl, one with character and and common sense. Whenever Jackie phoned for a date, she said she was busy. For months she fended him off. But one night, tired after a long rehearsal, she let him take her to dinner. He acted like a happy high-school kid. He told her his best stories and made her laugh. She forgot how exhausted she was and had a wonderful time. It was the beginning of a long, difficult romance.

Not long after their first date, Jackie broke his leg on his TV show and was taken to Doctors' Hospital. He set up an office there, supervising the show, okaying scripts and camera angles. One Sunday he relaxed in bed, his cast propped up, watching television. Marilyn sat in a chair beside him.

Suddenly Jackie's wife walked in. She glared at Jackie, then at Marilyn. Lips quivering with emotion, she began to yell. "You're nothing but a rat, taking advantage of an innocent girl! You ought to be ashamed of yourself!"

Then she turned to Marilyn, who kept staring at the television, not saying a word.

Jackie grabbed the phone and called his doctor. "Big trouble!" he yelled. "Get over here right away, Doc. Gen is here. So's Marilyn!"

The doctor persuaded Mrs. Gleason to leave. For many minutes afterward Jackie and Marilyn sat in silence. There was nothing for them to say. Gen had said it all.

To quiet the gossips, Marilyn quit Jackie's show, but their romance continued for several years, with Gleason promising that somehow he would "work things out." He never did. One summer he took her on a trip to Europe, but it was not a happy vacation. Both were increasingly aware that they faced an impossible future. Gen would never give Jackie a divorce. Finally, although their love never really cooled, Jackie and Marilyn stopped seeing one another.

Though his personal life was a mess, Gleason's career was never better. Buick signed him to the fattest TV contract in history—11 million for three years of performances. CBS signed him to a unique 15-year contract, including a promise to pay him $100,000 each year he *didn't* work.

The major record companies laughed when Jackie—unable to read a note of music—expressed a desire to compose and conduct musical works for them. Undaunted, he financed his first album himself, turning out a brand of lush romantic melodies which one critic described as "maple syrup poured over pizza." It sold so fantistically that the record companies implored Jackie to sign. He began to make $150,000 a year on the sale of such discs as *Melancholy Serenade* and *Music for Lovers Only*.

There was still another side to Gleason, seldom seen by the public. At times he could be extremely serious, generous, compassionate, even sentimental. Because he had painful memories of what it was like to be hungry, broke or bereaved, he could be quick to help those in need. When a Greenwich Village janitor committed suicide in despair, leaving an ailing widow, Gleason read the story, wiped a tear from his eye and called the New York *Daily News*. "Pal," he said, "I want to pick up the check for that funeral—and don't mention my name." It was done.

When the youngsters of the Dukes baseball team lacked uniforms, Gleason sent cash. A friend wrote him that St. Benedict's Church in Brooklyn had a collapsing ceiling. Jackie sent $1,000. Within a period of three weeks, he mailed $250 to a Salvation Army unit in Miami; $50 carfare to an old pal in New Orleans; $100 to a termite-infested school in the British West Indies, and a $500 check to a Chicago widow with five children.

Season after season he kept up an incredible pace, working all day, partying most nights. Inevitably his energy and his ratings slipped. The flashing feet in the $85 shoes felt like lead; large, dark pouches appeared under his snapping eyes. In the late Fifties, Art Carney left the show. Audrey Meadows and other regulars soon followed. Jackie kept going with such new people as Frank Fontaine. Sometimes the Gleason Show reached the hilarious heights of old; more often it didn't.

Frightened by his ratings, he monkeyed around with the show's format, cutting to a half-hour, filming it, then restoring it to an hour. Nothing helped. He gave it all up as hopeless, announcing that he was quitting TV for a long rest. Then—only a few days later—he saw the sensational ratings the show had received for a revival of *The Honeymooners*, co-starring Art and Audrey, whom he'd coaxed back for a one-nighter.

Jackie changed his mind again, announcing he'd be back for the 1966-67 season in a musical version of *Honeymooners*, with Carney and Sheila McRae.

Today, Gleason spends more time alone than ever before, a peculiar turnabout for a man who has always relished the attention of crowds. Now that he is past 50, he is moodier, more nervous, unable to sleep. The most sleep he gets is two or three hours at a stretch; he whiles away the long nights reading thick volumes on religion and ESP, trying to get a better understanding of himself and the people with whom he works. During his partying era, he often drank himself stupid to encourage sleep, but he was never an alcoholic—and still isn't. Today, when he feels anxious or insecure, he is more apt to glut himself on food, creating an inner solace as he stuffs himself on great slabs of roast prime beef au jus, steaks, Alaska king crablegs, strawberry shortcake and thick slices of rich cream pie.

Author Jim Bishop, who spent weeks with Gleason

while researching his biography, *The Golden Ham*, explains Jackie's unique unhappiness:

"He is one of the world's most tormented and fearful men. There are half a dozen Jackie Gleasons and they are not at peace. Gleason the businessman does not admire Gleason the playboy, Gleason the Catholic hates Gleason the connoisseur of blondes. Gleason the actor has little respect for Gleason the drinker. Gleason the brooding reader had no affection for Gleason the clown. Having seen the way his mother died, in agony and poverty, he has an abnormal fear of death, just as she did. This is one of the reasons he has remained a Catholic. Unable to run away from death, he prays that his religion will help discover what happens after death . . ."

Almost as much as dying, Jackie fears professional failure . . . and this is a never-ending source of insecurity and self-torment. After knocking around the clubs and theaters for more than 30 years, he has seen what happens to all the stars. Graying glamour queens are replaced by younger, sexier chicks. The great profiles give way to leading men with firmer cleft chins. And the funny comics lose their prized ratings, and their shows, to young nuts who are quicker with ad libs and prat falls.

One day 14 years ago, Gleason—wiser and more frightened than most top bananas—knew what to expect and prepared for it. That was the day of all great days when he received the contract moving from the local Du Mont network to fame and fortune with CBS. Dave Shelley, one of his pals, hurried over to Gleason's apartment, expecting a celebration party of booze, broads and hundred-dollar bills flying around like confetti.

Instead he found Jackie undressed, unshaved, alone, lying on his bed, staring sober-eyed at the ceiling. "What's the matter?" Shelley said. "This is a big wonderful day, and you look like a bum."

Gleason got up slowly, shaking his head. From a closet he dragged out an old trunk. He opened it and packed in his old suits, some fresh shirts, ties and underwear.

"My God," said Shelley, "what's going on?"

"Some day," said Gleason moodily, "I may find myself back at the old Adams Theater in Newark. I won't have a dime or a suit of clothes. So I'm sending all this stuff to the Adams right now, marking it JACKIE GLEASON—HOLD FOR ARRIVAL."

Shelley nodded. "Put a five or ten spot in each suit.

Then, if you reach in the pocket—you'll have eating money."

Jackie did it. As the trunk was being carried downstairs, he said: "No matter what happens in TV, I'll always have some place to go . . ."

He meant every word of it.